America Sings of War

# America Sings of War
American Sheet Music from World War I

Edited by
John Roger Paas

2014
Harrassowitz Verlag · Wiesbaden

Bibliografische Information der Deutschen Nationalbibliothek
Die Deutsche Nationalbibliothek verzeichnet diese Publikation in der Deutschen
Nationalbibliografie; detaillierte bibliografische Daten sind im Internet
über http://dnb.dnb.de abrufbar.

Bibliographic information published by the Deutsche Nationalbibliothek
The Deutsche Nationalbibliothek lists this publication in the Deutsche
Nationalbibliografie; detailed bibliographic data are available on the internet
at http://dnb.dnb.de.

For further information about our publishing program consult our website
http://www.harrassowitz-verlag.de
© Otto Harrassowitz GmbH & Co. KG, Wiesbaden 2014
This work, including all of its parts, is protected by copyright.
Any use beyond the limits of copyright law without the permission
of the publisher is forbidden and subject to penalty. This applies
particularly to reproductions, translations, microfilms and storage
and processing in electronic systems.
Printed on permanent/durable paper.
Typesetting and layout: Michael Fröhlich
Printing and binding: Memminger MedienCentrum AG
Printed in Germany
ISBN 978-3-447-10278-0

*For Bronwen, Hugo, and Monty,
whose greatgrandfather served on
the Western Front*

# TABLE OF CONTENTS

Preface .................................................................. ix

Introduction ............................................................ xiii

Songs of the Great War

    1914 .................................................................. 3

    1915 .................................................................. 17

    1916 .................................................................. 41

    1917 .................................................................. 59

    1918 .................................................................. 147

    1919 .................................................................. 271

    1920 .................................................................. 297

Color Plates

    Covers to Printed Songs (nos. 1-276) ................................. 301

    Additional Covers (nos. 277-441) ..................................... 334

Indexes

    Song Titles .......................................................... 354

    Songwriters .......................................................... 359

    Composers ............................................................ 362

    Performers ........................................................... 365

    Recording Artists .................................................... 366

    Artists .............................................................. 367

    Publishers ........................................................... 368

# PREFACE

When Paul McCartney performed in Red Square on 24 May 2003, his concert was enthusiastically received by those Russians who had grown up in the 1960s and for whom the music of the Beatles had proven to be an unexpected catalyst for change. Sergei Ivanov, Russian defense minister at the time of the concert and one of those youngsters from the '60s, was convinced that the Beatles had played a significant role in the dissolution of the Soviet Union.[1] The power that music can exert is undeniable, for music often has the ineffable ability to move people in ways that transcend any possible impact of purely intellectual reasoning. Martin Luther and his fellow reformers were clear on this point, as were organizers of the labor movement in America in the early twentieth century and anti-war protesters in the 1960s and '70s. What they all understood is that popular music, music that appeals to the broadest spectrum of listeners and frequently expresses common ideas and feelings, can exercise a powerful force on people.

Music is also something which can help to bond people together, and before the invention of radio, television, and computers, communal singing was a central social activity. Popular music, like movies today, reflects the culture in which it is produced at the same time that it may exercise a direct influence on that culture. Such was clearly the case in America during the First World War, when popular songs, issued as sheet music for piano and voice in editions that frequently numbered in the hundreds of thousands, enjoyed broad circulation. These songs gave expression to those common feelings and beliefs that motivated the actions of the American public and helped to define its attitude toward the European war.

The sheer magnitude of the output of popular music is striking. In 1909 alone more than 25,000 songs were entered for copyright registration.[2] Although not all songs copyrighted ever appeared in print as sheet music, it is noteworthy that during the First World War over 35,000 were registered.[3] The most comprehensive bibliography of sheet music from the war lists close to 10,000 pieces, but the actual number was significantly higher, since many songs were reprinted multiple times.[4] Considering the large number of songs that were actually published during the war, it is not surprising that they would have reflected the public's attitude toward America's involvement in the conflict.

These songs appeared not only in the form of individual pieces of sheet music but also as inserts in newspapers, as pocket-size songbooks such as *Songs the Soldiers and Sailors Sing* (at a cost of 15 cents) and *Popular Songs of the A.E.F*, and as single sheets issued by the Y.M.C.A.

---

1 Leslie Woodhead, *How the Beatles Rocked the Kremlin: The Untold Story of a Noisy Revolution* (New York: Bloomsbury, 2013), p. 154.

2 Russell Sanjek, *American Popular Music and Its Business: The First Four Hundred Years*, vol. 3: *From 1900 to 1984* (New York: Oxford University Press, 1988), p. 23. The year 1909 is mentioned, for as of 1 July of that year songwriters and composers were guaranteed by law a royalty if their songs were published.

3 Frederick G. Vogel, *World War I Songs: A History and Dictionary of Popular American Patriotic Tunes, with Over 300 Complete Lyrics* (Jefferson, NC: McFarland & Company, 1995), p. ix. The copyright records are maintained in the Library of Congress.

4 See Bernard S. Parker, *World War I Sheet Music: 9,670 Patriotic Songs Published in the United States, 1914-1920, with More than 600 Covers Illustrated*, 2 vols. (Jefferson, NC: McFarland & Company, 2007).

and at army camps throughout the U.S.A. One such small collection entitled *Liberty Songs* states on its cover: "Adapted for Camp, Home and Community Singing."[5] Another is an official *Army Song Book*—"For free distribution to all Officers and Men in the Army"—issued in 1918 by the War Department Commission on Training Camp Activities.[6] There also exists a folio-size collection of songs published in Paris for the A.E.F.[7] In addition to these collections aimed for use by soldiers, there were also selections of war songs issued specifically for civilians. One such song sheet with the "Pledge of Allegiance," "The American's Creed," and 13 songs was distributed to workers of Thomas A. Edison Industries, and on the front the following is printed: "Keep this for noon-day singing in Lakeside Avenue on Tuesdays and Fridays at 12.30 P.M." All of this leads to the obvious conclusion that public singing of war songs and other traditional patriotic songs was an integral part of American life during the First World War.

The songs that appeared as sheet music were a combination of words and music, and it was evident to people at the time that the lyrics were of primary importance. Music was also essential, but it played a secondary role and was meant to support the underlying message of the song. On the back of "My Belgian Rose" from 1918 (no. 223) is a full-page spread—reprinted from *The Saturday Evening Post*—extolling the power of popular songs in the time of war:

> A nation that sings can never be beaten—each song is a mile-stone on the road to victory.
>
> Songs are to a nation's spirit what ammunition is to a nation's army. The producer of songs is an "ammunition" maker. The nation calls upon him for "ammunition" to fight off fatigue and worry. The response has been magnificent. America's war songs are spreading through the world hailed by our allies as the omen of victory.

The conclusion drawn is unequivocal: "Therefore music is essential." The power of song at the time of war was echoed by the noted bandmaster John Philip Sousa in a full-page spread on the back of "We'll Build a Little Home in the U.S.A." (no. 292). In a reprint of an article from the 6 March 1916 issue of the *New York American*, Sousa, in speaking about the song "Wake up, America" (no. 38), makes the following point: "Lecture me, write

---

5 *Liberty Songs* (New York: Leo. Feist, Inc., 1918). Included among the 15 songs in the collection are "Over There" (no. 91), "Good-bye Broadway, Hello France" (no. 93), "My Belgian Rose" (no. 223), and "K-K-K-Katy" (no. 198). Soldiers had access not only to the printed lyrics of songs but also to acoustic recordings through the use of portable gramophones, which allowed them to listen to recordings while on the front lines. The British firm Decca even produced an aptly named "Trench Model." See: John Druesedow, "Popular Songs of the Great War: Background and Audio Resources," *Notes*, 65 (2008): 367.

6 This pamphlet has the lyrics to 85 songs, including "Over There" (no. 91), "Giddy Giddap, Go on, Go on" (no. 127), "Joan of Arc" (no. 85), and "Long Boy" (no. 128). At the back are two telling photographs emphasizing the extent of singing in the Army: "Ten thousand singing soldiers" and "The song leaders of a division." In addition to singing songs officially sanctioned by their superiors, soldiers enjoyed singing their own songs, many of them parodies of popular songs, and some quite raunchy, fatalistic, or cynical. A selection of these songs can be found in the following: John J. Niles, *Singing Soldiers* (New York: Charles Scribner's Sons, 1927); John J. Niles, Douglas S. Moore, and A. A. Wallgren, *The Songs my Mother never taught me* (New York: The Macaulay Company, 1929); Arthur Edward Dolph, *"Sound Off!": Soldier Songs from Yankee Doodle to Parlez vous* (New York: Cosmopolitan Book Corporation, 1929); and Max Arthur, *When this Bloody War is over: Soldiers' Songs of the First World War* (London: Piatkus, 2001).

7 *Popular Songs of the A.E.F. compiled for Use in the Huts of the Y.M.C.A.* (Paris: Editions Francis Salabert, 1918). This 86-page hardbound collection, which was "not for sale by the Trade," begins with "Good-bye Broadway, Hello France" (no. 93) and ends with "Smile, Smile, Smile (Pack up your Troubles)" (no. 32).

editorials at me, and I may be convinced that preparedness is necessary, but sing me a song that contains your message and I WILL BE won over at once!"

In explaining America's gradual movement from neutrality toward engagement, historians have traditionally relied on official records, diplomatic documents, memoires, and speeches by political leaders. As important as such primary sources are for our understanding of America's actions before and during the war, we should not overlook sheet music, a rich primary source which offers us the opportunity to gauge American feelings at the time.[8] Interestingly, however, sheet music has been virtually ignored by historians in their studies of the First World War. Despite the seminal role they played in helping to solidify American support for the war effort, they are left unmentioned in the permanent exhibitions in the major national war museums of Europe. Instead, when printed visual material is prominently exhibited, it is usually in the form of posters issued throughout the war.

The importance of posters during the First World War is undeniable. The Americans produced over 20 million copies of some 2,500 posters, whose primary purpose was propaganda for the war effort.[9] However, sheet music, too, was largely a form of printed propaganda. In connection with the relationship between popular music and current events, it has been said: "The music business dealt in musical journalism in a way, the emotional tabloid which told of the day to day events that stirred the public. It was above all, opportunistic, and for that very reason, it is one of the truest indices of the public and its desires."[10] It is hoped that this anthology will raise awareness of the importance of sheet music in the context of American involvement in the First World War and lead to an appreciation of the significant impact it had on public opinion.

When viewed in isolation and/or out of proper historical context, individual pieces of sheet music from the First World War are often at best little more than interesting musical artifacts. When they are published as groups, they have invariably been organized alphabetically, an arrangement which makes it difficult to follow the development of pubic sentiment over time. The arrangement of the songs in the present anthology is broadly by year of copyright, and within each year by the month of a song's appearance in the top 20, if known, or in connection with other songs of similar content.[11] All of the songs and other original material featured here are from the author's private collection of over 1000 pieces of sheet music and related material, and although not exhaustive, the collection is both comprehensive and representative.

The lyrics of each song are given in their entirety, but some silent editorial corrections

---

8 Timothy E. Scheurer has argued in chapter 5 in *Born in the U.S.A.: The Myth of America in Popular Music from Colonial Times to the Present* (Jackson and London: University Press of Mississippi, 1991) that the songs produced during the First World War reveal the national myths that helped Americans define themselves.

9 Walton Rawls, *Wake up, America!: World War I and the American Poster* (New York: Abbeville Press, 1988), p. 12.

10 Attributed to Chaim Berment in: Kenneth Aaron Kanter, *The Jews on Tin Pan Alley: The Jewish Contribution to American Popular Music, 1830-1940* (New York: Ktav Publishing House, 1982), p. 26. In the opinion of Isaac Goldberg, the way in which Tin Pan Alley, with its eye always on commercial success, reacted to changes of sentiment in the American public meant that it had "the soul—and callousness— of a professional propagandist." See: Isaac Goldberg, *Tin Pan Alley: A Chronicle of the American Popular Music Racket* (New York: The John Day Company, 1930), p. 216.

11 The information concerning the various songs' place among the top 20 is drawn from Edward Foote Gardner's compilation: *Popular Songs of the Twentieth Century: A Charted History*, vol. 1: *Chart Detail & Encyclopedia, 1900-1949* (St. Paul: Paragon House, 2000).

have been necessary. American English has evolved over the years, and, thus, the spelling of individual words has changed. In such cases, spelling has been modified as well as in cases of misspelling. Printers were also frequently quite careless with their punctuation, so where necessary, punctuation has been corrected to clarify the meaning of the lyrics.

In conclusion, I would like to acknowledge those people whose assistance was crucial in making this anthology possible. Early on several students helped to type the initial versions of the lyrics: Paul Carpenter, Aditi Krishna, Claire Pennington, and Eric Reich. All the retouching of the covers, some of which reveal significant wear through frequent use, was carefully undertaken by Mary Tatge. I am indebted to Michael Fröhlich at Harrassowitz Verlag for his constant assistance as he designed the layout and saw the book through publication. It is to my wife Martha, however, to whom I owe the most gratitude, for without her patience, constructive criticism, and steadfast support this book might never have become reality.

Carleton College
August 4, 2014

JOHN ROGER PAAS

# INTRODUCTION

The publication of individual songs as sheet music has a long tradition in Anglo-American culture that stretches back to the late seventeenth century. Over time there developed in the minds of music publishers a clear distinction between popular and art music, and throughout most of the nineteenth century the music scene in America was dominated by several established publishers in New York City and Boston who catered to a predominantly middle-class clientele. By the turn of the century, however, important new factors were contributing to a fundamental shift in the way popular music was produced and received in America. By the 1880s methods of mass production had helped to make the piano an item which not only the wealthy could afford, so that by 1900 the piano was the mainstay of musical home entertainment.[1] In 1909 alone 365,000 pianos were sold in America.[2] Piano parlor culture had come to be enjoyed by the less affluent, and the popular music they favored grew out of a rich multicultural tradition that was of scant interest to the big publishing firms. At the same time a new form of musical entertainment for the masses was emerging—vaudeville—where people heard catchy tunes and the joyous syncopated piano music known as ragtime.

A new group of entrepreneurs emerged in America to take advantage of the changes in the popular music scene. A number of the major new publishers were first- or second-generation Jewish immigrants who came to music publishing from other professions: the Witmarks started as amateur printers as teenagers; Joseph W. Stern (1870-1934) was a necktie salesman; Edward B. Marks (1865-1945) and Leo Feist (1869-1930) sold corsets; Maurice Shapiro (1873-1911) and Louis Bernstein (1879-1962) were retailers; Jerome H. Remick (1869-1931) was a businessman. Although not professional musicians themselves, they recognized a potential for profit in the publication of popular music and used their keen business and marketing skills to become extremely successful publishers specializing in the production of sheet music. While New York City became the center of this industry, firms also existed in other large cities such as Boston, Chicago, Detroit, Kansas City, San Francisco, and Seattle as well as in numerous small towns across the entire country.[3] By 1904 there were 45 music publishers in New York City alone, almost all in simple quarters located around West 28th Street, an area that came to be known as Tin Pan Alley.[4] The production of songs by Tin Pan Alley dominated

---

[1] *Piano 300: Celebrating Three Centuries of People and Pianos* (Washington: The National Museum of American History, 2001), p. 49.

[2] Russell Sanjek, *American Popular Music and Its Business: The First Four Hundred Years*, vol. 3: *From 1900 to 1984* (New York: Oxford University Press, 1988), p. 23. Of related importance was the widespread availability of phonographs, with over 500,000 produced in 1914. See: Craig H. Roell, *The Piano in America, 1890-1940* (Chapel Hill: University of North Carolina Press), p. 48. On sheet music covers (or inside) it was not uncommon to have a printed statement that the song could also be purchased as a recording.

[3] See, for example: Merle Irene Smith, *Seattle Had A Tin Pan Alley, Too!* (Seattle: Merle I. Smith, 1989).

[4] Sanjek, p. 16. The actual location of Tin Pan Alley varied over the years, for the publishers were quick to stay in close proximity to the theater district as it moved uptown. The exact meaning of the term "Tin Pan Alley" is still open to interpretation, but it appears to refer to the tinny sound the upright pianos made, which sounded like rattling pans.

the American popular music industry throughout the first half of the 20th century, and during its heyday sheet music maintained a relatively constant form irrespective of where it was printed.[5] It was not until the emergence of rock and roll and the rapid expansion of the record industry with plastic records in the 1950s that Tin Pan Alley lost its preeminent position as the purveyor of popular American music.[6]

The production of sheet music could be a very lucrative undertaking, and once the major publishers had gained the experience necessary to gauge their market accurately, large profits could be realized. By 1900 it was not uncommon for one million copies of a song to be printed, and during the first decade of the 20th century there were at least 100 such songs.[7] Some even had printings of over 2 million copies. The most successful song of the First World War was George M. Cohan's rousing patriotic call for American involvement in the war—"Over There" (no. 91)—with more than 1 million records and 2 million copies of sheet music in various editions sold. The publisher, Leo Feist, used the back of "Bring back my Daddy to me" from 1917 (no. 87) to advertise the fact that he had paid Cohan the unheard-of sum of $25,000 for the hit song, and he boasted:

> Soldiers, sailors, and citizens made it popular. They fight to it. They march to it. Sing it. Whistle it. Talk it. That's why we paid $25,000 to Geo. M. Cohan, who wrote it. It's the highest price ever paid for a song, but "Over there" is worth it.

To his mind, this song epitomized his company's motto: "You can't go wrong with any 'Feist' song."

As production increased and more and more songs were available in print, the cost of sheet music fell: from 40 cents in 1890 to about 25 cents in 1900 and to an average of 10 cents in 1910.[8] For the vast majority of songs published during the First World War the cover price varied from 10 cents to 60 cents, with most in the 25- to 50-cent range. Publishers received less through sales at department stores such as Woolworth, Kresge, Kress, McCrory, Kraft, Grant, and Metropolitan. Nevertheless, the publication of

---

5 Originally, a piece of sheet music consisted of six pages, namely, one large sheet (ca. 14 x 11 inches) folded once with an added one-page insert. Later, to reduce production costs, the inserted leaf was usually omitted. During the First World War rationing sometimes necessitated reduced-size editions of songs (ca. 10 x 7 inches).

6 The demise of Tin Pan Alley in the 1950s was not simply the result of a change in musical taste. Its success had always depended on the song itself, but by the late 1930s songs were increasingly associated with a specific performer, and as the star, rather than the song, became the marketable product, the publishers of Tin Pan Alley could no longer compete. See: Thomas S. Hischak, *The Tin Pan Alley Song Encyclopedia* (Westport: Greenwood Press, 2002), p. x.

7 In talking about success in the publication of sheet music, Harry Von Tilzer, one of the more prolific publishers, stated sometime in the 1920s: "Why, I've had 118 songs that sold over half a million copies apiece. Under that number I wouldn't dream of calling a piece a hit." Quoted in: Isaac Goldberg, *Tin Pan Alley: A Chronicle of the American Popular Music Racket* (New York: The John Day Company, 1930), p. 109. Von Tilzer was speaking as one of the main publishers of sheet music, but for much sheet music the market was limited and the profits mediocre, for often songs were self-published by the songwriters and/or composers.

8 Kenneth Aaron Kanter, *The Jews on Tin Pan Alley: The Jewish Contribution to American Popular Music, 1830-1940* (New York: Ktav Publishing House, 1982), p. 30. These figures reflect the prices that were being charged in department stores in the large chains. According to Sanjek, *American Popular Music and Its Business*, p. 34, by early 1918 Woolworth was selling 200 million pieces of sheet music a year. This was a 30% increase in sales since 1913. Photos of the exterior of a Woolworth store with advertising for sheet music and of the interior of another store with a sales counter for sheet music are reproduced in: David A. Jasen, *Tin Pan Alley: The Composers, the Songs, the Performers and their Times* (New York: Donald I. Fine, 1988), after p. 96.

sheet music remained a potentially very lucrative venture, for the publisher of a successful song could realize a profit of $100,000, this at the time when the average weekly take-home pay of a family of four was about $13.[9]

The publishers of popular sheet music conducted business in a different way than the long-established firms since their mainstay was not high-brow classical music. In order to be successful, they had to market their music aggressively, for they realized that popular hit songs are not born but made. As Hazel Meyer has pointed out, each song was its own advertisement, "either justifying or disavowing its publisher's faith in his ability to please a fickle public."[10]

One common strategy on the part of the publishers to advertise their songs was to hire "pluggers," singers who would publicly sing a firm's newest songs in vaudeville theaters, burlesque theaters, and music houses. To guarantee the regular performance of a song, these publishers routinely paid vaudeville stars to sing specific songs, and usually then a photograph of the singer became part of the sheet music cover—sometimes accompanied by the phrase "Introduced by." The use of featured singers was especially common with sheet music published during the First World War, with two of the clearest examples being "Where do We go from Here?" (no. 92 with over 30 different featured singers) and "I Didn't Raise my Boy to be a Soldier" (no. 13 with at least 10 different featured singers).

Publishers also took care to have their lithographed covers appear as attractive as possible; snappy song titles, bright colors, and engaging designs were essential for success. These covers are in essence an important, though largely forgotten, treasure trove of American popular art designed by a substantial number of graphic artists during the war. Except for isolated examples designed by artists such as Norman Rockwell (nos. 146 and 263), most covers were the work of often capable though lesser-known or anonymous artists. Those artists most actively engaged during the war were Albert Barbelle (1887-1957), Edward Henry Pfeiffer (1868-1932), André De Takacs (1880-1919), and the brothers William Austin Starmer and Frederick Waite Starmer, all of whom were based in New York City but occasionally also worked on commissions from other cities.

The images the artists created frequently sent very strong subliminal messages, which reflected public opinion and underscored the ideas expressed in the songs. Throughout the war the grey-haired mother appears (nos. 60, 78, 159 and 395), at first regretting to see her dear son going to fight and later proud that he is "over there." Following America's entrance into the war, cover after cover show columns of young men eagerly marching to engage the enemy (nos. 63, 104, 314, 342, 359, and 387). When the enemy—often personified as Kaiser Wilhelm—is depicted, it is with its hands raised to surrender or in shock that it is about to be overrun by courageous American soldiers (nos. 101, 192, 352, 420, and 433). The American flag also appears time and again with repeated references in the songs to the Red, White, and Blue, or Old Glory, which has never fallen. In some cases artists based their designs on iconic American images, such as "The Spirit of '76" (nos. 40, 289, and 432) or "Washington crossing the Delaware" (no. 185). In others, they depicted American heroes past and present: George Washington, Abraham Lincoln, Robert E. Lee, Ulysses S. Grant, Woodrow Wilson, and John J. Pershing. Despite the fact that many of the images on the covers could be rather hackneyed, they had a broad appeal and were influential in helping to solidify public opinion.

---

9 Jasen, *Tin Pan Alley*, p. xx.
10 Hazel Meyer, *The Gold in Tin Pan Alley* (Philadelphia and New York: J. P. Lippincott, 1958), p. 45.

Controlling public opinion was essential to the outcome of the European conflict, and when war broke out on 4 August 1914, one of the first actions undertaken by the British was to cut the transatlantic cable. This in effect gave the British a monopoly over the news supplied to America and allowed the Allies to shape public opinion in their favor.[11] It was clear from the very beginning that propaganda was to have a major role in determining the outcome of the war—and American sheet music would have a part to play. It was also clear to the British that they faced no easy task in winning over the American public, which in some quarters was at best apathetic and in others firmly anti-war.

Although the elite along the East Coast tended to be sympathetic toward the British cause, the general feeling in America was one of definite neutrality. Separated from the European conflict by an ocean and in no way feeling personally threatened, most Americans saw no compelling reason to become involved. On principle, American Socialists and members of the International Workers of World were opposed to being sacrificed by capitalists interested only in profit, and to underscore their total opposition to the war, the Socialists amended their constitution in 1915 to read: "Any member of the Socialist Party, elected to an office, who shall in any way vote to appropriate moneys for military or naval purposes, or war, shall be expelled from the Party."[12] The Socialists were joined in their opposition to the war by members of women's groups, who advocated the settlement of national disputes through negotiation rather than war.

In addition to common citizens, the American administration, viewing the war from a safe distance, looked askance at the imperialistic and nationalistic fervor of the Europeans and sought to remain aloof from the conflict. Woodrow Wilson, who had been elected president in 1912 as a reformer and who was intent on pursuing an ambitious social agenda, feared that any involvement might derail the progress of his program. Cognizant of the fact that the American immigrant population had relatives on both sides and would naturally favor one belligerent nation over the other, he exhorted all Americans to maintain an attitude of neutrality. Even after the sinking of the passenger liner *Lusitania* off the Irish coast in May of 1915 (no. 17), the most the president did was to issue threats to the Germans.

While many wished to stay out of the European conflict, others began to push for direct involvement and even went to Europe to join the fight with the Allies. One such American was Arthur Guy Empey (1883-1963), who at the time of the sinking of the *Lusitania* was serving as a recruiting sergeant in New Jersey. In the opening to his best-selling book *"Over the Top,"* he described his emotions as he read the newspaper headlines of the sinking at the same time that he heard the tune of the anti-war song "I Didn't Raise my Boy to be a Soldier" (no. 13) being played outside:

> The windows were open and a feeling of spring pervaded the air. Through the open windows came the strains of a hurdy-gurdy playing in the street—*I Didn't Raise my Boy to be a Soldier*.

---

11 In actuality, the American public had long received its news of Europe through a British perspective, for with few of their own correspondents reporting from Europe, American newspapers had long relied on British journalists for their news. See: H. C. Peterson, *Propaganda for War: The Campaign against American Neutrality, 1914-1917* (Norman: University of Oklahoma Press, 1939), p. 6.

12 Quoted in: Meirion and Susie Harries, *The Last Days of Innocence: America at War 1917-1918* (New York: Random House, 1997), p. 54.

> "*Lusitania* Sunk! American Lives Lost!"
> —*I Didn't Raise my Boy to be a Soldier*. To us these did not seem to jibe.[13]

Empey decided to act, joined the British infantry, was wounded at the Battle of the Somme, and when back in America wrote several songs (nos. 137, 158, and 178).

Empey was not alone in wishing his country to take firm action against Germany, but the reasoning that was growing in popularity in 1915 and 1916 was that the United States should at the very least prepare itself for the eventuality of war. One of the most forceful voices in the public debate was that of former President Theodore Roosevelt, who fervently supported the Allies and who traveled widely to criticize President Wilson's pacifist foreign policy. Even though the Democratic Party's slogan in Wilson's successful reelection campaign during 1916 was "He kept us out of war," the voices calling for U.S. involvement became ever more strident. The chorus in *Wake Up, America* from 1916 (no. 38) poses in simple terms the pertinent question that faced the nation:

> If we are called to war,
> Are we prepared to give our lives
> For our sweethearts and our wives?

There is little doubt what the answer would be, but the underlying issue in the many calls for preparedness was less about defense and more about honor and self-respect. The proponents of preparedness were unabashedly proud to be Americans, and they wanted the country to demonstrate its strength.

Stories of German atrocities—many of them blatantly fallacious—had circulated widely since the beginning of the war.[14] Now, as the carnage on the Continent continued unabated and the German resumption of unrestricted submarine warfare threatened American shipping interests, President Wilson came to the conclusion that the U.S.A. had no choice but to become engaged in the European conflict; on 2 April 1917 he went before Congress to ask for a declaration of war against Germany and its allies. Considering the ineffectual state of the American military establishment at the time, it was a bold decision. Neither the army nor the navy had either adequate manpower or sufficient equipment to lead an effective military campaign abroad, and it would be months before the situation began to change.

At the same time, public opinion in America remained divided. Recognizing the serious challenges he faced, Wilson quickly began to look for ways to gain the support of the American public for the war effort. Within a week of the declaration of war, he took a first step and established the Committee on Public Information, with George Creel (1876-1953) as head. Under Creel's energetic leadership the committee became a highly organized propaganda agency, which spared no efforts to convince all Americans that everything the country did was right and that it should be fully supported in its war efforts. Creel was convinced of America's moral superiority and conceived of its mission in the world in religious terms: "The world, hopeless, despairing, turned to us as the forlorn of Galilee turned to

---

13 *"Over the Top": By an American Soldier who went* (New York and London: G. P. Putnam's Sons, 1917), pp. 1-2. Empey's book enjoyed great success, with multiple editions and over a quarter of a million copies sold.

14 It was only after the war, when people began to view their actions and motivations more objectively, that the insidious role of propaganda became clear, and what had originally been a neutral term took on negative connotations and was ultimately changed to "public relations." It was in the interwar years that people began to study the negative aspects of the propaganda campaign during the war. See, for example: George Sylvester Viereck, *Spreading Germs of Hate* (London: Duckworth, 1931).

Christ, not knowing, but believing; not asking, but trusting."[15] The CPI never exerted direct influence on the music industry, yet the shift in American policy from one of neutrality to one of proud engagement is clearly mirrored in the sheet music of the time and reflects the goal of the CPI. Creel believed more in positive propaganda than in censorship, although if a song had the potential to undercut the war effort, he was not averse to suppressing it.[16] Tin Pan Alley, however, needed little encouragement to produce patriotic songs, and in the two years of America's involvement in the First World War, at least 80% of American war sheet music was published.[17]

---

15 *The War, the World and Wilson* (New York: Harper & Brothers, 1920), p. 3. Creel tells the full story of the activities of the CPI in his book *How We Advertised America: The First Telling of the Amazing Story of the Committee on Public Information that Carried the Gospel of Americanism to Every Corner of the Globe* (New York: Harper & Brothers, 1920). See also James R. Mock and Cedric Larson, *Words that won the War: The Story of The Committee on Public Information 1917-1919* (Princeton: Princeton University Press, 1939).

16 Two songs ran afoul of CPI intentions: "There'll be a Hot Time for the Old Men when the Young Men go to War" (no. 218) and "I Don't Want to Get Well (I'm in Love with a Beautiful Nurse")" (no. 122). Copies of both were confiscated, and public performances were banned. See: Hazel Meyer, p. 69.

17 Just as many of the publishers of sheet music were first- or second-generation Jewish immigrants, so too were many of the songwriters and composers. As John Shepherd has pointed out in *Tin Pan Alley* (London: Routledge & Kegan Paul, 1982), p. 49, these people felt the need to prove that they were loyal American citizens: "The First World War provided the immigrants of Tin Pan Alley with a tremendous opportunity to show what good Americans they were." Many of the songs themselves have their roots in Yiddish songs and synagogue melodies, as shown by Jack Gottlieb in *Funny, It Doesn't Sound Jewish: How Yiddish Songs and Synagogue Melodies Influenced Tin Pan Alley, Broadway, and Hollywood* (Albany: SUNY Press, 2004).

In the songs from 1917 and 1918 there is a marked difference in tone from that in earlier songs. Whereas before America's involvement in the war voices both pro and con could find expression in sheet music, dissenting voices were silenced as soon as the U.S.A. had entered the war. The government was intent on molding the American public into a unified nation wholeheartedly committed to war, and the arguments it used to convince people are the same ideas that found expression in sheet music: America was fighting for liberty; America was fighting for the defeat of autocracy and in support of democracy; America was fighting for the freedom of the seas; America was repaying a debt it owed Lafayette and the French. As song after song appeared, they drew on the common images of mother, family, home, and flag and expressed a clear sense of duty, which prepared people for the sacrifices they would have to make for the good of the country. For the country to achieve its commitment to the war, young men were encouraged—sometimes cajoled or bullied—to enlist, mothers were praised for sending their sons to war, and the general public was exhorted to do its share by either conserving resources or supporting the war effort through the purchase of Liberty bonds. These strategies found repeated expression in sheet music, and in many of the songs one finds pithy slogans from the CPI printed on the inside of the sheet music: "Food will win the war. Don't waste it;" "Food is ammunition—Don't waste it;" "Win the war with bread and lead;" "Eat More Fish, Cheese, Eggs, Poultry, And Save Beef, Pork and Mutton For Our Fighters."

As a result of the incessant propaganda distributed by the CPI and supported by the songwriters of sheet music, newspaper cartoonists, and movie producers an atmosphere of hysteria and xenophobia gripped the nation, with all things connected to German culture becoming suspect. The Germans, who had previously been admired for their culture and their work ethic, were now viewed as barbaric Huns. German newspapers were suppressed, German language instruction in schools was dropped, and German names in everyday usage were changed: German shepherds suddenly became police dogs, while sauerkraut became freedom cabbage. American citizens of German heritage or with German-sounding names feared being erroneously suspected of espionage.

In the pervasive atmosphere of strident nationalism, blind patriotism, vicious insults, and insulting caricature, the most blatant case of anti-German hysteria occurred in Collegeville, Illinois, in April of 1918. A baker's assistant with a German-sounding name was dragged from his home by a gang of local miners, who accused him of being a German spy and forced him to kiss the American flag. Then, despite his pleading his innocence, he was wrapped in the flag and lynched. Although brought to trial, the miners—appearing in court attired with red, white, and blue ribbons—were found to be innocent after a trial of only 25 minutes and were actually commended for having allowed the poor victim to write a farewell letter.[18]

Americans appeared incapable of recognizing their prejudices and blatant unfairness, for they were fully convinced that they were in the right. In the aftermath of the war, the noted German theologian and philosopher Ernst Troeltsch wrote of the Anglo-American spirit that it "does nothing without moral grounding and never pursues its own interests without being conscious simultaneously of it moral superiority."[19] This sense of moral superiority comes through repeatedly in the songs that were published, as well as in the images on the covers. Particularly telling is the cover to the military march "Pershing's Crusaders," published in New York City in 1918 by E. T. Paul Music Company (see p. 146). The design was used "by courtesy of Committee on Public Information" and depicts General Pershing astride a horse solemnly leading toward battle columns of soldiers as far as the eye can see. Behind him an American flag is held high, while on his right flank he is accompanied by medieval knights, who hover slightly above the troops. On other covers it is an angel who accompanies the columns of soldiers (nos. 221, 351, and 406). The clear message was that these American soldiers were involved in a sacred crusade to protect humanity.

In addition to the anti-German sentiment of the songs, other long-standing prejudices found expression. Racism was deeply ingrained in the American psyche. While the American government recognized that it needed African-Americans to join the army if the country was to have a strong fighting force (no. 232), it was not prepared to treat these Americans equally, and in many songs the African-Americans are depicted as weak and/or uneducated (nos. 71 and 284). Images on covers were also often based on unflattering stereotypes (nos. 72, 231, 233, 272, and 420 f.). Native Americans did not fare much better (nos. 131 and 204). Nor did young women. Whereas mothers were praised for the sacrifices they were making (nos. 64, 78, 120, 247, and 371), young women tended to be depicted as frivolous (no. 199).

At the same time that the songwriters expressed their prejudices or praised the young men in uniform and encouraged the public in its sacrifices, they also showed a lighter side when writing about the experience of the American soldiers off the battlefield in France. For many, the exposure to French culture, especially to the worldly life of Paris, was an

---

18 Stuart Gorman and Joachim Reppmann, *Triumph of Will. Printer's boy to publisher: The remarkable story of German immigrant Henry Finnern* (Davenport: Hesperian Press, 2009), p. 69.

19 *Spektatorbriefe. Aufsätze* über *die deutsche Revolution und die Weltpolitik 1918-1922*, ed. Hans Baron (Tübingen: J. C. B. Mohr, 1924), p. 320.

eye-opening experience that changed them forever. Many songwriters used this meeting between the naïve American boys and the sophisticated Parisians as material for their songs, most of them humorous (nos. 227 f., 261, 268 f., 400, 405, and 441). But there is also a poignant side to some songs, for when the war ended, many young men left behind the young women they had loved (nos. 262 f. and 435).

As social historians turn to new sources for insight into the First World War, these songs are valuable primary sources. The hopes, the concerns, the prejudices are all there and reveal the evolving attitudes of the American public toward the European conflict. Their success as commercial undertakings underscores their influence before, during and after American involvement in the war, and as historical documents they offer us a new and unique insight into American culture in the complex second decade of the twentieth century.

# Songs of
the Great War

# 1914

# WE STAND FOR PEACE WHILE OTHERS WAR

Lyrics: W. R. Williams
Music: W. R. Williams
Artist: Starmer

Chicago: Will Rossiter, 1914.

*The actual appeal is printed inside on the back of the cover. A note above the title of the song reads: "This 'Peace Poem' was inspired by President Wilson's appeal to Americans to remain neutral in thought and deed."*

The world's turned back a thousand years,
Since "War!" is now the cry.
The smile of progress turns to tears,
The helpless wonder why.
There's nothing worth the toll of life,
Before or since the flood:
Is so-called "honor" worth the price,
When rivers flow with blood?

**CHORUS**
  We stand for peace, while others war,
  Tho' war we know is sin;
  But Uncle Sam's a neutral pow'r,
  And we must stand by him.
  We can't take sides, for all the world
  Will suffer for this wrong.
  And we'll pray that ev'ry nation
  Right their wrongs by arbitration,
  And that "Home Sweet Home"
  Will be their national song.

Who said the world was civilized,
We'd found the dawn of day,
That education's star of hope
With love would find the way?
This war's effect on us depends
On what we do or say.
Our greatest help is self-control,
Till peace shall hold full sway.

**REPEAT CHORUS**

# LET US HAVE PEACE

Lyrics: Charles B. Weston
Music: Charles B. Weston

New York: Charles B. Weston, 1914.

*The cover design was used again in 1917 for a song by the same composer entitled "Uncle Sam's Awake."*

When our heroes heard the cry, "To arms, get ready!
You are wanted down in Mexico,"
One and all they quickly responded,
And with anxious hearts were ready for to go.
Always ready for to fight for dear Old Glory,
And they answer'd bravely to the call.
Then our grand old Uncle Sam
With his great and mighty hand sent his message to them all:

**CHORUS**
  "Shout aloud to all the nations,
  Ring it out from shore to shore,
  Let them hear the joyous tidings.
  We're not out for war.
  Raise aloft the dear Old Glory,
  Let all struggle cease,

For our noble president
Showed the world his good intent,
When he said,
'Let us all have peace'."

Now our Yankee boys are all a lot of fighters,
Yet they're never looking for a fight.
Always out for peace, love and freedom,
And you'll ever find them fighting for the right.
Now the Blue and Grey are solidly united
Underneath the Red, White and Blue,
Shouting peace and liberty o'er the land and o'er the sea
Ev'ry soldier brave and true

**REPEAT CHORUS**

# THE CALL TO PEACE

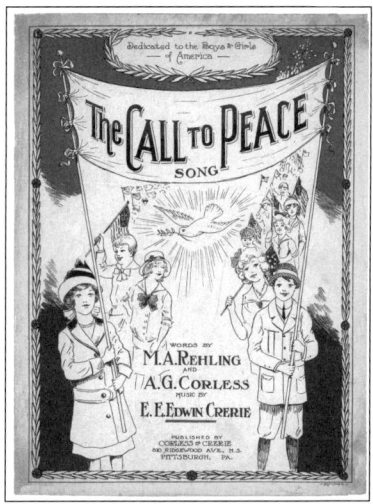

Lyrics: M. A. Rehling and A. G. Corless
Music: E. E. Edwin Crerie
Artist: E. S. Fisher

Pittsburgh: Corless & Crerie, 1914.

On bloody fields of battle,
Fighting has raged all day.
Hushed is the cannon's rattle;
Many in death now lay.
Here in a corner dying
One wounded soldier lies.
What is it he is crying,
Ere he must close his eyes?

**CHORUS**
 "Peace, my brothers, peace.
 Oh, lay your weapons down.
 Peace, my brothers, peace,
 Wherever man is found.

 The message is for all,
 It peals o'er land and sea:
 No more let battle's call
 Be heard by you and me."

Pick up this joyful tiding,
Pass it along the way.
Peace then shall be abiding,
O'er all the earth hold sway.
Hold out your hand, my brother,
Pledge now all strife to cease.
Help, as you can each other
Spread universal peace.

**REPEAT CHORUS**

# UNCLE SAM WON'T GO TO WAR

Lyrics: Casper Nathan
Music: F. Henri Klickmann

Chicago and New York: Frank K. Root & Co., 1914.

4

Little Bobbie, sitting on his father's knee
In the Land of the Free, says, "Daddy, tell me,
Why is Europe fighting, why are lands uniting
Just to whip old Germany?
Will our country join the parade?"
The father smiles upon his son
And says, "Don't be afraid."

**CHORUS**
   "Uncle Sam won't go to war,
   That's not what the U.S. got united for.
   Let all Europe fight, if they must,
   But the Yankee motto is, 'In God we trust.'
   When war clouds roll by once more,
   Things will be the same as before.
   Our country's always free.
   No matter what may be,
   Uncle Sam won't go to war."

From the top of Maine to Frisco's Golden Gate,
Yankee people don't hate; their love is too great.
So we're not excited, while we stand united.
We will love while others hate.
Peace will reign in our U.S.A.;
Tho' all the world may be at war,
Each Yankee's proud to say:

**REPEAT CHORUS**

# STAY DOWN HERE WHERE YOU BELONG

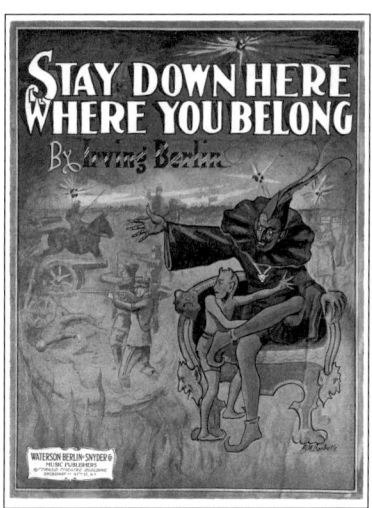

Lyrics: Irving Berlin
Music: Irving Berlin
Artist: Albert Barbelle

New York: Waterson, Berlin & Snyder Co., 1914.

Down below, down below
Sat the devil talking to his son,
Who wanted to go
Up above, up above.
He cried, "It's getting too warm for me down here and so,
I'm going up on earth, where I can have a little fun."
The devil simply shook his head and answered his son:

**CHORUS**
"Stay down here where you belong.
The folks who live above you don't know right from wrong.
To please their kings, they've all gone out to war,
And not a one of them knows what he's fighting for.
'Way up above they say that I'm a devil, and I'm bad.
Kings up there are bigger devils than your dad.
They're breaking the hearts of mothers,
Making butchers out of brothers.
You'll find more hell up there, than there is down below.

Kings up there, they don't care
For the mothers who must stay at home,
Their sorrows to bear.
Stay at home, don't you roam.
Although it's warm down below, you'll find it's warmer up there.
If e'er you went up there, my son, I know you'd be surprised.
You'd find a lot of people who are not civilized.

**REPEAT CHORUS**

# MY ALSACE LORRAINE (ON TO PARIS OR BERLIN)

Lyrics: L. Wolfe Gilbert
Music: Lewis F. Muir
Artist: André De Takacs

New York: F. A. Mills, 1914.

There's a big bound'ry line in my heart.
What to do I am puzzled to know.
There's my daddy, my ma and sweetheart.
They're apart, and it's grieving me so.
Alsace Lorraine holds me, sweetheart,
I don't know which way to go.

**CHORUS**
    Alsace Lorraine, on to Paris or Berlin,
    Come back again, there are hearts that call within.
    Berlin, my father's land,
    Paris, my mother's land,
    Oh, what a plight I am in!
    Alsace Lorraine, on to Paris or Berlin.

If I could, then I would please them all.
That's a thing that is so hard to do.
If I should go and pay one a call,
I'd be grieving the dear other two.
Alsace and Berlin and Paris,
I'll bring them all over here.

**REPEAT CHORUS**

# THE FATHERLAND, THE MOTHERLAND THE LAND OF MY BEST GIRL

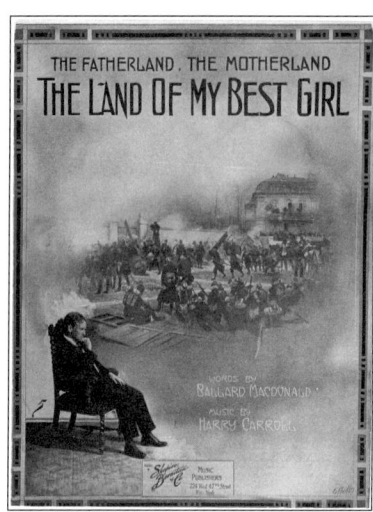

Lyrics: Ballard Macdonald
Music: Harry Carroll
Artist: E. H. Pfeiffer

New York: Shapiro, Bernstein, & Co., 1914.

I'm blue thru and thru,
And I don't know what to do.
In my heart a battle's raging,
All my sympathies engaging.
My mother comes from sunny France,
My daddy from Berlin,
And just across the Channel lies
The land my girl lives in:

**CHORUS**
There's the Fatherland, the Motherland,
And the land of my best girl.
They're all calling me,
And I love the three,
But make up my mind I can't,
For in my heart's a *triple entente*
That beats for one, and beats for all,
Till my poor head's awhirl
Over the Fatherland, the Motherland,
And the land of my best girl.

By day and by night,
All the allies rage their fight,
'Gainst my heart their forces sending,
Gen'ral Love its fort defending.
On one side waves red, white, and blue,
On one red, white, and black,
And yet another side displays
The proud old Union Jack:

**REPEAT CHORUS**

# WE ARE ALL AMERICANS

Words: O. S. Grinnell
Music: O. S. Grinnell
Artist: Glazier Lyceum Print

Chicago: F. G. Dickerson, 1914.

*This is the second printing of ten thousand, as stated on the cover. Also stated on the cover is a dedication: "Dedicated to Those Unemployed as a result of War."*

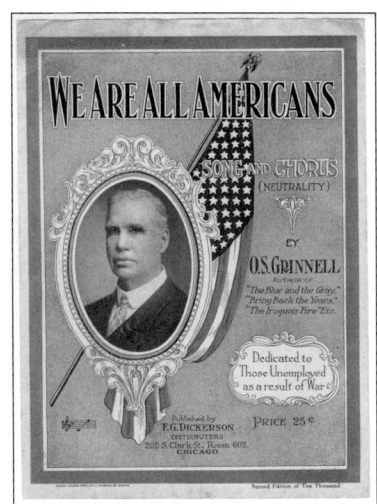

There are feelings in the heart that may cause the tear to start,
As we think what may befall humanity;
Many nations go to fight, and we know not which is right,
Or their plea for cruel war, whate'er it be.

**CHORUS**
   We are all, all, all Americans,
   And neutrality the hour demands,
   Though the clash of arms be heard on land and sea;
   May our country take a final stand
   With a noble purpose, and demand
   That all wars forevermore shall cease to be.

There are many peoples too, some are false and others true,
Coming to United States from all the lands;
Though they speak a different tongue, they are brothers, every one;
'Neath the stars and stripes they're all Americans.

**REPEAT CHORUS**

What our differences may be, what our sympathies may see,
We'll not use, or cause to use, in any way,
To engender mortal strife, mar the nation's peace and life,
Lead to war, an awful war, some future day.

**REPEAT CHORUS**

Money we should freely send, and our doctors, nurses send,
Giving aid to starving, dying misery;
May our country take the stand with full purpose, and demand
That all wars forevermore shall cease to be.

**REPEAT CHORUS**

## THE FINEST FLAG THAT FLIES

Lyrics: Joseph H. Hughes
Music: Harry Richardson

Saginaw: Jos. H. Hughes, 1914.

*This song was reprinted with the same cover design in 1916 and 1917.*

My father said to me one day with teardrops in his eyes,
As I was leaving our old home, he came to say goodbye.
He said, "My boy, now you must know wherever you may roam,
You'll find no land beneath the sun that you would call your home."

**CHORUS**
  "You may be in darkest Russia,
  You may be in sunny Spain,
  You may be in dear old London,
  But you'll long for home again.
  And no matter where you wander,
  You will ever realize
  That this dear old land of Uncle Sam
  Has the finest flag that flies."

There's things I saw so strange to me while I o'er the sea:
Drank beer in dear old Germany, absinthe in gay Paree.
When our old flag I chanced to spy which thrilled me with delight,
I booked my trip for U.S.A. and sailed right home that night.

**REPEAT CHORUS**

# THE WAR IN SNIDER'S GROCERY STORE

Lyrics: "Hank" Hancock, Ballard MacDonald, and Harry Carroll
Music: "Hank" Hancock, Ballard MacDonald, and Harry Carroll
Artist: D

New York: Shapiro, Bernstein & Co. Inc., 1914.

Hans Gustav Snider, a local provider
Of groceries, canned goods and such,
Had read of the war, till himself and the store
Were both what is known as "In Dutch."
His brains he'd been feeding on so much war reading,
He woke up one night in a fright:
He rushed down the stairs, fell over two chairs,
And turned up the groc'ry store light:

**CHORUS**
   There were eggshells bursting near and far
   Above the Russian caviar
   A Bismarck herring by itself
   Was pushing all the French peas off the shelf.
   An Irish potato started to cry,
   When a Spanish onion hit its eye.
   Frankfurters fighting all over the floor,
   Howling and growling: "We're the dogs of war!"

There was "Sunny Jim," upon his horse,
Swooping down with all his "force."
The paprika growing weaker, shouted out:
"Won't you open that door?"
And a couple of tough Vienna rolls,
Shot a poor Swiss cheese all full of holes,
In the terrible war in Snider's groc'ry store.

Dutch pumpernickel had joined a dill pickle
Attacking the fresh navy beans.
A Limburger cheese greatly strengthened the breeze,
And anchovies, prunes and sardines
Were fighting an army of dago salami.
And that's only half what he saw.
He jumped into bed, put ice on his head,
And went on the wagon once more.

**REPEAT CHORUS**

# SISTER SUSIE'S SEWING SHIRTS FOR SOLDIERS

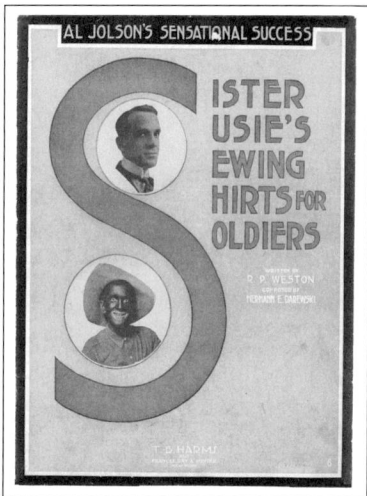

Lyrics: R. P. Weston
Music: Hermann E. Darewski

New York: T. B. Harms and Francis, Day & Hunter, 1914.

*This song was in the top 20 from December 1914 to May 1915 and reached number 9 in February and March. It was performed on stage by Al Jolson and recorded by Billy Murray.*

Sister Susie's sewing in the kitchen on a "Singer,"
There's miles and miles of flannel on the floor and up the stairs,
And father says its rotten getting mixed up with the cotton
And sitting on the needles that she leaves upon the chairs.
And should you knock at our street door, Ma whispers, "Come inside."
Then when you ask where Susie is, she says with loving pride:

**CHORUS**
  "Sister Susie's sewing shirts for soldiers.
  Such skill at sewing shirts our shy young sister Susie shows!
  Some soldiers send epistles, say they'd sooner sleep in thistles
  Than the saucy, soft, short shirts for soldiers sister Susie sews."

Piles and piles and piles of shirts she sends out to the soldiers,
And sailors won't be jealous when they see them, not at all.
And when we say her stitching will set all the soldiers itching,
She says our soldiers fight best when their back's against the wall.
And little brother Gussie, he who lisps when he says "yes,"
Says, "Where's the cotton gone from off my kite? Oh, I can gueth!"

**REPEAT CHORUS**

I forgot to tell you that our sister Susie's married,
And when she isn't sewing shirts, she's sewing other things.
Then little sister Molly says, "Oh, sister bought a dolly.
She's making all the clothes for it with plenty bows and strings.
Says Susie, "Don't be silly," as she blushes and she sighs.
Then mother smiles and whispers with a twinkle in her eyes:

**REPEAT CHORUS**

# HURRAH! HURRAH FOR THE CHRISTMAS SHIP

Lyrics: Henry S. Sawyer
Music: Henry S. Sawyer

Chicago and New York: McKinley Music Co., 1914.

*A special note is printed at the bottom of the cover: "This is the Great 'Children's Rally Song' of the Nation-Wide Movement for the Children of America to send a Shipload of Toys and gifts to the Children of Europe made Orphans and Homeless by the Great War."*

Come, boys and girls, just listen to
This news for you and me:
They're going to send a Christmas Ship
Across the great blue sea!
It's going to be all filled with gifts
For families abroad
Who've suffered in this cruel war
From fire, gun and sword.
Now all the boys and all the girls
Will ev'ry effort bend
To see how many useful things
They to the ship can send;
But *I* was thinking we could do
About as much *real* good
By sending money from our banks
As *well* as clothes and food.

**CHORUS**

   Hurrah! hurrah for the Christmas Ship
   As it starts across the sea
   With its load of gifts and its *greater* load
   Of loving sympathy.
   Let's wave our hats and clap our hands
   As we send it on its trip;
   May many a heart and home be cheered
   By the gifts in the Christmas Ship!

The paper says there's thousands who
Are homeless thro' the war;
That Santa Claus can't *half* get 'round
As he has done before.
So this year *we'll* help Santa Claus
Remember each poor child,
And bring a smile of happiness
Amid those terrors wild.
Let Dorothy and Mary send
A pair of shoes apiece,
And little Jane can send the dime
She got from Aunt Bernice,
While Tom and all the boys and girls
Are eager to pitch in
To make this Christmas time the best
The world has ever seen.

**REPEAT CHORUS**

1915

# I DIDN'T RAISE MY BOY TO BE A SOLDIER

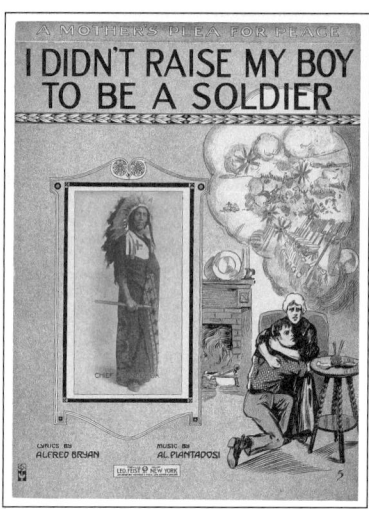

Lyrics: Alfred Bryan
Music: Al Piantadosi
Artist: Rosenbaum Studios

New York: Leo Feist, Inc., 1915.

*A note above the title of the song reads: "Respectfully dedicated to Every Mother — Everywhere." This song was in the top 20 from January to July 1915 and reached number 1 in March and April. Other featured singers include the American Comedy Four (twice), Josephine Davis, Mae Francis, Gene Greene, McCormack & Irving, Ed Morton, (twice), Ruby Raymond & Fred Heider, Chee Toy, and Will Ward (twice). The song was recorded by both Morton Harvey and the Peerless Quartet.*

Ten million soldiers to the war have gone
Who may never return again.
Ten million mothers' hearts must break
For the ones who died in vain.
Head bowed down in sorrow
In her lonely years,
I heard a mother murmur thro' her tears:

**CHORUS**
"I didn't raise my boy to be a soldier,
I brought him up to be my pride and joy.
Who dares to place a musket on his shoulder,
To shoot some other mother's darling boy?
Let nations arbitrate their future troubles,
It's time to lay the sword and gun away.
There'd be no war today,
If mothers all would say,
'I didn't raise my boy to be a soldier.'"

What victory can cheer a mother's heart,
When she looks at her blighted home?
What victory can bring her back
All she cared to call her own?
Let each mother answer
In the years to be,
"Remember that my boy belongs to me!"

**REPEAT CHORUS**

# I DIDN'T RAISE MY DOG TO BE A SAUSAGE

Lyrics: Chas. McCarron
Music: Herman Paley
Artist: Starmer

New York and Detroit: Jerome H. Remick & Co., 1915.

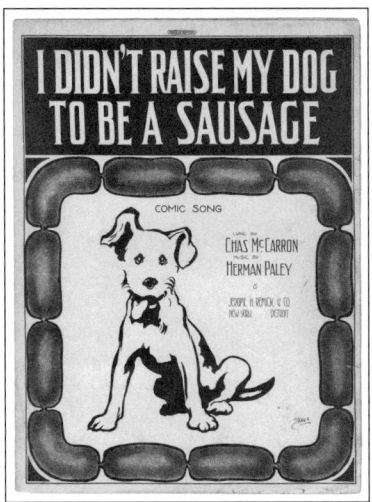

14

Mary Noodle had a poodle and she loved him so!
Mary'd never go out with any beau.
Fellows called, but Mary stalled, it wasn't any use;
At the door she'd always meet them with the same excuse:
"I can't go out with you, but this is what I'll do:"

**CHORUS**
  "I'll let you take my dog out for a ramble,
  But you be sure and bring him back to me.
  I raised him from a pup and now that he's grown up,
  I know he'll want to chase the chickens when he's free.
  Among the fields of clover, let him gambol,
  Why you can even trust him on a bridge!
  But never let him hop
  Into a butcher's shop.
  I didn't raise my dog to be a sausage!"

Mary Noodle's little poodle swam across the sea.
Landed in Paree, "Dog of war" was he.
"Gen'ral Lala" bought a collar, said, "This dog is mine,"
And to keep him safe, he tied him to the firing line.
Amid the shot and shell a soldier heard him yell:

**CHORUS**
  "I'll let you take my dog out on a ramble,
  But you be sure and bring him back to me.
  Steer clear of Bertha Krupp, she'll blow the poor pup up.
  I know he likes to chase the chickens when he's free.
  Among the fields of clover let him gambol,
  Why you can even trust him on a bridge!
  But look out, he is French!
  Don't go near a German trench!
  I didn't raise my dog to be a sausage!"

# DON'T TAKE MY DARLING BOY AWAY

Lyrics: Will Dillon
Music: Albert Von Tilzer
Artist: André De Takacs

New York: Broadway Music Corporation, 1915.

*This song was reprinted at least once.*

A mother was kneeling to pray
For loved ones at war far away,
And there by her side
Her one joy and pride
Knelt down with her that day.
Then came a knock on the door,
"Your boy is commanded to war."
"No, Captain, please,
Here on my knees
I plead for one I adore."

**CHORUS**
   "Don't take my darling boy away from me,
   Don't send him off to war.
   You took his father and brothers three,
   Now you come back for more.
   Who are the heroes that fight your wars?
   Mothers, who have no say.
   But my duty's done, so for God's sake leave one,
   And don't take my darling boy away.

A hero is now laid to rest,
A hero and one of the best.
She fought with each son,
The battles he'd won,
And the battles that proved a test;
Tho' she never went to war,
She was the hero by far.
They gave the guns
But who gave the sons?:
M-O-T-H-E-R.

**REPEAT CHORUS**

# LAY DOWN YOUR ARMS

Lyrics: Louise Small
Music: Charles James
Artist: André De Takacs

New York: The Cadillac Music Co., 1915.

In the hearts of many mothers there is sorrow,
On the eyes of many mothers there are tears,
On the lips of many mothers and the lips of many others
There's a prayer for those held precious all these years.
If their mother's voice could reach them far away,
They'd seem to hear their dear old mother say:

**CHORUS**
"Lay down your arms, my boy, my boy,
Let us have universal peace.
God only knows there has been bloodshed enough,
It's time the shot and shell should cease.
Mothers are weeping day by day
For their pride and joy.
Your father lost his life that way.
If he was here right now he'd say,
'Put that sword and gun away,
Lay down your arms my boy.'"

In the homes of many mothers there's a picture,
In the eyes of many soldiers he was brave.
But today that dear old mother she must place beside the other
A picture of the son she could not save.
Now if years ago the mothers had their say,
They'd have their darling boy with them today.

**REPEAT CHORUS**

# WHEN THE LUSITANIA WENT DOWN

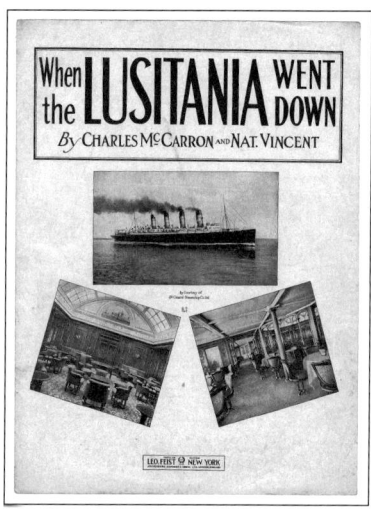

Lyrics: Charles McCarron and Nat Vincent
Music: Charles McCarron and Nat Vincent

New York: Leo. Feist, Inc. 1915.

*This song was also issued without any photographs on the cover.*

The nation is sad as can be,
A message came over the sea.
A thousand or more, who sailed from our shore,
Have gone to eternity.
The Statue of Liberty high
Must now have a tear in her eye.
I think, it's a shame,
Someone is to blame,
But all we can do is just sigh!

**CHORUS**
"Some of us lost a true sweetheart,
Some of us lost a dear dad,
Some lost their mothers, sisters and brothers,
Some lost the best friends they had.
It's time they were stopping this warfare,
If women and children must drown.
Many brave hearts went to sleep in the deep,
When the Lusitania went down."

A lesson to all it should be,
When we feel like crossing the sea.
American ships that sail from our slips
Are safer for you and me.
A Yankee can go anywhere,
As long as Old Glory is there.
Altho' they were warned,
The warning they scorned,
And now we must cry in despair:

**REPEAT CHORUS**

# WE'RE ALL WITH YOU, MISTER WILSON

Lyrics: Bernie Grossman, Herman Jacobson, and Maurice Abrahams
Music: Bernie Grossman, Herman Jacobson, and Maurice Abrahams
Artist: Albert Barbelle

New York: Maurice Abrahams Music Co. Inc., 1915.

From shore to shore we sorrow for
Those who forever sleep.
With sadness and sighs we turn our eyes
To one who our honor will keep.
United we stand, a great mighty land,
Our faith in you we'll show.
Whatever you do, we'll follow you,
We're here to let you know.

**CHORUS**
We're all with you, Mister Wilson, in ev'ry
   thing you do,
Waiting your call, you'll find us all,
Steady and ready, whate'er befall.
Just like our fathers before us,

We're here to dare and do
For our country's cause and right.
If we must, then we will fight.
Mister Wilson, we're with you.

We hope and pray that we will stay
Peaceful with all the world,
That our flag that flies high in the skies,
In war it shall not be unfurled.
Although if we must, our cause it is just,
We'll give our ev'ry best.
No matter what's done, we'll be as one,
To prove through ev'ry test.

**REPEAT CHORUS**

# GO RIGHT ALONG, MISTER WILSON
# (AND WE'LL ALL STAND BY YOU)

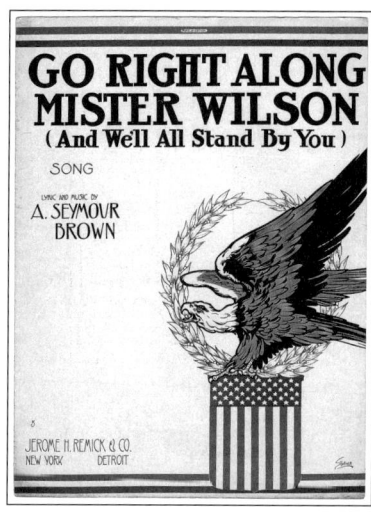

Lyrics: A. Seymour Brown
Music: A. Seymour Brown
Artist: Starmer

New York and Detroit: Jerome H. Remick & Co., 1915.

Dark clouds gather in the eastern sky,
People are excited ev'rywhere;
Wise men shake their heads and heave a sigh,
There's a spirit of war in the air.
But down in Washington is a man,
Who is watching night and day:
He'll do his best for ev'ryone,
And I think ev'rybody should say:

**CHORUS**
 "Go right along, Mister Wilson,
 We're all for you strong.
 You speak for us as a nation,
 And we're for the nation right or wrong.
 In war or peace it's just the same,
 We'll leave that up to you.
 We know that you will do the best that can be done,
 For it is one for all; and all are for that one,
 And so you go right along, Mister Wilson,
 And we'll all stand by you."

Those who lose upon the battlefield,
Never will return to us again;
Wilson knows the sorrows of a war,
And he's trying to spare us the pain.
But even he may have to call on you,
And so prepare to play your part:
Polish your gun while you pray for peace,
And say to him with all your heart:

**REPEAT CHORUS**

# I THINK WE'VE GOT ANOTHER WASHINGTON (AND WILSON IS HIS NAME)

Lyrics: George Fairman
Music: George Fairman
Artist: Einson

New York: Kendis-Brockman Music Co. Inc., 1915.

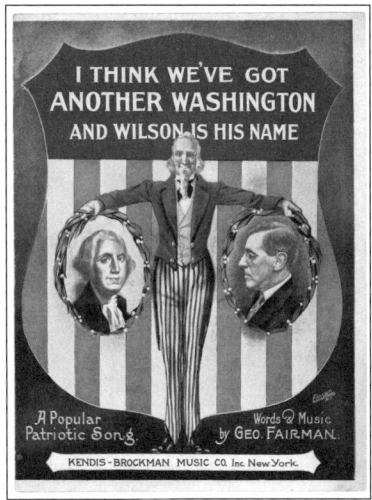

20

When Yankee Doodle came to town,
He brought a man of great renown
And called him Georgie Washington.
When things are mighty blue,
He knew just what to do
To save the old Red, White, and Blue.
Conditions are about the same today,
And I'm mighty proud to say:

**CHORUS**
 "I think we've got another Washington,
 Someone who's just as good as he can be.
 He's called the man of peace, no matter
   where he goes.
 He's just the one for me.

 It takes a little time for him to make up his
   mind,
 But he get's there just the same.
 I think we've got another Washington,
 And Wilson is his name."

I can't forget George Washington.
The things that he has said and done
Have all gone down in history.
To set our country free,
He fought for you and me;
He fought for peace and liberty.
And if our Yankee fathers lived today,
Ev'ryone I'm sure would say:

**REPEAT CHORUS**

# WE'RE GOING TO CELEBRATE THE END OF WAR IN RAGTIME
# (BE SURE THAT WOODROW WILSON LEADS THE BAND)

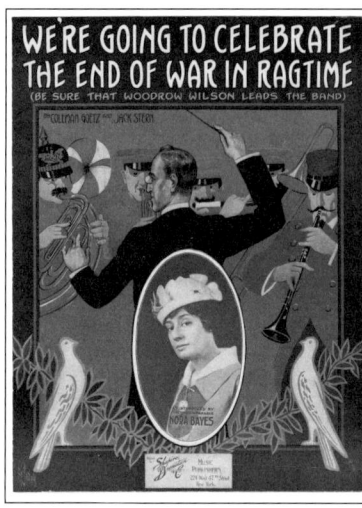

Lyrics: Coleman Goetz and Jack Stern
Music: Coleman Goetz and Jack Stern
Artist: André De Takacs

New York: Shapiro, Bernstein & Co. Inc., 1915.

Ev'rybody's asking when
We will be at peace again.
Ev'rybody wants prosperity.
I hear many people say,
"Lay the sword and gun away,"
But still they're fighting 'cross the sea.
The end must come, it's true,
That's why I say to you:

**CHORUS**
   "We're going to celebrate the end of war in
      ragtime.
   Ev'ry nation soon will sing in rag rhyme,
   England, France, and Germany,
   Even folks from Italy.
   The Aristocrats,
   And the Diplomats,
   Marching arm in arm,

   See them tip their hats
   To a raggy melody (so pretty);
   Ev'rywhere there's harmony,
   So when we celebrate the end of war in
      ragtime,
   Be sure that Woodrow Wilson leads the
      band."

Ev'ryone will feel so gay
There'll be one long holiday,
When each nation claims neutrality;
There'll be lots of waving flags
Waving to the raggy rags.
Each one will have their liberty.
With peace in ev'ry land,
I trust you'll understand:

**REPEAT CHORUS**

# WE'LL NEVER LET OUR OLD FLAG FALL

Lyrics: Albert E. MacNutt
Music: M. F. Kelly
Artist: Starmer

New York: Chappell & Co., Ltd., 1915.

*This song was printed at least two other times: both without the various prices stated, with one also lacking the musical notation at the very top.*

22

Stars and Stripes, the emblem of our nation,
Grand old flag of strength and unity,
Best old flag that waves in all creation,
Our Stars and Stripes, the flag of liberty.
Stars and Stripes, our flag of grace and
  beauty,
Each brave heart will answer to thy call.
Hand in hand, we stand, to do our duty,
And we'll never let the old flag fall.

**CHORUS**
  We'll never let our old flag fall,
  For we love it best of all.
  We don't want to fight to show our might,
  But when we start, we'll fight, fight, fight.
  In peace or war, our voices ring.

  "My country, 'tis of thee," we sing.
  At the sound of her call,
  We'll show them all,
  We'll never let our old flag fall.

Stars and Stripes, wave on, wave on, forever,
O'er a land of peace and purity,
Bond of love that discord cannot sever,
Our dear old emblem of security.
Stars and Stripes, our flag of fame and story,
Each heart throbs, in answer to thy call.
Side by side, we'll fight for our Old Glory,
And we'll never let the old flag fall.

**REPEAT CHORUS**

# IF THEY WANT TO FIGHT, ALL RIGHT
# (BUT "NEUTRAL" IS MY MIDDLE NAME)

Lyrics: Jack Frost and James White
Music: Jack Frost and James White

Chicago and New York: Frank K. Root & Co., 1915.

I heard the newsboys crying latest war news of the day,
I saw the people buying and the crowds begin to sway,
But what seemed to me so funny in that big crowd that I spied
Were English, French and Germans there, all standing side by side.
The German said, "Zwei tausend uf dem Enklish kilt — dot's fine."
The English said, "I hear they've pawned the watch upon the Rhine;"
And little old yours truly of the good old U. S. A.
Said, "It's a sad, sad story, but here's all I've got to say:"

**CHORUS**
"If they want to fight, all right, all right,
I'm over here, they're over there,
So I don't care;
Over here in America, I heard somebody say
That he who fights and runs away
Will live to fight some other day.
For I'm here and they're there,
So what do I care,
Because it's 'Home, Sweet Home' just the same.
While I'm as happy as can be
Behind the Statue of Liberty,
For 'neutral' is my middle name."

Said Mike McDever, "Did you ever hear the likes o' these?
They say the Frenchmen shot the holes we see in Sweitzercheese."
Then said someone to McDever there, "Say, Mike, why do you frown?"
Said he, "Because old Pilsner beer goes up instead of down.
The army with the longest legs is what I'm betting on,
For when it comes to battle they can do some marathon;
And I'll believe most anything that anybody tells
But that the Frenchmen saw the 'English' on the German shells."

**CHORUS**
  "If they want to fight, all right, all right,
  I'm over here, they're over there,
  So I don't care;
  Over here in America, I heard somebody say
  That he who fights and runs away
  Will live to fight some other day.
  For I'm here and they're there,
  So what do I care,
  Because it's 'Home, Sweet Home' just the same.
  The enemy can do their worst,
  But believe in safety first,
  For 'neutral' is my middle name."

## I'D BE PROUD TO BE THE MOTHER OF A SOLDIER

Lyrics: Charles Bayha
Music: Charles Bayha
Artist: André De Takacs

New York: Shapiro, Bernstein, and Co., Inc., 1915.

Seated 'round the table were mother and dad,
And their darling lad.
He was all they had.
"It's not right that men should fight,"
He wisely shook his head.
"Each soldier brave, his nation's slave, goes out to die," he said.
His mother sadly smiled and sighed,
And as she took him in her arms, replied:

**CHORUS**
  "You'd do the same thing, if it should come tomorrow,
  You'd do the same thing, altho' you'd cause me sorrow.
  Just like your dad before, you'd march away to war,
  And the same as any other, leave your sweetheart and your mother.

Now that the others are fighting, I pray for peace, it's true,
But it would be a diff'rent story,
If they trampled on Old Glory.
I'd be proud to be the mother of a soldier."

While the father listened, his heart filled with pride.
"You're right, dear!" he cried.
"Now to keep peace we've tried,
But the game we'll play the same
As Washington would do,
And if we must, we will or bust for old Red, White, and Blue.
Let's hope we'll never see the day,
But still I'm glad to hear your mother say:"

**REPEAT CHORUS**

# YOU'LL BE THERE!

Lyrics: J. Keirn Brennan
Music: Ernest R. Ball
Artist: Dunk

New York, Chicago, and London: M. Witmark and Sons, 1915.

Our forefathers came across the sea,
Pioneered the way to liberty,
Builded up a country state by state
From the Hudson to the Golden Gate,
Fought and wrought for us a wondrous land,
Formed a nation with a master hand.
If to tear it down someone should try,
Would you stand idly by?

**CHORUS**
If the time should come when we must go to war,
You'll be there,
You'll be there!
You will go just like your daddy did before.
If they dare, we'll prepare,
For our race was never known to run.
Should they come, we'll meet them gun to gun,
North and south, yes, ev'ry mothers's son,
You'll be there!
You'll be there!

Pilgrim fathers came with heart and hand,
Hewed their homes from out a savage land,
Left the fire of freedom burning clear
From New England to the last frontier,
Crossed a continent in wagon trains,
Spreading peace beyond the farthest plain.
If this peace were threatened by some foe,
To stop them, would you go?

**REPEAT CHORUS**

## WHO'LL TAKE CARE OF THE HAREM WHEN THE SULTAN GOES TO WAR?

Lyrics: Jimmie Kaufmann and Archie Mayer
Music: William J. Lewis
Artist: E. H. Pfeiffer

New York: Maurice Richmond Music Co. Inc., 1915.

I can't sleep a wink at night, I'm worried all the day;
To find out a certain thing I've tried in ev'ry way.
I have even gone so far to cable 'cross the sea,
Just to see if there's a way to solve this mystery.

**CHORUS**
Who'll take care of the harem
When the Sultan goes to war?
He's gone out in a world of harm,
Leaving behind a poultry farm.
He would die for Turkey,
But he loves his chicken more.
That's the job I'd like to get, I wish it were for keeps,
And I would do more in one day than Paul did in three weeks,
If he'd let me mind his harem,
When the Sultan goes to war

I know why dear Turkey was the last to go to war.
If the Sultan had no harem, he'd been there before.
He tried hard to get a man to take care of his wives.
Over here they look for jobs like that all thru their lives.

**CHORUS**
Who'll take care of the harem
When the Sultan goes to war?
He's gone out in a world of harm,
Leaving behind a poultry farm.
He would die for Turkey,
But he loves his chicken more.
If I were his majesty, in leaves I'd dress them all
And then I'd close the window when the leaves began to fall,
If he'd let me mind his harem,
When the Sultan goes to war.

# WHEN GERMANY LICKS ENGLAND OLD IRELAND WILL BE FREE

Lyrics: Charles A. Meyers
Music: Charles A. Meyers

Kenosha: Independent Music Publishers, 1915.

When Germany licks England, old Ireland will be free,
And mighty proud we'll be of dear old Germany.
The jinx is on the Belgians, the French and Russians, too,
And England's best like all the rest, they don't know what to do.
Defeated soon they'll be, they're all up in a tree,
For Germany spells victory on any land or sea.

**CHORUS**
   Oh, Germany, oh, Germany,
   Fight on to victory.
   'Tho you may be on land or sea,
   Old Ireland's by your side.
   So strain each gun and make them run,
   Pull down their haughty pride.
   Then dear old Ireland will be free
   So fight on to victory.

We're proud that there's a country like dear old Germany.
That conquers when it fights like Ireland for its rights.
The "Johnny Bulls," the Belgians, the French and Russians, too,
They all may fight, but Germany has told us what she'll do.
She'll set old Ireland free, so take this tip from me.
With just one gun the Kaiser is the man that makes them run.

**REPEAT CHORUS**

# AMERICA, I LOVE YOU

Lyrics: Edgar Leslie
Music: Archie Gottler
Artist: Albert Barbelle

New York: Kalmar, Puck & Abrahams Consolidated, Inc., 1915.

*This song was in the top 20 from November 1915 to April 1916 and reached number 2 in January. Other featured singers with this cover design include Abbott & White, Murray Bennett, Granis & Granis, and Evelyn Phillips. Other printings with a similar cover design feature singers including Amy Butler, Anna Chandler, Larry Comer, Wellington Cross, Thomas Potter Dunne, Daisy Leon, Madge P. Maitland, Genia Raie, Eshell Roberts, Sophie Tucker, Tom Ward & Dolly McCue, Fannie Watson, and Elsie White. The song was recorded by both the American Quartet and Sam Ash.*

Amid fields of clover,
'Twas just a little over
A hundred years ago,
A handful of strangers,
They faced many dangers
To make their country grow.
It's now quite a nation
Of wond'rous population,
And free from ev'ry king.
It's your land, it's my land,
A great do-or-die land,
And that's just why I sing:

**CHORUS**
"America, I love you,
You're like a sweetheart of mine.
From ocean to ocean
For you my devotion
Is touching each bound'ry line.
Just like a little baby
Climbing its mother's knee,
America, I love you,
And there's a hundred million others like me."

From all sorts of places,
They welcomed all the races
To settle on their shore.
They didn't care which one,
The poor or the rich one,
They still had room for more.
To give them protection
By popular election,
A set of laws they chose.
They're your laws and my laws,
For your cause and my cause,
That's why this country rose.

**REPEAT CHORUS**

# THE LITTLE GREY MOTHER WHO WAITS ALL ALONE

Lyrics: Bernard Grossman
Music: Harry De Costa

New York, Chicago et al.: M. Witmark & Sons, 1915.

*This song was in the top 20 from November 1915 to February 1916 and reached number 11 in December. It was reprinted at least once and was recorded by both Jim Doherty and James Reed & James F. Harrison.*

The toys that brought joy to her little boy
Are scattered about on the floor;
The sword that his father before him had used
Is gone from its place by the door.
The lad, like his dad, now is sleeping.
Far away, night and day, someone's weeping.

**CHORUS**
There's a little grey mother who waits all alone
In a chill, dreary spot that was once Home, Sweet Home.
While gen'rals are saying, "This fight must be won!"
She's sadly praying, "Please send back my son!"

When the battles are over and peace once more reigns,
When the cost and the lost will be known,
Will kings give a thought to the heartaches they've brought
To that little grey mother alone?

Each pray'r that she'd make was just for his sake,
She shared all his joys and his tears;
At thought of his manhood her heart beat with pride
While dreaming of sweet future years.
But now there's a brow marked with yearning
For the boy who will ne'er be returning.

**REPEAT CHORUS**

# DON'T BITE THE HAND THAT'S FEEDING YOU

Lyrics: Thomas Hoier
Music: Jimmie Morgan

New York: Leo. Feist, Inc., 1915.

*This song was in the top 20 from February to April of 1916 and reached number 10 in March. It was reprinted at least four times, each time with the same photograph of Ed Morton and was recorded by both Irving Kaufman and Albert Campbell & Henry Burr.*

Last night, as I lay a-sleeping,
A wonderful dream came to me.
I saw Uncle Sammy weeping
For his children over the sea;
They had come to him, friendless and starving,
When from tyrant's oppression they fled,
But now they abuse and revile him,
Till as last in just anger he said:

**CHORUS**
  "If you don't like your Uncle Sammy,
  Then go back to your home o'er the sea,
  To the land from where you came,
  Whatever be its name,
  But don't be ungrateful to me!

If you don't like the stars in Old Glory,
If you don't like the Red, White, and Blue,
Then don't act like the cur in the story,
Don't bite the hand that's feeding you!"

"You recall the day you landed,
How I welcomed you to my shore?
When you came here empty handed,
And allegiance forever you swore,
I gathered you close to my bosom.
Of food and of clothes you got both,
So, when in trouble I need you,
You will have to remember your oath:"

**REPEAT CHORUS**

# WHEN OUR MOTHERS RULE THE WORLD

Lyrics: Alfred Bryan
Music: Jack Wells
Artist: Starmer

New York and Detroit: Jerome H. Remick & Co., 1915.

31

Camp fires gleaming
Soldiers are dreaming
Sobs one lonesome lad:
"I left her sighing, I left her crying;
She was all I had.
While men rule our nations,
Sweethearts and mothers must cry.
Men in their madness caused all the sadness."
And then they heard him sigh:

**CHORUS**
   "There would be no sweethearts crying,
   If our mothers had their say.
   There would be no lovers dying
   In the trenches far away.
   There would be no armies marching
   And no battle flags unfurled.
   Let us kneel and pray
   We'll live to see the day
   When our mothers rule the world."

Up spoke another,
"I'm with you brother.
All you say is right.
Where is the mother would see another
Send her boy to fight?
Men made all those cannons;
Men made the shot and the shell.
While men are slaying, mothers are praying,
Praying that all is well."

**REPEAT CHORUS**

# PACK UP YOUR TROUBLES IN YOUR OLD KIT-BAG AND SMILE, SMILE, SMILE

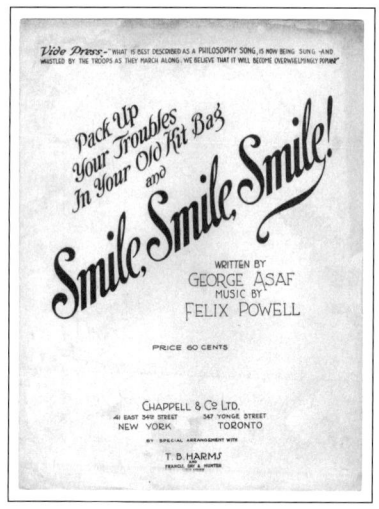

Lyrics: George Asaf
Music: Felix Powell

New York and Toronto: Chappell & Co. Ltd., 1915.

*This song was first performed in London in 1915 and subsequently became a standard marching song in the army. In America it was featured in the show* Her Soldier Boy, *which opened in December 1916. It was in the top 20 from February to September 1917 and reached number 2 in June. It was recorded by Edward Hamilton, the Victor Military Band, James F. Harrison, Murray Johnson, Reinald Werrenrath, and the Knickerbocker Quartet.*

Private Perks is a funny little codger
With a smile, a funny smile.
Five feet none, he's an artful little dodger
With a smile, a funny smile.
Flush or broke he'll have his little joke,
He can't be suppress'd.
All the other fellows have to grin,
When he gets this off his chest,
Hi!

**CHORUS**
  "Pack up your troubles in your old kit-bag,
  And smile, smile, smile;
  While you've a lucifer to light your fag,
  Smile, boys, that's the style.
  What's the use of worrying?
  It never was worthwhile, so
  Pack up your troubles in your old kit-bag,
  And smile, smile, smile."

Private Perks went a-marching into Flanders
With his smile, his funny smile.
He was lov'd by the privates and the
  commanders
For his smile, his funny smile.
When a throng of Bosches came along,
With a mighty swing,
Perks yell'd out, "This little bunch is mine!
Keep your heads down, boys, and sing,
Hi!"

**REPEAT CHORUS**

Private Perks he came back from Bosche
  shooting
With his smile, his funny smile.
Round his home he then set about recruiting
With his smile, his funny smile.
He told all his pals, the short, the tall,
What a time he'd had;
And as each enlisted like a man
Private Perks said, "Now my lad,
Hi!"

**REPEAT CHORUS**

# KEEP THE HOME-FIRES BURNING (TILL THE BOYS COME HOME)

Lyrics: Lena Guilbert Ford
Music: Ivor Novello

New York: Chappell & Co. Ltd., 1915.

*This song, entitled "'Till the Boys Come Home," was first published in London in October 1914. It was in the top 20 from February to April 1916 and again from July 1917 to April 1918, reaching number 7 in October and November. It was recorded by John McCormack, Frederick J. Wheeler and Reed Miller & Frederick Wheeler.*

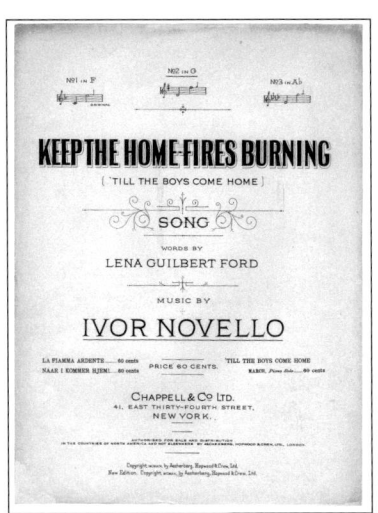

They were summoned from the hillside,
They were called in from the glen,
And the country found them ready
At the stirring call for men.
Let no tears add to their hardship,
As the soldiers pass along,
And although your heart is breaking,
Make it sing this cheery song:

**CHORUS**
  "Keep the home-fires burning,
  While your hearts are yearning.
  Though your lads are far away
  They dream of home;
  There's a silver lining
  Through the dark cloud shining.
  Turn the dark cloud inside out,
  Till the boys come home."

Over seas there came a pleading,
"Help a nation in distress!"
And we gave our glorious laddies;
Honour made us do no less,
For no gallant son of freedom
To a tyrant's yoke should bend,
And a noble heart must answer
To the sacred call of "Friend."

**REPEAT CHORUS**

1916

# WE ARE A PEACEFUL NATION

Lyrics: Darl MacBoyle
Music: R. Kenneth Dawson
Artist: USA

Newark: Francklyn Wallace, 1916.

The mighty sound of battle
Can be heard across the sea,
And to every nation fighting,
We all give our sympathy.
Although our tears are falling,
We are not cowards but men,
But there's some who have forgotten,
And they must be told again.

**CHORUS**
  We are a peaceful nation,
  But lest they misunderstand,
  Just say the dove and eagle,
  They both nest in Yankee land,

For each one would answer ready,
As his daddy did before,
And from Maine to California,
There's a hundred million more.

Across the briney ocean
Sailed the Pilgrim Fathers bold,
And they brought to us a treasure
That is greater far than gold.
The only king we'll bow to
Is the one on heaven's throne,
But we'll stay a peaceful nation,
If they just let us alone.

**REPEAT CHORUS**

# THE BATTLE CRY OF PEACE

Lyrics: Bert Sherry
Music: Sammy Powers

Boston and New York: Daly Music Publisher Inc., 1916.

35

In Europe they've taught us the meaning of war,
Battle without cease;
The burst of the shrapnel, the cannon's roar
Teach us the lesson of peace.
We have seen the fire and pillage
In ev'ry Belgian village,
We've heard the call for help across the sea.
But now that we have seen
What war may really mean,
Let us prepare to keep our nation free.

**CHORUS**
   "Put your gun on your shoulder, be ready for war."
   That's the battle cry of peace.
   For we can't stand back when the foes attack,
   Striving for our home and country.

We need an army to fight for our flag
And a larger navy too.
With peace forever, we'll still be able to shout out
The battle cry of freedom.

When foeman shall come with their millions of men,
Ships and cannon too,
If we've not made our defences then
What is our nation to do?
Will we bow before the raider,
And yield to the invader,
Or will we stand and see our cities burn?
For when the awful war
Shall reach our peaceful shore,
It will be too late for us all to learn.

**REPEAT CHORUS**

# I'M GOING TO RAISE MY BOY TO BE A SOLDIER AND A CREDIT TO THE U.S.A.

Lyrics: J. Will Callahan
Music: Leo Friedman

Chicago and New York: Frank K. Root & Co., 1916.

A father and a mother fondly watching
The playful antics of their only son,
A manly lad of seven proudly marching
Around the hall with soldier suit and gun.
"I hate to think someday the call of battle
Will take our darling boy," the father sighed.
The mother drew him near,
Her eyes grew dim with tears,
Yet bravely to his father she replied:

**CHORUS**
  "I'm going to raise my boy to be a soldier,
  To serve his country when and where he can.
  I'll teach him to be true to the old red,
    white, and blue,
  I want him to be ev'ry inch a man.
  If war should come, my heart would break
    with sorrow,
  And yet I'd proudly bid him march away.
  I'm going to raise my boy to be a soldier,
  And a credit to the U.S.A."

With measured step and brown eyes brightly
  flashing,
The youthful hero once more faced the foe;
In silent pride the parents watched their
  loved one,
Within their tear-dimmed eyes their love
  aglow.
"God grant that war may never take him
  from us,"
The father spoke again and bowed his head.
"My heart repeats that pray'r,"
The mother whispered there,
Yet with a steady voice again she said:

**REPEAT CHORUS**

# ARE YOU HALF THE MAN YOUR MOTHER THOUGHT YOU'D BE

Lyrics: Leo Wood
Music: Harry De Costa
Artist: Rosenbaum Studios

New York: Leo. Feist, Inc., 1916.

Have you ever stopped to think of how you sat at mother's knee,
While she planned your future with you, pictured what man you'd be?
And you threw your arms around her, promised all you'd do someday,
The happiness you'd bring to her, when she was old and grey?

**CHORUS**
Have you kept your promise to her
That you made while on her knee?
Can you truly say
You're half the man today
That she always thought you'd be?
Is she proud to be your mother?
Is it joy or sorrow in her eyes you see?
Are you all she planned and prayed for,
All she raked and scrap'd and slaved for?
Are you half the man your mother thought you'd be?

There are times, when first a thought of her and days that used to be,
Make you wish that you were half that man she longed to live to see;
Though she may not be with you, still she's watching from above
To see if you are going to repay her for her love.

**REPEAT CHORUS**

# WAKE UP, AMERICA!

Lyrics: George Graff, Jr.
Music: Jack Glogau
Artist: Rosenbaum Studios

New York: Leo. Feist, Inc., 1916.

*This song was reprinted at least twice.*

Have we forgotten, America,
The battles our fathers fought?
Are we ashamed of our history
In the peace that fighting brought?
Must we be laughed at, America,
While our swords turn weak with rust?
Is the blood of our fathers wasted?
And how have we treated their trust?
Is Columbia the gem of the ocean?
Is Old Glory the pride of the free?
Let's forget ev'ry selfish emotion,
United forever let's be!

**CHORUS**
  Wake up, America!
  If we are called to war,
  Are we prepared to give our lives
  For our sweethearts and our wives?
  Are our mothers and our home worth
    fighting for?

  Let us pray, God, for peace, but peace with
    honor,
  But let's get ready to answer duty's call.
  So when Old Glory stands unfurled,
  Let it mean to all the world
  America is ready, that's all!

Do you remember George Washington
That winter at Valley Forge?
Jackson and Custer and Farragut,
And of Perry at Fort George?
McKinley and Lincoln were fighting men,
And the heroes our country knew,
Simply crowd thru our hist'ry pages,
Just think what they're done all for you!
Made Columbia the gem of the ocean,
Made Old Glory the pride of the free.
Shall we fail in our test of devotion?
Oh! What is our hist'ry to be?

**REPEAT CHORUS**

# GIVE YOUR HAND TO UNCLE SAM

Lyrics: W. S. Steege
Music: Eddie Miller

Harrisburg, IL: Steege Miller Co., 1916.

39

In this favored land of peace and plenty,
Which we all for years have shared,
It is only right and justly fitting,
That we now should be prepared.
Not to harbor hate, nor yet to plunder,
Not to glory, nor to boast,
But to protect our own country from the
Lakes to gulf and coast to coast.

**CHORUS**
  Give your hand to Uncle Sam, boys,
  He's the one that's tried and true,
  Ready to fight, to stand up for right,
  To protect the red, white, and blue.
  While all other nations battle,
  He is working to prepare,
  To fight in need, but never for greed,
  But freedom and happiness to share.

While we sit around the cozy fireside
Of our happy homes today,
Let us not forget our brave forefathers,
And the price they had to pay.
Let us not forget our solemn duty,
To those men who fought and died
That we might enjoy the glorious freedom
Of our country's joy and pride.

**CHORUS**
  Rally to the grand old flag, boys,
  Never let it drag in shame.
  In God to trust, to always be just,
  To honor your country and His name.
  When a helpless nation's calling,
  May your vigil never cease.
  Give him your hand and then with him stand
  For freedom, for happiness, and peace.

# LET'S BE READY! THAT'S THE SPIRIT OF '76

Lyrics: Charles Bayha and Rubey Cowan
Music: Charles Bayha and Rubey Cowan

New York: Rubey Cowan Music Publishing Co., 1916.

Some want peace, and notes they will write for it.
Others want it so bad they'll fight for it.
Peace at any price,
May be good advice,
But our forefathers thought a diff'rent way.
Just remember, you're an American;
Don't forget that they were the very men
Who fought side by side
And who gladly died
To put us where we are today. So

**CHORUS**
    Let's be ready, let's be ready,
    That's the Spirit of Seventy-six.
    And if they decide to begin it then,
    We'll be on the job like the minute men
    Down in Lexington,
    Just like Washington,
    One for all and all for one,
    No more riot,
    Peace and quiet.
    That may be a wonderful plan,
    But if they force us into war,
    There's lots here worth fighting for.
    So let's be ready, strong and steady,
    That's the Spirit of Seventy-six.

Tho' our parents may come from diff'rent lands,
We're here now, so we may as well join hands.
Wives and sweethearts true,
Our dear mothers too,
May need protection from the foe someday.
We want battleships that can rule the foam,
Guns and areoplanes to protect our home.
Then all kings will see
That Miss Liberty
Has come to Yankee Land to stay.

**CHORUS**

# AMERICA FIRST IS OUR BATTLE CRY! 'TIS THE LAND WE LOVE!

Lyrics: J. Will Callahan
Music: Eddie Gray

Chicago and New York: Frank K. Root & Co., 1916.

America will always hold a welcome hand
To those who come across the seas from ev'ry land;
She offers them the sacred rights of liberty
Beneath the starry emblem of the brave and free.
She bids them say, "Whate'er befall,
America is first of all."

**CHORUS**
  "The star spangled banner
  We always will defend,
  The standard of freedom
  Until all time shall end.
  No pow'r shall o'erthrow it
  While God reigns high above;
  'America first' is our battle cry,
  'Tis the land we love!"

America will always be a land of peace,
Americans will always pray that war shall cease;
But if the time should ever come to stand for right,
Americans will not be found afraid to fight,
But ringing clear o'er land and sea
Will sound this song of liberty:

**REPEAT CHORUS**

# PREPARE THE EAGLE TO PROTECT THE DOVE

Lyrics: Harry T. Bunce
Music: Will Donaldson

New York: F. B. Haviland Pub. Co. Inc., 1916.

America, America,
You are the queen of earth.
It seems to me that sometimes
We don't realize your worth.
Your history of victory
In days so long gone by
Is one to be proud of
And sing right out loud of,
So let this be our cry:

**CHORUS**
"Prepare the Eagle to protect the Dove"
Is the battle cry of peace.
A mighty army and a mighty navy,
We need both of these.

If we prepare, no foe would dare,
To touch our flag so fair;
"Prepare the Eagle to protect the Dove,"
That's the battle cry of peace.

Washington, our Washington,
The father of this land,
In days of old with words of gold
Spoke to his valiant band:
"Be ready for all cruel war,
And peace reign supreme."
So let us respect it,
And always protect it,
And this must be our theme:

**REPEAT CHORUS**

# AMERICA PREPARE

Lyrics: Elizabeth Herbert Childs
Music: Ribé Danmark
Artist: LPN

New York and Detroit: Jerome H. Remick & Co., 1916.

You've seen our soldiers drill on their parade grounds,
You've watch'd them marching on the avenue,
You know how gay the military band sounds,
You thrill with love of country through and through;
But now you like to know that we are neutral,
You feel secure because you're far away,
But let a submarine appear,
Or a Zeppelin be near,
You would realize the price we'd have to pay.

**CHORUS**
   Let ev'ry man know how to fight in battle;
   That does not mean that we will have a war.
   Let ev'ry man know how to hold a weapon,
   A peace back'd by preparedness means more.
   We stand by what is right in ev'ry nation,
   We take no part in Europe's deadly fights;
   We must show that we're not scar'd of a war,
   For we're prepar'd to force the world to recognize our rights.

Americans, you're there when duty calls you.
It is not this that causes us to fear.
In case of need each man of you would answer
Unto your country's call with "I am here."
What good would you be going into action
When few of you know how to hold a gun?
You would take so long to train
That so many would be slain.
Is it not a pity something can't be done?

**REPEAT CHORUS**

The aeroplane and submarine and gases
Have made of modern warfare one long hell.
What chance would you men have against such forces?
The loss of life we'd scarcely like to tell,
So why not come out strong for preparation?
In knowing how, we have our greatest might.
Preparedness will show just what way to meet a foe,
And perhaps keep us from getting in the fight.

**REPEAT CHORUS**

# THAT'S THE MEANING OF UNCLE SAM

Lyrics: Frank Davis
Music: Win Brookhouse
Artist: Dunk

New York: Shapiro, Bernstein & Co. Inc., 1916.

A little lad of six one day climbed on his father's knee.
"Tell me, daddy, what they mean by Uncle Sam," said he.
"It's a name our fathers gave to dear old Yankee land;
I'll spell it out for you, my boy, and then you'll understand:"

**CHORUS**
   "U" means our Union forever,
   "N" is our Navy so bold,
   "C" means the Cause that we fought so long for,
   "L" stands for Liberty, and
   "E" our Emblem old;
   "S" means the Star Spangled Banner,
   "A" is our Army so grand,
   "M" means we're Mighty,
   A hundred million mighty.
   That's the meaning of "Uncle Sam."

The little lad has now grown up to be a bold brave man,
Commander of a great big fleet, protecting Uncle Sam.
When he's home, he always takes his son upon his knee.
Just listen how he teaches him his little A-B-C.

**REPEAT CHORUS**

# HANDS OFF THE U.S.A.

Lyrics: George Garrett
Music: Ralph Keefer
Artist: E. Hurst

Syracuse: George R. Garrett, 1916.

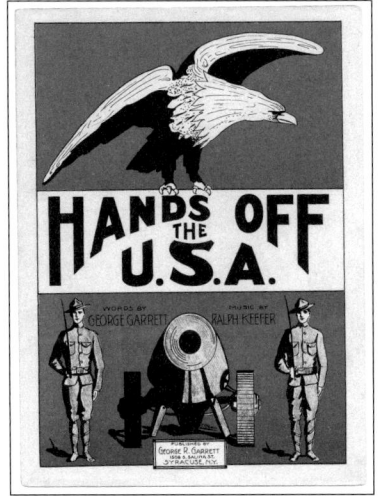

45

We have heard a lot about invading hosts,
And attack by a lurking foe,
But where lies the land with so reckless a hand,
That she dares aim at us a blow?
A thing or two we've taught John Bull and Mexico and Spain,
And if anyone should care to try again,
When the old bugle sounds, and the war drum resounds,
Just see what happens then.

**CHORUS**
Oh! Say can you see
Those millions and millions of men marching by,
Hear that old eagle scream,
See those bay'nets agleam,
While the cheers for Old Glory mount to the sky?
From the Land of Cotton to the old Great Lakes,
From the tip of Maine to Frisco Bay,
Each mighty cannon's roar, echoes to the farthest shore,
"Hands off the U. S. A."

When George Washington chased all the redcoats out,
He chased them out to stay.
And not one thing from Kaiser or king,
Have we feared even to this day.
Our dreadnought fleets with bristling guns patrol the rolling seas,
And our forts are manned with watchful, fearless men.
When the old bugle sounds, and the war drum resounds,
Just see what happens then.

**REPEAT CHORUS**

# I LOVE MY U. S. A.

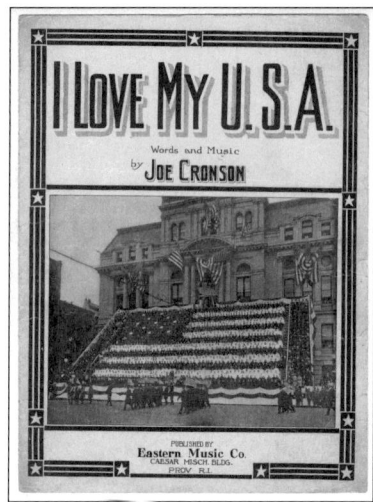

Lyrics: Joe Cronson
Music: Joe Cronson

Providence: Eastern Music Co., 1916.

Last night as I lay a-dreaming,
I'll tell you the things I saw:
I dream't that they came to our hometown
And said, "Boys, you've got to go to war."
We all got up and said, "We're ready,"
As they gave us our uniforms of blue;
Then we shouted loud "America,
We'll fight and we'll die for you."
When we left our hometown right after
  sundown
Saying our last good-byes,
I heard a laddie say
When he went on his way
As the tears rolled from his big blue eyes:

**CHORUS**
  "Gee! It's great to be a soldier,
  And you don't know how proud I am;
  That means a true American
  In the land of old Uncle Sam.
  My country, 'tis of thee,
  It's for peace on earth we pray.
  I'll give my life for you
  Red, White, and Blue
  For I love my U. S. A."

While 'cross the sea they are fighting
And peace reigns in this great land,
The stars and the stripes in "Old Glory"
For our freedom and liberty will stand.
We must prepare and then protect you,
For the flag that our fathers had to fight
Is a story of life's devotion.
The stand that they took was right;
Our mothers and sisters they need protection,
Those that we love the best,
And ev'ry mother's son must learn to hold a
  gun,
And say if put right to the test:

**REPEAT CHORUS**

# I'M SATISFIED WITH UNCLE SAM

Lyrics: Marvin Lee and Terry Sherman
Music: Marvin Lee and Terry Sherman

Chicago: F. J. A. Forster Music Publisher, 1916.

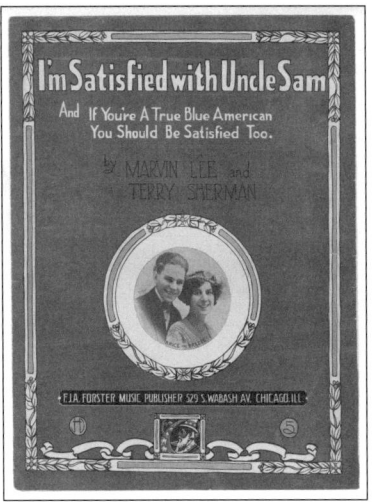

In a land of plenty we are living,
And there's surely room enough for all;
Still a lot of people are complaining
Who would never heed our nation's call.
Uncle Sammy never looks for trouble,
But if trouble e'er should come his way,
Any foe will find that he's a fighter,
And we'll be standing by him in a fray.

**CHORUS**
　I'm satisfied with Uncle Sam,
　He's good enough for me;
　I'm for Sammy, you can bet I am,
　Just like a son ought to be.

I'm satisfied that he's all right,
He's on the square thro' and thro'.
And if you're a true-blue American,
You should be satisfied too.

Lincoln, Grant, and Lee, and Gen'ral Sherman
Were a few of Uncle Sammy's sons,
And altho' no chips were on their shoulders,
There they carried Uncle Sammy's guns.
Don't forget the father of our country,
Washington, who set our nation free;
If Uncle Sam was good enough for those men,
He must be good enough for you and me.

**REPEAT CHORUS**

# IN DUTCH

Lyrics: E. J. Lake
Music: E. J. Lake

Los Angeles: E. J. Lake, 1916.

Said the Eagle to the Lily, "I'm the real live wire."
Said the Lily to the Eagle, "You are something of a liar."
In diplomatic language these few remarks were passed
And back and forth the repartee was flying thick and fast.
Who will be—

**CHORUS**
    In Dutch, in Dutch, I wonder who will be,
    In Dutch in that fight away across the sea.
    Your Uncle Sam is watchful waiting, and he'll try to never be
    In Dutch in that fight away across the sea.

When the Eagle saw the land where the lilies grew,
He said, "I'll clean the bunch up in a day or maybe two."
But the lilies never drooped a head and stood so tall and straight,
That the Eagle screamed and turned his tail and flew to call his mate.
Lest he be—

**CHORUS**
    In Dutch, in Dutch; the people, don't you see,
    Are in Dutch in that fight across the sea?
    Your Uncle Sam is mighty lucky that he didn't have to be
    In Dutch in that fight away across the sea.

The Bull and Bear and others too, tho't they would join the fray,
And the Beasts and Birds from ev'ry clime just couldn't keep away
Till the Eagle's backed against the wall and fo't with beak and claw,
And the feathers flew and blood began to flow from the Bear's maw.
Now who was—

**REPEAT CHORUS**

When a feather from an Eagle hit the Dago in the eye,
He wiped away the tears and said, "I'll get-a you bye and bye."
He watched the fight until he tho't one Bird was almost dead.

Then picking out that Bird for his, he swelled his chest and said.
I'll put-a you—

**REPEAT CHORUS**

"Gott mit uns," screamed the Eagle; "Mon Dieu," the Lilies cried,
And from both was heard the battle cry, "The Lord is on my side."
But the gates of hell flew open and the devil danced with glee,
For the earth was heaped with corpses as far as you could see.
Now who was—

**REPEAT CHORUS**

The Bull made for a Turkey, who was looking kind o' sick,
To land him in the Bosphorus with just one little kick.

But the Turkey dodged and ran around and filled the air with yells,
And Johnny missed the Turk and tumbled in the Dardenelles.
Where he was—

**REPEAT CHORUS**

And now the war is over; there is neither friend nor foe;
The Beasts and Birds are silent, but the world is full of woe.
A million homes are empty and a million fathers dead,
And the curses of the people, instead of prayers are said.
For they are—

**REPEAT CHORUS**

# U.S.A.
# LIBERTY WALTZ

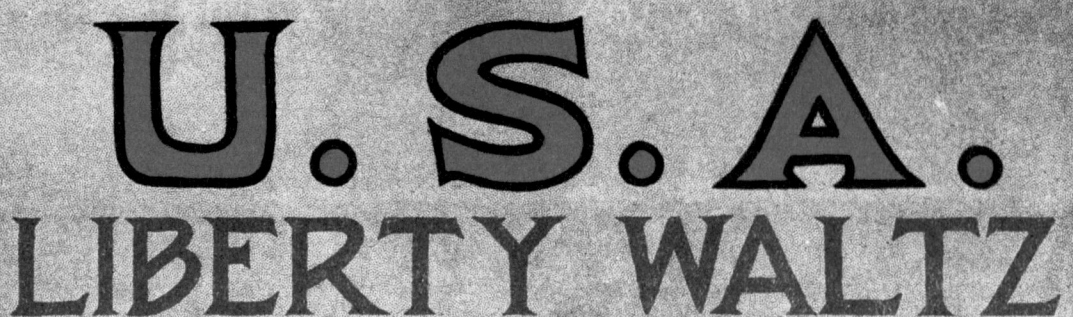

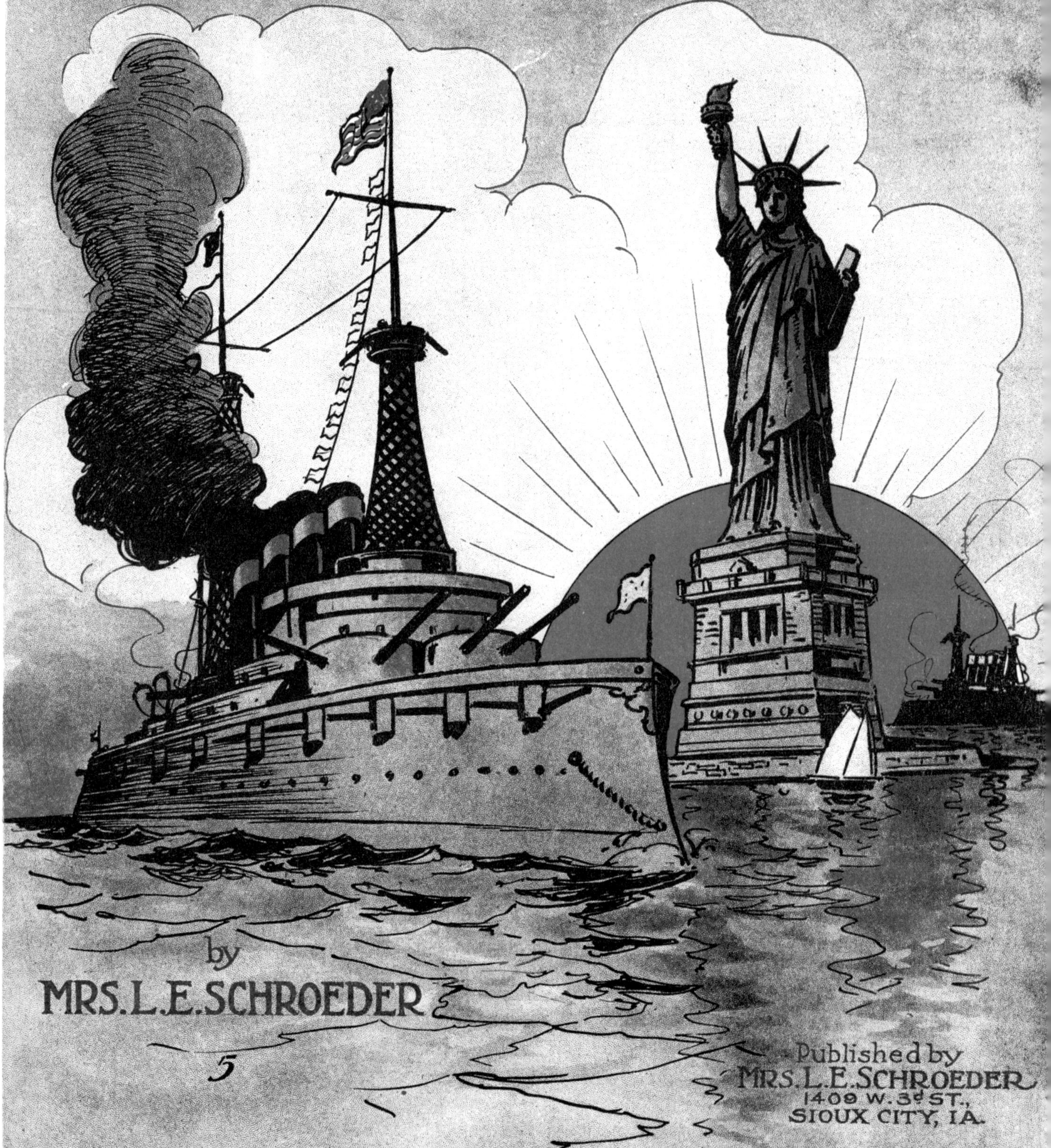

by

MRS. L. E. SCHROEDER

5

Published by
MRS. L. E. SCHROEDER
1409 W. 3rd ST.,
SIOUX CITY, IA.

1917

# THE U.S. OF THE WORLD

Lyrics: Kathrine Oliver McCoy
Music: John E. Thomas

Los Angeles: Edw. L. Ballenger Music Publishing Co., 1917.

We have found a way in the U.S.A.
To make ev'rybody feel at home.
From whatever place,
No matter what race,
Or country they called their own.
We don't have space for the whole blame race,
But they're welcome to our cue.
To get on with one another
We treat ev'ry one as a brother
'Neath the old Red, White, and Blue.

**CHORUS**

   For it's a good way, it's a good way,
   It's a good, good way to do,
   For this good old friendly spirit
   Means an awful lot to you.
   It will work with nations, too.
   With free men, free men ev'rywhere
   All the kinks would get uncurled,
   By helping one another be a big or little brother,
   In the U.S. of the world.

When all men are free, they live cheerfully
And learn to put on the smile that wins,
For they know that their wrists
Must control their fists,
Where their neighbor's nose begins.
Old Glory stands for friendly hands,
And we're sure when she's unfurled,
That it doesn't matter whether
You are this or that or tother.
She is glad to serve the world.

**REPEAT CHORUS**

Then salute each flag tho' a tattered rag,
And say when they all have been unfurled.
All nations must be
Like brothers, you see,
In a sane and a Christian world,
For states, like folks, are bloomin' blokes,
When you stir up all their hates,
But they'd live with one another
Like the children of one mother
In a world United States.

**REPEAT CHORUS**

# LOYALTY IS THE WORD TODAY, LOYALTY TO THE U. S. A.

Lyrics: Dee Dooling Cahill
Music: J. E. Andino
Artist: E. H. Pfeiffer

New York: Dee Dooling Cahill, 1917.

50

North, South, East and West, your country calls you
To swear you'll be true to the Red, White and Blue.
United, we stand, divided, we fall;
A free sea and land means freedom for all.
Then show your colors bravely, each maid and man,
A true united nation, proud American;
With loyalty, with courage, and pride we say,
"We stand by our flag and our country today!"

**CHORUS**
   Loyalty is the word today,
   Loyalty to the U. S. A.;
   "Peace with honor," the nation cries,
   Peace without, the nation dies!
   Now's the time for hearty action
   Without fear and without faction.
   Loyalty is the word today,
   Loyalty to the U.S.A.!

'Tis no time for doubt, 'tis no time to pause;
With love and with faith we'll be true to our cause.
Defending our land, protecting our trust,
For freedom we'll fight, and die if we must.
Then show your colors bravely, each maid and man,
A true united nation, proud American;
With loyalty, with courage, and pride we say,
"We stand by our flag and our country today!"

**REPEAT CHORUS**

# FOR OLD GLORY (UNCLE SAM, WE ARE PREPARING)

Lyrics: Walter Irving
Music: Walter Irving
Artist: E. H. Pfeiffer

New York: American Junior Naval and Marine Scout, Inc., 1917.

*This song was reprinted at least once.*

To be a Junior Naval Marine Scout,
Live an upright manly life.
Do a good turn day by day,
Believe in what your parents say;
Help others in this sad old world of strife.
You are taught loyalty to God and country,
And trained morally to go life's way.
All of the boys of the glorious movement
Will hold up their heads and proudly say:

**CHORUS**
 "Uncle Sam, we are preparing,
 Uncle Sam, we'll soon be through.
 We can hear the nation calling
 To protect our homes and you.
 Soon we'll be in line of marching,
 There to answer your call.
 Ev'ry boy with gun in hand
 Will march at your command,
 For Old Glory and you, Uncle Sam."

Boys, join the Junior Naval Marine Scout,
It's a movement that calls to you
Through the forest, o'er the hills,
On the water with its thrills,
Prepares a boy for what he cares to do.
He is taught it's a scout's sacred duty
To be ready for the President's call.
America will cherish your devotion,
For you will do your duty, that's all.

**REPEAT CHORUS**

# WHAT KIND OF AN AMERICAN ARE YOU?

Lyrics: Lew Brown and Charles McCarron
Music: Albert Von Tilzer

New York: Broadway Music Corporation, 1917.

52

This land of the free is for you and for me
Or for anyone at all who is seeking liberty.
We welcome ev'ry stranger,
And we help him all we can.
And now that we're in danger,
We depend on ev'ry man.
The Stars and Stripes are calling you to lend a helping hand.
If you're true blue, it's up to you to show just where you stand.

## CHORUS

What kind of an American are you?
It's time to show what you intend to do.
If they trample on Old Glory will you think they are right,
Or will you stand behind your land and fight with all your might?
What kind of an American are you?
That's a question you'll have an answer to.
If the Star Spangled Banner don't make you stand and cheer,
Then what are you doing over here?

This country's been dared, but they'll find us prepared,
And to try and gain our aim not a penny will be spared.
We are a friendly nation,
And we always look for peace.
We've waited and we've waited,
Hoping this war would cease.
The enemy across the sea won't take our good advice,
So now it's up to ev'ry man to make some sacrifice.

**REPEAT CHORUS**

# FOR YOUR COUNTRY AND MY COUNTRY

Lyrics: Irving Berlin
Music: Irving Berlin
Artist: Albert Barbelle

New York: Waterson, Berlin & Snyder Co., 1917.

53

We know you love your land of liberty,
We know you love your U.S.A.
But if you want the world to know it,
Now's the time to show it;
Your Uncle Sammy needs you one and all.
Answer to his call.

**CHORUS**
  It's your country, it's my country,
  With millions of real fighting men;
  It's your duty, and my duty,
  To speak with the sword, not the pen.

If Washington were living today,
With sword in hand he'd stand up and say:
"For you country and my country,
I'll do it all over again."

America has opened up her heart
To ev'ry nationality,
And now she asks of ev'ry nation
Their appreciation.
It makes no diff'rence now from where you came,
We are all the same.

**REPEAT CHORUS**

# WE'RE ALL WITH YOU, DEAR AMERICA

Lyrics: Lew Schaeffer and Phil Leventhal
Music: Lew Schaeffer and Phil Leventhal

New York: Lew Schaeffer Music Co., 1917.

54

We're with you, strong for you, Uncle Sammy,
With that spirit of do or die.
We are surely with you, dear Sammy,
We'll be there with a steady eye.
We're with you right or wrong,
One hundred million strong.

**CHORUS**
　We're all with you, dear America,
　And we'll do just as you say.
　We're all with you, dear America,
　Now that you are in this fray.

O'er the top we will go for you,
Even if what Sherman said was true.
We're all with you, dear America,
Three cheers for the Red, White, and Blue.

We will fight for our right, Uncle Sammy,
With that Spirit of Sev'nty-six.
We'll go over for you, dear Sammy,
With the foe we will gladly mix.
Been with you right or wrong,
And for you we are strong.

**REPEAT CHORUS**

# WHEN A YANKEE ROLLS UP HIS SLEEVES

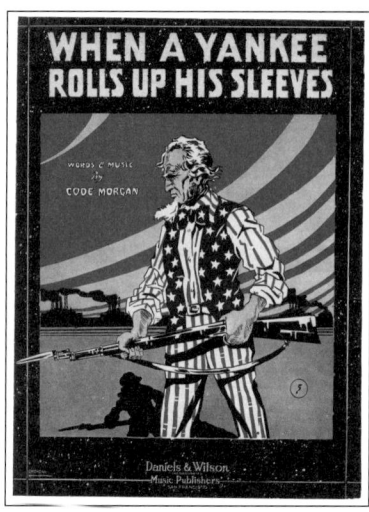

Lyrics: Code Morgan
Music: Code Morgan
Artist: Le Morgan

San Francisco: Daniels & Wilson Music Publishers, 1917.

There is a great commotion
Just now across the ocean,
All the way from Netherlands to Greece,
For there's a big tall fellow
Who ne'er showed a streak of yellow,
And he much prefers the pipe of peace.
But they've forced him into action,
He'll soon get satisfaction.
When he starts to scrap, someone grieves,
For it's an awful breezy story,
Mighty short but full of glory,
When a Yankee rolls up his sleeves.

**CHORUS**
 The "Y" is for the years that he's been victor,
 The "A" is for the arm that's feared by all.
 The "N" is for a nation not afraid of all creation,
 The "K" is for the kick behind the ball.
 The double "EE" makes Yankee.

Now they've got him good and cranky;
From his drubbing no one ever retrieves,
For history shows that he can do it.
You bet someone will rue it,
When a Yankee rolls up his sleeves.

They all admit the truth,
It was way back in his youth,
This Yankee lad just cleaned up all his foes.
And then when he'd grown older,
Now and then someone got bolder,
Only to retire deep in woes.
His last victory to gain,
Was to avenge the dear old *Maine*.
There'll soon be one more nation that believes
That history simply will repeat,
For it's impossible to beat
A Yankee when he rolls up his sleeves.

**REPEAT CHORUS**

# LET'S ALL BE AMERICANS NOW

Lyrics: Irving Berlin, Edgar Leslie, and George W. Meyer
Music: Irving Berlin, Edgar Leslie, and George W. Meyer
Artist: Albert Barbelle

New York: Waterson, Berlin and Snyder Co., 1917.

*This song was reprinted at least once.*

56

Peace has always been our pray'r,
Now's there's trouble in the air;
War is talked of ev'rywhere,
Still in God we trust.
We're not looking for any kind of war,
But if fight we must.

**CHORUS**
It's up to you!
What will you do?
England or France may have your sympathy,
Or Germany.
But you'll agree
That now is the time,
To fall in line.
You swore that you would,
So be true to your vow.
Let's all be Americans now.

Lincoln, Grant, and Washington,
They were peaceful men, each one.
Still they took the sword and gun,
When real trouble came.
And I feel somehow, they are wondering now,
If we'll do the same.

**REPEAT CHORUS**

# LIKE A BABY NEEDS ITS MOTHER THAT'S HOW UNCLE SAM NEEDS YOU

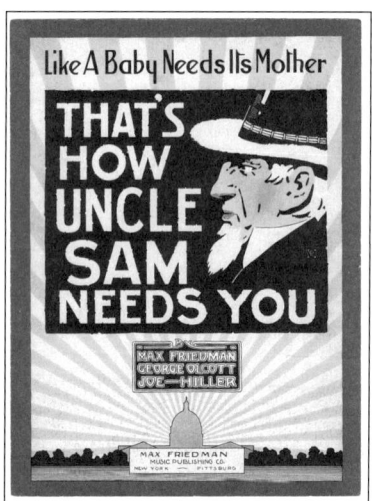

Lyrics: Max Friedman, George Olcott and Joe Hiller
Music: Max Friedman, George Olcott and Joe Hiller

Pittsburgh and New York: Max Friedman Music Publishing Co., 1917.

The time of war has come,
And ev'ry mother's son
Should be glad to go and do this share.
So let's get ready now,
And live up to our vow,
And show them Uncle Sam is there.
When bugles sound their call,
Be ready one and all.

**CHORUS**
  Our fathers before us did their duty,
  They fought 'mid shot and shell.
  Their battles still reflect
  How they fought to gain respect.
  Their hardships we all remember well.
  The present war is teaching us preparedness,
  We must defend the old Red, White, and Blue.
  Like a baby needs its mother,
  That's how Uncle Sam needs you.

Our Congress passed a law
That we prepare for war
To defend the old Red, White, and Blue.
We tried to maintain peace.
Their abuse they would not cease,
So there's only one thing to do.
Get ready one and all,
To answer duty's call.

**REPEAT CHORUS**

# GOOD-BYE, MOTHER! SO LONG, DAD! HELLO, UNCLE SAM!

Lyrics: W. E. Browning
Music: C. A. Grimm

Chicago: Lyceum Music Publishers, 1917.

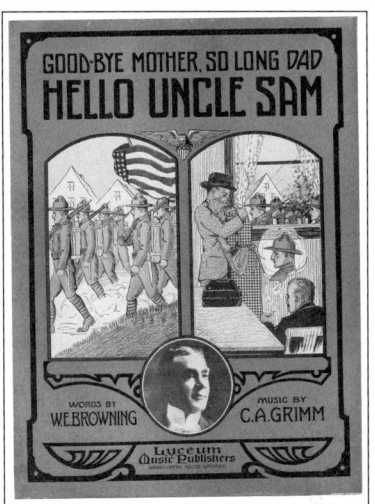

58

The Sammies are going across the deep seas,
And, Mother, I must go too,
For it's my country that's calling.
In line I'll be falling,
And fight for the Red, White, and Blue.
To poor bleeding France we will soon pay our debt,
It's a debt we've owed for years.
Now dear, Mother, do not cry,
Kiss your soldier boy goodbye.
There'll be millions of volunteers.

**CHORUS**

Goodbye, Mother, so long, Dad, hello, Uncle Sam.
I'm only one of your loyal sons,
Who honor and obey your command.
Our great-granddaddies fought for liberty,
And it's up to all of us to lend a hand,
For now that we're in this fight,
My country wrong or right.
So, goodbye, Mother, so long, Dad, hello, Uncle Sam.

When this war is over and we are at peace,
Come back to your dad and me,
But now you know that they need you.
Go, lad, and God speed you,
For soon we must have victory.
My country, we give you our one darling boy,
That's as much as we can do.
Do your bit and never fear.
Fight for all that you hold dear.
The whole world will be watching you.

**REPEAT CHORUS**

# I'D FEEL AT HOME IF THEY'D LET ME JOIN THE ARMY

Lyrics: Jack Mahoney
Music: Albert Gumble
Artist: Emmons

New York and Detroit: Jerome H. Remick & Co., 1917.

Some men are getting married so they won't be called to war,
But if they want to dodge it, what do they get married for?
It takes about a year or more to train a soldier right.
A year of married life will make them all know how to fight.

**CHORUS**
   Oh, give me a gun and away I'll run
   To fight the foreign foe.
   I'm not afraid the shot and shell will harm me,
   For ever since I took a wife,
   I've been in battles all my life,
   And I'd feel at home, if they'd let me join the army.

They'll have to force the single men to go to war I fear;
The married men all want to go, they always volunteer.
It takes the bravest of the brave to bear the battle's brunt.
That's why they always find the married men way out in front.

**CHORUS**
   Oh, give me a gun and away I'll run,
   To fight the foreign foe.
   The sound of rifle fire would not alarm me,
   For since my wife had twins, you see,
   Each night I lead the infantry,
   And I'd feel at home, if they'd let me join the army.

Since I got married, my wife charges ev'rything to me,
But I'd reverse the charges and change the enemy.
I'm always on the firing line of that there is no doubt,
When she invites her company, I'm always muster'd out.

**CHORUS**
    Oh, give me a gun and away I'll run,
    To fight the foreign foe.
    A trip up in the aeroplane would charm me.
    Since I got married, I declare,
    I've always been up in the air,
    And I'd feel at home, if they'd let me join the army.

My house is a recruiting station for her family.
They're first in war and first in peace and first for lunch you see.
Now I treat them to anything and ev'rything I get,
But like a gallant army they have not retreated yet.

**CHORUS**
    Oh, give me a gun and away I'll run,
    To fight the foreign foe.
    The life out in the trenches wouldn't harm me.
    They're small but I am used to that,
    Living in a Harlem flat,
    And I'd feel at home, if they'd let me join the army.

# YOUR COUNTRY NEEDS YOU NOW

Lyrics: Al Dubin
Music: Rennie Cormack

New York: M. Witmark & Sons, 1917.

60

Volunteer, volunteer, volunteer.
Can't you hear, can't you hear, can't you hear?
Uncle Sammy is calling you,
What are you goin' to do?
Must he call in vain?
Fall in line, fall in line, fall in line.
Now's the time, now's the time, now's the time.
Don't be a slacker, son,
Go get yourself a gun.
Your country needs you now.

**CHORUS**

Your country needs you,
Now what will you do?
It's time to stand together
For the Red, White, and Blue.
Sweethearts and mothers
Want you to keep your vow.
They love you, I know,
But they want you to go,
For your country needs you now.

March away, march away, march away.
Don't delay for a day, don't delay.
Are you ready to do and dare,
Ready to do your share?
Join the ranks today.
Shoulder arms, shoulder arms, shoulder arms.
We have heard, we have heard war alarms.
Don't stand aside and cheer.
What are you doing here?
Your country needs you now.

**REPEAT CHORUS**

# IT'S TIME FOR EVERY BOY TO BE A SOLDIER

Lyrics: Alfred Bryan
Music: Harry Tierney
Artist: LPN

New York and Detroit: Jerome H. Remick and Co., 1917.

*This song was reprinted at least twice and was recorded by Charles Hart.*

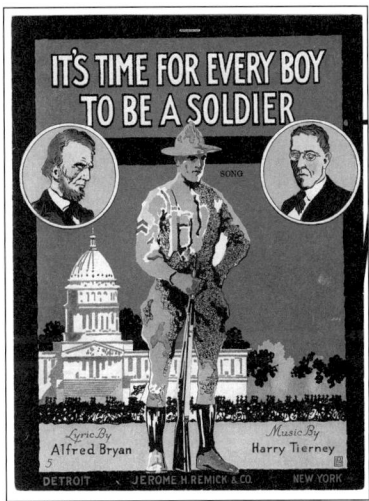

61

Most ev'ry fellow has a sweetheart,
Some little girl with eyes of blue;
My daddy also had a sweetheart,
And he fought to win her, too.
There'll come a day when we must pay
The price of love and duty.
Be there staunch and true.

**CHORUS**
It's time for ev'ry boy to be a soldier,
To put his strength and courage to the test;
It's time to place a musket on his shoulder
And wrap the Stars and Stripes around his breast.
It's time to shout those noble words of Lincoln
And stand up for the land that gave you birth:
"That the nation of the people by the people for the people
Shall not perish from the earth."

Boys of America, get ready,
Your motherland is calling you;
Boys of America, be steady
For the old Red, White, and Blue.
When Yankee Doodle comes to town
Upon his little pony,
Be there staunch and true.

**REPEAT CHORUS**

# IF I HAD A SON FOR EACH STAR IN OLD GLORY (UNCLE SAM, I'D GIVE THEM ALL TO YOU)

Lyrics: J. E. Dempsey
Music: Joseph A. Burke
Artist: Rosenbaum Studios

New York: Leo. Feist, Inc., 1917.

*Other featured singers with this cover design include Brice & King (twice) and Ben Davis.*

Uncle Sam, is that somebody calling,
Someone calling you from far away?
Don't you hear that gentle mother's voice?
Listen, this is what she seems to say:
"While I'm only one of the million other mothers,
I speak for all the U.S.A."

**CHORUS**
"Though God never made men for soldiers,
Now the clouds of war have burst,
We must pray for the best,
And prepare for the test.
Our country must come first.

Tho' I've but one boy to offer,
He's yours when you call.
That's all a mother can do,
But if I had a son for each star in Old Glory,
Uncle Sam, I'd give them all to you!"

Uncle Sam, I'll paint a picture for you,
Frame the scene, in battle clouds of gray,
Count the dead and dying soldier boys,
Call the picture, "What a price to pay!"
And over each son place a brokenhearted mother,
Too sad to weep, yet proud to say:

**REPEAT CHORUS**

# THERE'S A SERVICE FLAG FLYING AT OUR HOUSE

Lyrics: Thomas R. Hoier and Bernie Grossman
Music: Al W. Brown
Artist: Starmer

New York: Joe Morris Music Co., 1917.

*This song was reprinted at least once.*

See the people running
Hear the rum-tum-tuming.
Military music fills the air.
Ev'ry one is waiting,
Hearts are palpitating,
Flags are flying ev'rywhere.
Of ev'ry allied nation,
From nearly all creation
Their banners wave from ev'ry staff and dome.
But the one I love to see,
That means so much to me,
Is the flag that's flying at home.

**CHORUS**

There's a service flag flying at our house,
A blue star in a field of red and white.
Father is so proud of what his boy has done,
There's a tear in mother's smile and she murmurs, "My son."

Perhaps he may return with fame and glory,
But if by chance we lose him in the fight,
There'll be a service flag flying at our house
And a new star in heaven that night.

There beside Old Glory
Telling all our story
Until the end, that flag is going to fly.
We are proud to show it,
Want the world to know it,
We will do or we will die.
There's a million others
Giving sons and brothers,
And proudly watch them as they march away.
And although their hearts may ache,
Although their hearts may break,
There's a million glad they can say:

**REPEAT CHORUS**

# AMERICA, HERE'S MY BOY

Lyrics: Andrew B. Sterling
Music: Arthur Lange
Artist: André De Takacs

New York: Joe Morris Music Co., 1917.

*This song was reprinted at least four times.*

There's a million mothers knocking at the nation's door,
A million mothers, yes, and there'll be millions more;
And while within each mother's heart they pray,
Just hark what one brave mother has to say.

**CHORUS**
"America, I raised a boy for you.
America, you'll find him staunch and true.
Place a gun upon his shoulder,
He is ready to die or do.
America, he is my only one,
My hope, my pride and joy,
But if I had another, he would march beside his brother.
America, here's my boy."

There's a million mothers waiting by the fireside bright,
A million mothers, waiting for the call tonight;
And while within each heart there'll be a tear,
She'll watch her boy go marching with a cheer.

**REPEAT CHORUS**

# AMERICA NEEDS YOU LIKE A MOTHER
# (WOULD YOU TURN YOUR MOTHER DOWN?)

Lyrics: Grant Clark
Music: Jean Schwartz
Artist: Albert Barbelle

New York: Kalmar, Puck, and Abrahams Consolidated Inc., 1917.

*Other featured singers with this cover design include Clara Howard, Rae Samuels, and Jimmy Hussey & Billy Worsley. It was also issued with a different cover design by Albert Barbelle.*

65

I seem to see a picture of a mother
With her children by her side;
Some her own and some that she's adopted,
Still she looks at all with pride.
Now it seems the mother is in trouble
And she needs her children's aid;
Some are coming forth to help her,
But there's some who seem afraid.

**CHORUS**
   America has been a mother
   To the children of the world.
   She has taken to her bosom
   Ev'ry homeless boy and girl.
   Now we find that she's in trouble,
   Danger's lurking all around.
   America, she needs you like a mother,
   Would you turn your mother down?

We know that there are diff'rent kinds of children,
There are some who love to roam;
Then again there's some who love their mother,
They would rather stay at home.
Still, with all our many faults and failings,
She remains our only friend.
Just like many loyal children,
We should help her to the end.

**REPEAT CHORUS**

# ANSWER MR. WILSON'S CALL

Lyrics: Billy Gould
Music: Billy Gould
Artist: Albert Barbelle

New York: A. J. Stasny Music Co., 1917.

66

Dear Old Glory is in danger,
Our own dear Red, White, and Blue.
So Yankee Doodle Dandies,
It's clearly up to you.
Let's remember George Washington,
Dear old "Honest Abe" and Lee,
And show our might, preserve our right
To sail upon the sea:

**CHORUS**
Your Uncle Sam is calling you,
Calling you and I;
Let's all be real Americans,
Ready to do or die,
For our country shall be free,

Though every man must fall.
We've suffered abuses,
So now don't make excuses,
But answer Mr. Wilson's call.

Now our Eagle's loudly screaming,
With its wings spread to the sky;
So, Yankee Doodle Dandies,
It's up to you and I.
Let's remember dear old Bunker Hill,
Sherman's march down to the sea.
Each lad be glad, this chance he's had,
To fight for humanity:

**CHORUS**

# CAN'T YOU HEAR YOUR COUNTRY CALLING

Lyrics: Gene Buck
Music: Victor Herbert

New York: T. B. Harms and Francis, Day & Hunter, 1917.

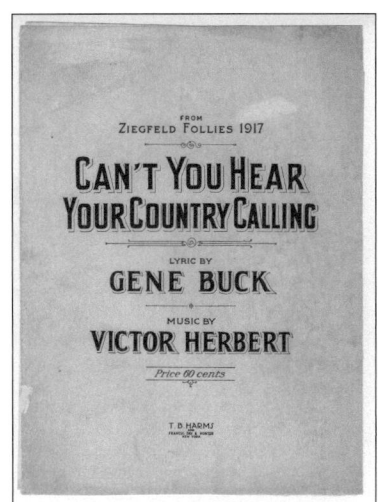

Now all the world's a stage, they say,
And we all have a part to play;
Our greatest role is called today,
The President will lead you.
Before you, humbly, I appear
And play the modern Paul Revere
To warn you all that war is here.
You must awake, we need you.

**CHORUS**
Can't you hear your country calling, calling
   to fight for peace?
Help on land and sea
For humanity.
Rise in might to shield our honor.
Can't you see your country needs you?
Answer the call today!
Now we all must stand by our dear beloved
   land
The U. S. A.

# COME ON, BOYS

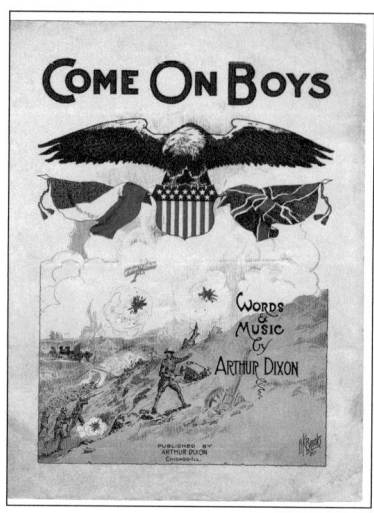

Lyrics: Arthur Dixon
Music: Arthur Dixon
Artist: H. K. Brooks

Chicago: Arthur Dixon, 1917.

U.S. army, U.S. navy on the land or on the sea,
Fighting for the cause of justice,
What a vict'ry it will be;
Guided on by those who love us,
We will fight to win the day;
As we march along to vict'ry,
We will watch and we will pray.

**CHORUS**
  Rally 'round, boys,
  Rally 'round, boys,
  Now's the time to do or dare.
  See the Stars and Stripes are flying,
  You can see them ev'rywhere.

  See Old Glory now is waving,
  And we'll never let her fall.
  For the cause of right and justice
  We'll uphold you one and all.

With the Stars and Stripes above us
We will gaily march along,
Fighting for the ones who love us,
Vict'ry always is our song;
With the banner floating o'er us,
Proud and faithful we will be;
We will show them we are coming,
On the land and on the sea.

**REPEAT CHORUS**

# I'M RAISING MY BOY TO BE A SOLDIER TO FIGHT FOR THE U. S. A.

Lyrics: Leo J. Ryan
Music: Mrs. Leo J. Ryan

South Groveland, MA: Ryan & Bradley Pub. Co., 1917.

A sweet-faced mother sitting by the fireside,
Her boy has gone to fight for Uncle Sam.
Her eyes are bright with tears although she's smiling
As she listened to the military band.
Her thoughts go back to when he was a baby,
His dad gone when duty called to him.
He always called her Uncle Sammy's Lady
When she sung this song to Sonny Jim.

**CHORUS**

"I'm raising my boy to be a soldier
To fight for the U.S.A.
I'm raising my boy to be a soldier,
He is growing every day.
Tenting tonight, preparing to fight,
They'll be off at the break of day.
I'm raising my boy to be a soldier
To fight for the U.S.A."

The soldier boy upon the field of battle
Dear mother's face sweet memories would bring.
He would think of days when childish prattle
Would stop to hear his dear old mother sing.
These thoughts of home and mother made him tearful,
But bravely he would march on once again.
And when the bombs and guns begin to rattle
My mother's song to victory I'll bring.

**REPEAT CHORUS**

# AH DIDN'T RAISE MAH BOY TO BE A SLACKER

Lyrics: Al Hart
Music: Al Hart

Omaha: The Hospe Music Co., 1917.

Steven Jackson Washington
Was a-hidin' in a load of hay;
De town folks drillin' in de public square,
And dey's new ones everyday;
De soldier boys am a-marchin' by,
De band am a-playin' and a-steppin' high.
His father pulled young Steven out,
And he talked to him dis way:

**CHORUS**
  "Ah didn't raise mah boy to be a slacker.
  Dey's a molly coddle, sissy, dear,
    A-hangin' to der mammy's apron string,
      A-shakin' in der boots of fear.
  Your dad was a soldier in sixty-two,
  He fought for his country and you should,
      too.
  Steven Jackson Washington,
  If you'se gwine to be a slacker,
  Den you ain't mah son."

Steve got up and looked around,
He's a feelin' kinda stiff and sore.
His Uncle Sammy is a-callin' him,
But he ain't no use for war.

He told his ma he's a-feelin' blue,
And he thought he'd ask her what he ought
    to do.
She roasted him, and shamed him, too,
And she said to him once more:

**REPEAT CHORUS**

He went to see his honey-girl,
Miss Arabella Phoebe Snow.
She's dressed up fancy like a millionaire,
And he said, "Ah love you so,
So let's get married dis very day,
'Cause ah'se in a hurry for to get away."
But Phoebe said, "Hold on, dere man,
Dey's a few things you don't know:"

**CHORUS**
  "Ah never could get married to a slacker.
  Dey's a molly coddle, sissy, dear,
    A-hangin' to der mammy's apron string,
      A-shakin' in der boots of fear.
  Your dad was a soldier in sixty-two,
  He fought for his country and you should,
      too.

So, Steve, I'll tell you what I'll do.
If you'se gwine to join th army,
Den I'll marry you."

Steven's blood was a-boilin' now,
For everybody turned him down.
He got a rifle and a uniform,
And he marched right through the town.
He joined the army as you may know,
And he wed Miss Arabella Phoebe Snow.
De neighbors had a jubilee,
And dey came from miles around.

**CHORUS**
"Ah didn't raise mah boy to be a slacker.
Dey's a molly coddle, sissy, dear,
A-hangin' to der mammy's apron string,
  A-shakin' in der boots of fear.
Your dad was a soldier in sixty-two,
He fought for his country and you should,
  too.
So, boys, I'll say dis ain't no fun;
If you'se gwine to be a slacker,
Den you'se no man's son.

# NIGGER WAR BRIDE BLUES

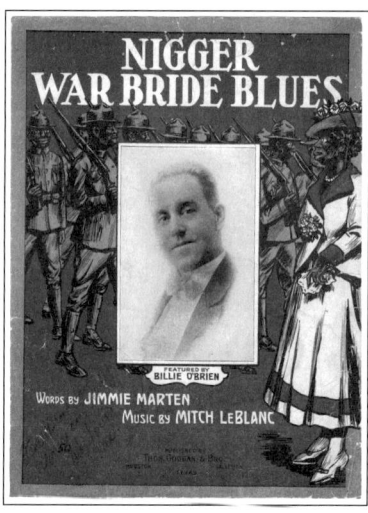

Lyrics: Jimmie Marten
Music: Mitch LeBlanc

Houston and Galveston: Thos. Goggan & Bro., 1917.

71

Listen folks, I'm going to tell you,
Oh, baby's gone an' I'm feelin' awfull terribly blue,
Done j'ined the war an' lef' me all alone that's true,
Oh, I'm blue.
He lef' a note, it was all edged in black,
Jes' tellin' me that he never was a-comin' back,
Jes' staten' he was never, never comin' back,
Now that's fact.

**CHORUS**
    Easy greasy breezy John,
    Easy breezy greasy John,
    Makes me blue an' sick
    An' out an' down, out an' down.
    Easy easy easy breezy greasy John,
    Down the road just as far as I could see,
    Thought I saw my dear old used to be,
    Thought I heard my Johnnie callin' me.

Engine whistled like it neverer whistled before,
Saw him walk inside, turn around and shut the door;
I felt so bad I nearly fell down on the floor,
An' what's more,
Two sixteen done carried poor John away.
"It's a long way," so I heard mos' all the white folks say,
Yes, two-sixteen done took my lovin' Johnnie away,
T'other day.

**REPEAT CHORUS**

# JEFFERSON BROWN

Lyrics: Adrian Metzger
Music: Gertrude Voorheis
Artist: Le Morgan

San Francisco: Clark-Levy Co., 1917.

72

Jefferson Brown left his hometown
For a job of twenty bucks a day and all found;
It looked all right as well it might,
Till he found he had to handle dynamite.
Jefferson Brown, he looked aroun',
A shaky feeling hit his spine and jiggled 'way down;
He sees the belles a-making shells,
Grabs his hat in panic and he loudly yells:

### CHORUS
"Just keep your job, please, ah'm goin' away,
No kind of money kin make me stay.
No ammunition's in my ambition.
Somethin' is tellin' me, 'Be on your way.'
Maybe a streak's in mah black and tan.
This ain't no job fo' no cullud man.
It's lot o' money but mah stummuck's funny;
Ah'm a-goin' while the goin' am good."

But just before he reached the door
Tons and tons of high explosives wheeled 'cross the floor;
Too scared to stop, 'fraid they might drop,
Made the nearest window with a ten-foot hop.
Brown was rash, he raised the sash,
Took one leap that cleared him from that big pile of trash.
A sentry called to stop and halt,
But Jefferson, he says, "To catch me, you'll shoo need salt."

### REPEAT CHORUS

# DO YOUR LITTLE "BITTY-BIT" RIGHT NOW

Lyrics: F. Belohlavek and C. C. Perkins
Music: Edmund Braham

Chicago: Frances-Clifford Music Publishing Co., 1917.

The battle's on, "Somewhere in France,"
Our boys are over there;
They are fighting for our own U.S.
On land, on sea, in air.
What are we doing at home
For our security?
We each must do our little "bit."
It's up to you and me.

**CHORUS**
　Do your little "bitty bit" right now,
　Do your little "bitty bit" somehow;
　Either buy a bond or fight
　For all that's just and right,
　And help your dear old Uncle Sam.

　Do your little "bitty bit" right now,
　Do your little "bitty bit" somehow;
　With our Yankee "pep" and "vim"
　We will pitch right in and win.
　Do your little "bitty bit" right now.

The battle's o'er, the cause is won,
Our boys are homeward bound.
They fought the fight for liberty,
With victory were crowned.
We'll greet them all when they return,
And with them make a "hit,"
When they find out we didn't "slack,"
But did our little "bit."

**REPEAT CHORUS**

# THE MAN BEHIND THE HAMMER AND THE PLOW

Lyrics: Harry Von Tilzer
Music: Harry Von Tilzer
Artist: E. H. Pfeiffer

New York: Harry Von Tilzer Music Publishing Co., 1917.

America, the world is calling you;
America, it needs you badly, too.
The nations o'er the sea
Cry out for liberty.
The Stars and Stripes can save and make them free.
The sons of Uncle Sam can win the fray,
And here's the man that has to save the day.

**CHORUS**
It's the man behind the hammer and the plow
Who made this country what it is today;
It's the man behind the hammer and the plow,
The gift of God's creation,
The builders of the nation.

Mechanic and the engineer, all honest sons of toil,
The backbone of the world today,
The man who tills the soil.
It's up to him to win the battle now,
The man behind the hammer and plow.

America, we know you'll do what's right;
America, you've never lost a fight.
You're bound to do your share
And do it on the square,
And when there's peace at least you will be square;
Now, working man, today you have the pow'r
To win for Uncle Sam, this is your hour.

**REPEAT CHORUS**

# PLANT A LITTLE GARDEN IN YOUR OWN BACK YARD

Lyrics: Walter Hirsch and Bert Lewis
Music: Walter Leopold

Chicago: Forster Music Publisher Inc., 1917.

I've been reading in the papers that the price of food is high;
"Cut the prices, cut the prices" is the nation's cry.
Now I've got a dandy little scheme that you all should try:
Go and raise the things you need, the things too high to buy.

**CHORUS**
  Plant a little garden in your own back yard,
  Where the green grass used to grow.
  Plant some nice potatoes, and some red tomatoes.
  Buy a rake and hoe.
  You'll have plenty for the wife and kiddies bye and bye.

You should worry if the prices go up to the sky.
Take my advice
And plant a little garden in your own back yard.

There's a saying in the Bible that you all have heard a heap,
Just get busy, just get busy, don't you fall asleep.
Never mind the man across the street, your own council keep;
The Bible says that as you sow, that is the way you'll reap.

**REPEAT CHORUS**

# HOE YOUR "LITTLE BIT" IN YOUR OWN BACK YARD.
# WHERE THE BOY SCOUTS GO, 'TIS HOE, HOE, HOE!

Lyrics: Dee Dooling Cahill
Music: J. E. Andino
Artist: E. H. Pfeiffer

New York: Great Aim Society, 1917.

76

Lay down the playin' and take up the hoe,
For that is the way to make things grow;
The life of the world will now be at stake,
The best way to help is with hoe and rake.

**CHORUS**
  Boys in the trenches cannot fight, you know,
  Without the boys at home with the hoe;
  For sharp is the hoe and straight is the row,
  Where the Boy Scouts go, 'tis hoe, hoe, hoe!
  Feeding the soldiers, ev'ry scout should know,
  Means the boys at home must hoe, hoe, hoe!
  The way to make a hit, is to hoe your "little bit."
  Hoe your "little bit" in your own back yard.

Now comes our trial for this our test,
So show us the ground, we'll do the rest;
The eyes of the world will look out, 'tis true,
Upon these brave boys and what they will do.

**REPEAT CHORUS**

# BUY A LIBERTY BOND FOR THE BABY

Lyrics: Eddie Moran
Music: Harry Von Tilzer
Artist: E. H. Pfeiffer

New York: Harry Von Tilzer Music Pub. Co., 1917.

Have you got a baby boy?
Or a girlie bunch of joy?
There is something you can buy far better than a toy,
Something just as good as gold.
We all should own a few.
Something they can have and hold;
Right now it's up to you.

**CHORUS**
  Buy a Liberty Bond for the baby.
  Tell him it's a bond of love.
  That's the best gift you'll ever make
  Both for his and liberty's sake.
  Buy a Liberty Bond for the baby.
  Help our cause across the pond.

Do it now; don't wait, whatever you do.
If he could, he'd buy it for you.
Someday he'll be glad,
He'll be proud of dad,
If you buy a Liberty Bond.

Baby will grow up someday.
He'll be mighty proud to say,
"My old dad bought this for me and for the U.S.A."
Maybe there'll be some boy near
Whose dad has not bought one.
In his eye there'll be a tear,
Don't let that be your son.

**REPEAT CHORUS**

# THAT'S A MOTHER'S LIBERTY LOAN

Lyrics: Mayo & Tally and Clarence Gaskill
Music: Mayo & Tally and Clarence Gaskill

New York, Chicago et al.: M. Witmark and Sons, 1917.

*This song was reprinted at least twice.*

There's a lonely little mother
In a lonely home tonight;
She's thinking of her soldier boy,
Who marched away to fight.
Though she's only one in millions,
And she has no gold to spare,
Her tear-dimmed eyes just seem to say:
"I think I've done my share!"

**CHORUS**
  "I gave my boy to Uncle Sam,
  To fight for you and me,
  Just like his dad at Gettysburg,
  In Eighteen Sixty-three.
  If life must pay for liberty,
  I'm giving all I own,
  And when battle's won,
  I'll then take back my son.
  That's a mother's liberty loan!"

Ev'ry night this lonely mother
Has a dream that makes her sad;
She seems to see her soldier boy
When he was but a lad.
He is playing with his soldier toys,
They're scattered o'er the floor;
She never thought that someday he
Would hear the call of war.

**REPEAT CHORUS**

# AMERICA TO-DAY

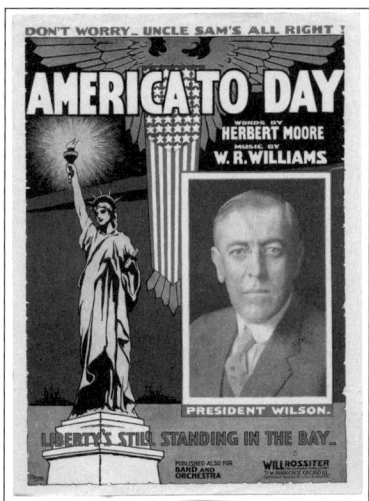

Lyrics: Herbert Moore
Music: W. R. Williams
Artist: Starmer

Chicago: Will Rossiter, 1917.

79

The hist'ry of America is wonderful,
Its chapters tell of men with hearts of gold;
Their names we'll always cherish,
Their fame will never perish,
Their splendid deeds will live for years untold;
But if we dwell on bygone days, there's danger
That we'll forget the qualities that last;
Place laurel on each great man's brow,
But don't forget the men of now.
Don't think that all the good lies in the past.

**CHORUS**
  Don't say that all the statesmen died with Lincoln,
  Don't think that all the heroes died with Grant;
  You'll find we've still the pow'r
  To produce men of the hour;
  Because they've had no call, don't say they can't.

Remember we've a heritage of glory,
And Liberty's still standing in the bay;
As in his former days of might,
Don't worry, Uncle Sam's all right!
We'll fight for America today.

We have the mem'ry of the Revolution,
And we've the memory of Sixty-one;
We tell in song and story
They battled for Old Glory,
And we'll protect the victories they won.
We're strong for peace, if it is peace with honor,
But don't forget, we're stronger still for right;
Whatever future days may bring,
Our country first, that's *the* big thing.
United to a man we still can fight.

**REPEAT CHORUS**

# SONS OF AMERICA (AMERICA NEEDS YOU)

Lyrics: Arthur F. Holt
Music: William T. Pierson
Artist: Dunk

Washington and New York: W. T. Pierson & Co., 1917.

80

Hark to the call, high over all!
Hark to grim war's alarms!
Our Uncle Sam, as perils befall,
Sounds the loud call, "To Arms!"
Rally, brave sons, your land to defend;
Stand to your guns and nobly contend;
You are the ones on whom we depend;
Valorous sons, "To Arms!"

**CHORUS**

   Sons of America, America needs you.
   Protect your country's flag, the old Red,
     White, and Blue.
   Fight for America, home of the free.
   United stand to guard the land of liberty.

Fight for the flag, glorious flag,
Banner of stripe and star.
When it's assailed, what coward will lag?
Come with a loud hurrah,
Boldly to fight, the foeman defy,
"Freedom and right" your rallying cry;
You are our might, on you we rely,
Sons of America!

**REPEAT CHORUS**

# OUR SAMMY BOYS

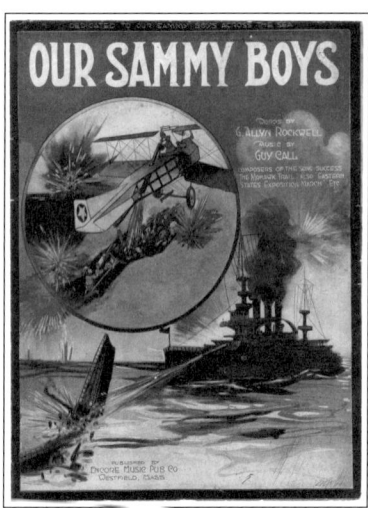

Lyrics: G. Allyn Rockwell
Music: Guy Call
Artist: E. H. Pfeiffer

Westfield, MA: Encore Music Pub. Co., 1917.

Our Sammy boys have crossed the sea,
God spare them all we pray;
They're fighting for our country's flag
That we may win the day.
They've gone to join the Allies
To end this world of wars,
And bring about democracy,
Our great and noble cause.

**CHORUS**
   Sammies on the ocean,
   Sammies in the air,
   Sammies in the trenches,
   Sammies everwhere,

Fighting for our country,
It will be no sham.
By golly, we will show them
They can't fool our Uncle Sam.

We'll sweep the seas of all U-boats,
To end this cruel war,
And bring about a lasting peace
Of international law.
We'll stop this awful slaughter,
Give freedom to the sea,
To ev'ry flag that floats aloft,
Make ev'ry country free.

**REPEAT CHORUS**

# WE HAIL FROM THE U.S.A.

Lyrics: Daisy Theresa Meyer
Music: Daisy Theresa Meyer
Artist: Dunk

New York: National Music Company, 1917.

We are in it, now we're in it,
This world is full of woe;
We've been driven to the limit,
But it's not our fault, you know;
We have tried to sooth the Kaiser,
His acts he'll surely rue;
He'll drop his reign when our aeroplanes
Show him a thing or two.

**CHORUS**

Oh, say, can you see,
We hail from the U.S.A.
Let's all join in this chorus,
We hail from the U.S.A.
The time is now ripe for us
To sink ev'ry U-boat we might see
And end his would-be majesty.
We hail from the U.S.A.,
And right and might are with us.

We are ready, yes, now ready
To fight with all our might.
Though we'll spend a lot of money
We shall always do what's right;
Our President is loyal,
He will guide us quite aright.
Yes, Germany's autocracy
We'll wipe clean out of sight.

**REPEAT CHORUS**

Our army, too, is ready
It's duties to fulfill,
And our regulars and engineers
Will prove American skill;
Yankee cavalry to back them,
Oh, won't those horses prance
When our Sammies bring the Stars and Stripes
To the firing line in France.

**CHORUS**

Oh, say, can you see.
We hail from the U.S.A.
Let's all join in this chorus,
We hail from the U.S.A.
The time is now ripe for us
To sink ev'ry U-boat we might see
And end his would-be majesty.
We hail from the U.S.A.,
And right and might are with us.
When Hohenzollerns meet the fate
Of Romanoff of Russia,
We'll shout "Hurrah" and say "Amen"
To the government of Prussia.

# LORRAINE (MY BEAUTIFUL ALSACE LORRAINE)

83

Words: Alfred Bryan
Music: Fred Fisher
Artist: André De Takacs

New York: McCarthy and Fisher Inc., 1917.

*This song was in the top 20 from April to June 1918 and reached number 6 in May. It was reprinted at least three times and was recorded by both Henry Burr and Reinald Werrenrath.*

Beside a campfire gleaming,
A grenadier was dreaming;
His thoughts went back again to other years.
Night shadows found him,
And as they gathered around him,
Tenderly he murmured through his tears:

**CHORUS**
　"Lorraine, Lorraine,
　My beautiful Alsace Lorraine,
　You're in my heart forever to remain.
　I see your village steeple,
　Your quaint old-fashioned people,
　And I wouldn't care if I could be there again.
　Lorraine, heart of France, part of France,
　Someday when all my worries are through,
　I'm coming to you;
　Lorraine, Lorraine,
　Oh, welcome me home once again.
　To live and die in my Alsace Lorraine.

He dreamt that he was straying
Among the children playing,
And often kissed his mother's tears away.
But ah, the waking!
How his sad heart it was breaking,
How he wished that he could dream for aye.

**REPEAT CHORUS**

# I'M HITTING THE TRAIL TO NORMANDY SO KISS ME GOOD-BYE

Lyrics: Charles Snyder and Oscar Doctor
Music: Charles Snyder and Oscar Doctor
Artist: E. H. Pfeiffer

New York and Chicago: Snyder Music Pub. Co., 1917.

*This song was also printed with a similar cover design featuring the singer Paul Elwood.*

84

Come, dear, kiss your boy goodbye,
Look me in the eye, promise you'll not cry.
Keep love's fire burning bright,
And Uncle Sam will see that things come right.
If I know that you are brave, I'll beat the foe.
So smile and, honey, kiss me ere I go.

**CHORUS**
    For I'm hitting the trail to Normandy, so kiss me goodbye;
    After we get the enemy, back home to your arms I'll fly.
    I'll come back to your shack, 'neath the sycamore tree,
    So, honey, keep your love and kisses waiting for me,
    'Cause I'm hitting the trail to Normandy,
    So kiss me goodbye.

Oh, hon, I will miss you so,
When away I go to battle with the foe;
Each night, I promise, in your sleep
I'll come to you across the briny deep.
Your smile will spur me like the flag unfurled.
One kiss for you, and I can free the world.

**REPEAT CHORUS**

# JOAN OF ARC, THEY ARE CALLING YOU

Lyrics: Alfred Bryan and Willie Weston
Music: Jack Wells
Artist: Albert Barbelle

New York: Waterson, Berlin and Snyder Co., 1917.

*A French version by Liane Held Carrera is printed below the English version. This song was in the top 20 from July 1917 to April 1918 and reached number 4 in November and December. It was reprinted at least six times and was recorded by Henry Burr, Willie Weston, and Vernon Dalhart.*

While you are sleeping,
Your France is weeping;
Wake from your dreams, Maid of France.
Her heart is bleeding,
Are you unheeding?
Come with the flame in your glance
Through the gates of heaven, with your sword in hand.
Come your legions to command.

**CHORUS**
Joan of Arc, Joan of Arc,
Do your eyes, from the skies, see the foe?
Don't you see the drooping fleur-de-lis?
Can't you hear the tears of Normandy?
Joan of Arc, Joan of Arc,
Let your spirit guide us through.
Come, lead your France to victory;
Joan of Arc, they are calling you.

Alsace is sighing,
Lorraine is crying.
Their mother, France, looks to you.
Her sons at Verdun,
Bearing the burden,
Pray for your coming anew;
At the gates of heaven, do they bar your way?
Souls that passed through yesterday.

**REPEAT CHORUS**

# AU REVOIR, BUT NOT GOOD-BYE, SOLDIER BOY

Lyrics: Lew Brown
Music: Albert Von Tilzer
Artist: E. E. Walton

New York: Broadway Music Corporation, 1917.

*This song was reprinted at least three times and was recorded by the Peerless Quartet.*

Though you're leaving me today, never fear;
In my thoughts you'll always be ever near.
There's a tear in ev'ry eye,
As the boys go marching by,
But they're out to do or die, hear them cheer.
All the things you planned to do
I am sure they will come true,
And I'll watch and wait for you, over here.

**CHORUS**
    Au revoir but not goodbye, soldier boy.
    Brush that teardrop from your eye, soldier boy.
    When you're on the deep blue sea,
    Will you sometimes think of me?
    I'll be waiting anxiously, soldier boy.

Tho' we're many miles apart, soldier boy,
Keep my picture near your heart, soldier boy.
When you've won your victory,
God will bring you back to me;
Au revoir but not goodbye, soldier boy.

Though your mother old and grey 'waits you here,
I will comfort her each day, never fear.
We all love you and you know
That we're proud to see you go,
But we're goin' to miss you so, over here.
When your fighting days are through
For the old Red, White, and Blue,
We'll be here to welcome you, with a cheer.

**REPEAT CHORUS**

# BRING BACK MY DADDY TO ME

Lyrics: William Tracey and Howard Johnson
Music: George W. Meyer
Artist: Rosenbaum Studios

New York: Leo. Feist, Inc., 1917.

*This song was in the top 20 from April to July 1918 and reached number 15 in June. It was reprinted at least once and was recorded by both Robert Lewis and Harry McClaskey.*

A sweet little girl, with bright golden curls
Sat playing with toys on the floor;
Her dad went away to enter the fray
At the start of the this long bitter war.
Her mother said, "Dear, your birthday is near.
Tomorrow your presents I'll buy."
The dear little child quickly looked up and smiled,
And said with a tear in her eye:

**CHORUS**
  "I don't want a dress or a dolly,
  'Cause dollies get broken 'round here.
  I don't want the skates, the books, or the slates
  You bought for my birthday last year.

  If you'll bring the present I ask for,
  Dear Mother, how happy I'll be;
  You can give all my toys
  To some poor girls and boys,
  But bring back my daddy to me!"

Her ma softly sighs and tears fill her eyes
As she hears her dear baby's plea.
She answers, "My dear, if daddy were here,
What a wonderful present 'twould be."
How many homes yearn for some one's return,
With honor, and justice and right?
There are more little girls in this grief-stricken world,
All saying the same thing tonight.

**REPEAT CHORUS**

# LIBERTY BELL (IT'S TIME TO RING AGAIN)

Lyrics: Joe Goodwin
Music: Halsey K. Mohr
Artist: Albert Barbelle

New York: Shapiro, Bernstein and Co. Inc., 1917.

*This song briefly reached the top 20 in May 1918. It was reprinted at least four times and was recorded by both the Peerless Quartet and Arthur Fields.*

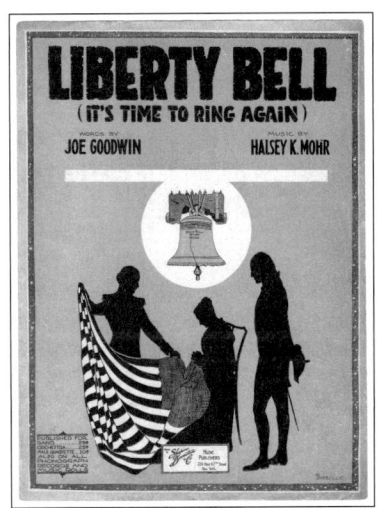

88

You have rested, Liberty Bell,
For a hundred years and more;
End your slumber, Liberty Bell,
Ring as you did before.
It's time to wake 'em up,
It's time to shake 'em up,
It's a cause worth ringing for:

**CHORUS**
   Liberty Bell, it's time to ring again,
   Liberty Bell, it's time to swing again,
   We're in the same sort of fix
   We were in Seventy-six.
   And we are ready to mix and rally 'round
     you

Like we did before, oh, Liberty Bell;
Your voice is needed now, Liberty Bell.
We'll hear your call one and all.
Though you're old and there's a crack in you,
Don't forget Old Glory's backin' you.
Oh! Liberty Bell, it's time to ring again.

Once you rang out, Liberty Bell,
As we watched Old Glory wave;
You have made us, Liberty Bell,
Land of the free and brave.
It's time to sing again,
It's time to ring again
For the cause you've got to save:

**REPEAT CHORUS**

## I'M GOING TO FOLLOW THE BOYS

Lyrics: Howard Rogers
Music: James V. Monaco

New York, Chicago et al.: M. Witmark and Sons, 1917.

*This song was in the top 20 from April to August 1918 and was number 4 in June. It was reprinted at least twice and was recorded by Elizabeth Spencer & Henry Burr.*

I've always had a lot of boys around me;
Wherever boys were, that's the place you found me.
Now I'm lonesome most ev'ry night,
There's not a single fellow in sight.
I miss the smiles of Billy, Jack, and Harry;
Percy was a dear;
I never felt so blue, but I know what to do.
I've got a great idea.

**CHORUS**
   I'm going to follow the boys over there,
   Anywhere, I don't care.
   I'm just dying for one little dance,
   But all my dancing partners are "Somewhere in France."
   I never nursed anyone, I'll admit,
   But I'm strong to do my bit,
   And if one little kiss or more
   Can help them in the war,
   Why, I'm going to follow the boys!

I don't know much about the military,
Still I can help them if it's necessary.
I don't know a thing about war,
I don't see what they're having it for,
But when it comes to things like osculation,
That's where I'd be missed,
If they should ever send, a suffrage regiment,
I'd hurry to enlist.

**CHORUS**
   I'm going to follow the boys over there,
   Anywhere, I don't care.
   I'd just love to be hugged by someone,
   But ev'ry fellow's right arm is holding a gun.
   I've never nursed anyone, I'll admit,
   But I'm strong to do my bit.
   There's a feeling down in my heart
   That I'm a Joan of Arc,
   So, I'm going to follow the boys!

**EXTRA CHORUS**
   I'm going to follow the boys over there,
   Anywhere, I don't care.
   Submarines have no terrors for me,
   One hard look from me and they'll go under the sea.
   I never nursed anyone, I'll admit,
   But I'm strong to do my bit.
   Lack of sugar won't worry me,
   Love's a necessity,
   So, I'm going to follow the boys!

# THE GIRLS OF THE U.S.A.

Lyrics: David Kohn
Music: A. L. Williams

Chicago: Ideal Music Publishing Co., 1917.

90

With our soldiers side by side
We will march with martial pride,
Hear the bugle loudly call,
Salute the flag girls one and all.
Listen, hear the fife and drum,
Look, the soldiers here they come.
Red, White, and Blue,
We'll stand by you
At home or in the fray.
Ev'ry girl that's in the land
Will join at thy command.
We're the girls of the U.S.A.

**CHORUS**
America, we hold thy banner high;
Old Glory we dignify.
My country 'tis of thee,
Sweet land of liberty,
We sing of thee both night and day.
Uncle Sam, to defend thy name
We will serve with might and main.
We're the girls of the U.S.A.

Dearly do we love our land;
We will give a helping hand
In the Red Cross ev'rywhere,
To give the soldiers tender care.
Whether on the land or sea,
We will with our heroes be.
Soldiers so brave,
The flag does wave;
Duty we must obey.
Ev'ry girl that's in the land
Will join at thy command.
We're the girls of the U.S.A.

**REPEAT CHORUS**

## OVER THERE

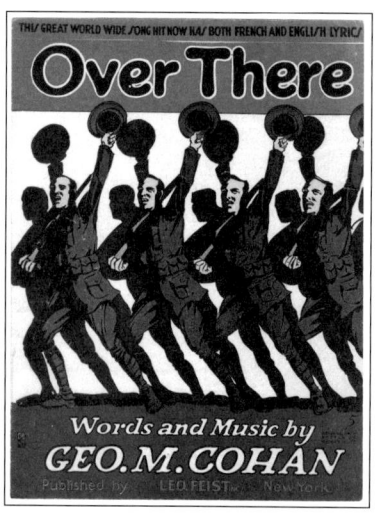

Lyrics: George M. Cohan
Music: George M. Cohan
Artist: Rosenbaum Studios (after a sketch by Henry Hutt)

New York: Leo. Feist Inc., 1917.

*This song was in the top 20 from July 1917 to May 1918 and remained at number 1 from August 1917 to January 1918. It was frequently issued by Feist: with the same cover design (with William J. Reilly as the featured singer) and with a cover design by Norman Rockwell. It was also issued several times in New York by William Jerome Publishing Corporation with various featured singers: Nora Bayes (with cover art by Albert Barbelle), William J. Reilly, and Harry Ellis (with cover art by Albert Barbelle). The song was also recorded by Enrico Caruso, Nora Bayes, the American Quartet, and the Peerless Quartet.*

Johnnie, get your gun, get your gun, get your gun.
Take it on the run, on the run, on the run.
Hear them calling you and me,
Ev'ry son of liberty.
Hurry right away, no delay, go today.
Make your daddy glad to have had such a lad.
Tell your sweetheart not to pine,
To be proud her boy's in line.

**CHORUS**
  Over there, over there,
  Send the word, send the word over there
  That the Yanks are coming, the Yanks are coming,
  The drums rum-tumming ev'rywhere.
  So prepare, say a pray'r,
  Send the word, send the word to beware.
  We'll be over, we're coming over,
  And we won't come back till it's over, over there.

Johnnie, get your gun, get your gun, get your gun.
Johnnie show the Hun you're a son-of-a-gun.
Hoist the flag and let her fly,
Like true heroes do or die.
Pack your little kit, show your grit, do your bit.
Soldiers to the ranks from the town and the tanks,
Make your mother proud of you,
And to liberty be true.

**REPEAT CHORUS**

# WHERE DO WE GO FROM HERE?

Lyrics: Howard Johnson and Percy Wenrich
Music: Howard Johnson and Percy Wenrich
Artist: Rosenbaum Studios

New York: Leo. Feist, Inc., 1917.

*This song was in the top 20 from July to December 1917 and was number 3 in September and October. Other featured singers with this cover design include the Avon Comedy Four, Frank Bessinger, Dorothea Brenner, Claire & Dorothea, Larry Comer, Josephine Davis, Collins & Harlan, Brice & King, Harry Ellis, Eleanor Fisher, Jackson & Wahl, the Klein Brothers, Beatrice Lambert, Neil McKinley, Artie Mellinger, Frank Mullane, Lewis C. Piotti, Santly & Norton, Blossom Seeley, Moe Thompson, Jack Wise, and the Watson Sisters. The song was recorded by both Arthur Fields and the American Quartet.*

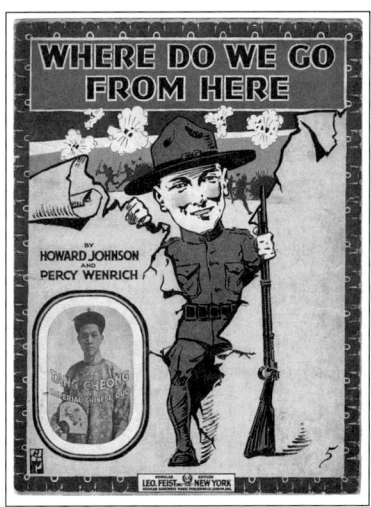

92

Paddy Mack drove a hack up and down Broadway;
Pat had one expression and he'd use it ev'ry day;
Anytime he'd grab a fare, to take them for a ride,
Paddy jumped up on the seat, cracked his whip, and cried:

**CHORUS**
"Where do we go from here, boys,
Where do we go from here?
Anywhere from Harlem to a Jersey City pier."
When Pat would spy a pretty girl, he'd whisper in her ear,
"Oh joy, oh boy,
Where do we go from here?"

One fine day, on Broadway, Pat was driving fast,
When the street was blown to pieces by a subway blast;
Down the hole poor Paddy went, a-thinkin' of his past,
Then he says, says he, "I think these words will be my last:"

**CHORUS**
"Where do we go from here, boys,
Where do we go from here?"
Paddy's neck was in the wreck, but still he had no fear;
He saw a dead man next to him and whispered in his ear,
"Oh joy, oh boy,
Where do we go from here?"

First of all, at the call, when the war began,
Pat enlisted in the army as a fighting man;
When the drills began, they'd walk a hundred miles a day.
Tho' the rest got tired, Paddy always used to say:

**CHORUS**
"Where do we go from here, boys,
Where do we go from here?
Slip a pill to Kaiser Bill and make him shed a tear;
And when we see the enemy, we'll shoot them in the rear,
Oh joy, oh boy,
Where do we go from here?"

# GOOD-BYE BROADWAY, HELLO FRANCE!

Lyrics: C. Francis Reisner and Benny Davis
Music: Billy Baskette
Artist: Rosenbaum Studios

New York: Leo. Feist, Inc., 1917.

*This song, featured as the finale in* Passing Show of 1917, *was in the top 20 from July 1917 to January 1918 and was number 2 from September to November. It was reprinted at least ten times and was recorded by both the Peerless Quartet and the American Quartet. A note at the end of the song states that the name of any city may be substituted for Broadway, if desired.*

Goodbye, New York town, goodbye, Miss Liberty.
Your light of freedom will guide us across the sea.
Ev'ry soldier's sweetheart bidding goodbye,
Ev'ry soldier's mother drying her eye.
Cheer up, we'll soon be there,
Singing this Yankee air:

### CHORUS
"Goodbye, Broadway, hello, France,
We're ten million strong.
Goodbye, sweethearts, wives, and mothers,
It won't take us long.
Don't you worry while we're there,
It's for you we're fighting, too;
So goodbye, Broadway, hello, France,
We're going to square our debt to you."

"Vive Pershing!" is the cry across the sea.
We're united in this fight for liberty.
France sent us a soldier, brave Lafayette,
Whose deeds and fame we cannot forget.
Now that we have the chance,
We'll pay our debt to France.

### REPEAT CHORUS

# I'M OFF FOR A PLACE SOMEWHERE IN FRANCE
# (BUT I'M COMING BACK FROM BERLIN)

Lyrics: Alex C. Fortner
Music: Kitt G. Sapp
Artist: Livezey

Kansas City, MO: Sapp-Fortner Pub. Co., 1917.

Goodbye, Yankee land, goodbye,
Don't cry, little girl, don't cry.
So long, old hometown,
Farewell, eyes of brown,
I'll soon return to you:
Goodbye, Yankee rocks and rills,
Farewell, fancy frocks and frills.
Smile, Mother, smile and remember all the while
The fight will soon be thru.

### CHORUS
I'm off for a place somewhere in France,
But I'm coming back from Berlin.
'Mid the battle's din I take my chance,
'Neath the Star Spangled Banner,
somewhere in France.

With the French tricolor and the British Jack,
"Old Glory" will triumph or never come back.
I'm off for a place somewhere in France,
But I'm coming back from Berlin.

No tears, eyes of brown, no tears,
No fears, Yankee land, no fears.
So long, dear old pals,
Take care of the gals,
I leave them all to you.
Goodbye, land of liberty,
The home of the brave and free.
And, Mother mine, we soon will cross the Rhine.
Then all will soon be thru.

### REPEAT CHORUS

# HOMEWARD BOUND

Lyrics: Howard Johnson and Coleman Goetz
Music: George W. Meyer
Artist: Rosenbaum Studios

New York: Leo. Feist, Inc., 1917.

*Other featured singers with this cover design include Belle Brooks, Harry Cooper, Dooley & Nelson, Eddie Mortan, Miss Pielert of Pielert & Scofield, and Claire Rochester. This song was also reprinted at least twice with a brown cover with a photograph of Emma Carus and at least once with a brown cover with a photograph of Dorothy Jardon.*

Somewhere far away,
Somewhere in the fray,
Many boys are over the sea,
Fighting for you, fighting for me.
They're all proud to carry a gun.
Their work will soon be done.

**CHORUS**

"Homeward Bound."
Someday they'll hear that welcome sound,
For while the shot and shell are flying,
For the ones at home they're sighing;
And tho' the skies seem grey,
There's bound to be a brighter day,
For when the dove of peace flies over the land,
They all will hear the general give the command,
"We are 'Homeward Bound'."
That's a wonderful, wonderful sound.

When the moon looks down
On the battleground,
By the campfires' flickering gleams,
They think of home in all their dreams.
Of the future naught can they learn.
Let's pray for their return.

**REPEAT CHORUS**

AD LIB. RECITATION:
"Homeward bound."
There's so much meaning in the sound
To all those faithful ones, those noble sons, upon the battleground,
For tho' their minds are on their duty
And the fight that must be won,
There are times they can't help wishing,
That their mighty task were done.
Even tho' you're not a soldier, tho' you're not across the sea,
There is something in these words that takes you back to mother's knee,
So let's keep the home fires burning, with the hope in every heart,
That they soon will be returning to us, nevermore to part.

# 'ROUND HER NECK SHE WEARS A YELLER RIBBON
# (FOR HER LOVER WHO IS FUR, FUR AWAY)

Lyrics: George A. Norton
Music: George A. Norton
Artist: E. H. Pfeiffer

New York and Denver: Theron C. Bennett, 1917.

Susie Simpkins in the village paper
Read about the soldiers' manly capers
And made up her mind
That a soldier's bonnie bride she'd be.
Volunteers were called a little later;
Big Si Hubbard stopped a-hoeing taters,
Fell right into line
And mustered with a company.
She cried and kissed him when he marched away,
And she vowed to keep him in her mind each day.

**CHORUS**

'Round her neck she wears a yeller ribbon,
She wears it in the winter and the summer, so they say.
If you ask her, "Why the decorations?"
She'll say, "It's fur my lover, who is fur, fur away.
Fur away, fur away."
If she is milkin' cows or mowing hay,
'Round her neck, she wears a yeller ribbon;
She wears it fur her lover, who is fur, fur away.

Months rolled by and patiently she waited,
Read the war news, greatly agitated.
No word from her boy
Till a letter from his Captain said,
"Your beau, Silas, he went out a-gunnin',
Soon he had the enemy a-runnin'."
Susie wept for joy,
Tho' further on the letter read,
"The enemy can run some you can bet,
But they couldn't capture Si, he's runnin' yet."

**REPEAT CHORUS**

## ARE WE DOWNHEARTED? NO! NO! NO!

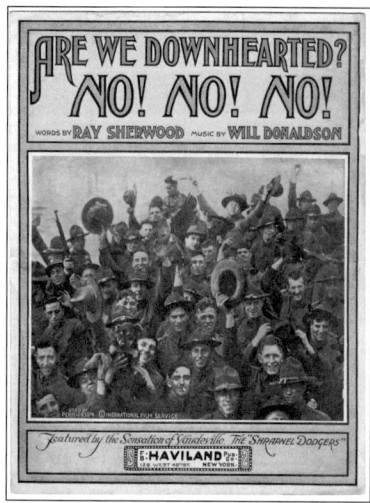

Lyrics: Ray Sherwood
Music: Will Donaldson

New York: F. B. Haviland Pub. Co. Inc., 1917.

"Cheer up, cheer up, cheer up ev'ryone,"
Said a soldier boy one day.
"Cheer up, cheer up, let us have some fun,
Before it's time to go away.
Ev'rybody sing, let your voices ring;
We'll march away with a song."

**CHORUS**
"Are we downhearted? No! No! No!
We are ready to go, go, go.
Goodbye, sweetheart, for a little while,
Goodbye, mother, let me see you smile.
Soon the bugle will blow, blow, blow.
Duty calls, we know;
And we'll hang the Kaiser to a sour apple tree.
Are we downhearted? No! No! No!"

"Dearie, dearie, now's the time to dance,
Soon the band will start to play.
Dearie, dearie, over there is France,
I won't forget this happy day.
Tho' we go to fight, still our hearts are light.
Cheer up, it's time to be gay."

**REPEAT CHORUS**

## AFTER THE WAR IS OVER WILL THERE BE ANY HOME SWEET HOME?

Lyrics: E. J. Pourmon and Joseph Woodruff
Music: Harry Andrieu
Artist: Pfeiffer Illustrating Co.

New York: Joe Morris Music Co., 1917.

*This song was reprinted at least twice with the same cover design and at least twice with the same cover design but different placement of the publisher's name. It was also issued at least twice by Broad & Market Music Company in Newark.*

98

Angels they are weeping o'er the foreign war,
Transports are sailing from shore to shore;
Brave heroes are falling to arise no more,
But still the bugle's calling ev'ry man to war.

**CHORUS**
After the war is over and the world's at peace,
Many a heart will be aching after the war has ceased.
Many a home will be vacant,
Many a child alone,
But I hope they'll all be happy
In a place called "Home Sweet Home."

Changed will be the picture of the foreign lands,
Maps will change entirely to diff'rent hands;
Kings and queens may ever rule their fellow man,
But pray they'll be united like our own free land.

**REPEAT CHORUS**

# WE'RE GOING TO TAKE THE GERM OUT OF GERMANY

Lyrics: Arthur J. Lamb
Music: Frederick V. Bowers
Artist: E. H. Pfeiffer

New York: Frederick V. Bowers Inc., 1917.

*This song was reprinted at least once.*

There's a song the boys are singing ev'rywhere,
You can hear the echoes ringing over there;
It must be right, for it can't be wrong.
They sing this song as they march along:

**CHORUS**
  "We're going to take the germ out of Germany,
  And a happy land 'twill be.
  We're going to take the germ out of Germany,
  As all the world will see.

  Sweet flowers will bloom where the cannons boom;
  Eternal peace will be planned.
  And when we take the germ out of Germany,
  They'll all love the fatherland."

Tho' they think that we may blunder, we don't care.
You can bet the Germans wonder, over there.
But they'll find out, as they will see,
We're fighting the cause of liberty.

**REPEAT CHORUS**

# WE'LL KNOCK THE HELIGO – INTO HELIGO – OUT OF HELIGOLAND!

Lyrics: John O'Brien
Music: Theodore Morse
Artist: Rosenbaum Studios

New York: Leo. Feist, Inc., 1917.

*Other featured singers with this cover design include Emma Carus, Harry Cooper, Dooley & Nelson, Hudler, Stein & Phillips, Billy Murray, Florence Timponi, Willie Weston, and Walter Winchell & Rita Greene.*

The bos'n blew and a Yankee crew
Had stopped to hear him say:
"My lads, get under way,
We're leaving port today, hooray!
We're going to meet the German fleet
And blow them inside out."
Each sailor boy was filled with joy
And all began to shout:

**CHORUS**
"We're on our way to Heligoland
To get the Kaiser's goat.
In a good old Yankee boat,
Up the Kiel Canal we'll float.
I'm a son-of-a-gun, if I see a Hun
I'll make him understand,
We'll knock the Heligo, into Heligo,
Out of Heligoland.
Yip!"

The anchor's hauled as the captain called.
The crew are standing by,
Each man to do or die,
When shells began to fly, goodbye!
"We're going to go and let them know
We hit with all our might,
I'd like to bet when we have met,
They'll know they had a fight."

**REPEAT CHORUS**

## WE'RE AFTER YOU

Lyrics: Jeff Branen
Music: Evans Lloyd
Artist: Rosenbaum Studios

New York: Jeff Branen Publisher, 1917.

*This song was reprinted at least once.*

The town is full of soldiers, see them here and there;
They're headed for the other side, you all know where.
They're singing as they march along,
It's just another soldier song.
Join in the chorus, ev'rybody, loud and strong:

**CHORUS**
"We're after you, two million strong, you bet.
And there are five or ten or twenty millions yet
To fight for dear old France that gave us Lafayette.
Better beat it, Bunco Bill, because we're after you."

Just see that line of transports sailing down the bay
All loaded down with soldiers who are on their way.
They're not afraid of anything,
Just listen to their voices ring.
Come on, now, ev'ryone of you, and help us sing:

**CHORUS**
"We're after you, to square that little debt
We owe to dear old France that gave us Lafayette;
When we get through with you, you'll be nobody, yet,
Better beat it, Bunco Bill, because we're after you."

# WE'RE COMING OVER AFTER YOU

Lyrics: Charles E. Henderson
Music: Norman Nathan

Salt Lake City, New York, and San Francisco: H & N Music Publishers., 1917.

102

Come along, Old Timer,
And we'll get aboard a liner,
And take a little journey far across the sea,
And perchance we will land in France,
And then we'll go to Germany.
There we'll meet old William
With our great big hundred million,
And show him we're Americans, you bet.
We'll defend our sacred rights
With the good old Stars and Stripes.
Oh, you Kaiser, we will get you yet.

**CHORUS**
  We know you don't like the United States,
  We know you hate the Red, White, and Blue.
  You'd like to rule over land and sea,
  But take a little message from the land of
    the free:
  Old Uncle Sammy and his million boys
  Are going to show what they can do.
  It will be a different story
  When we make you kiss Old Glory.
  We're coming, coming over after you.

Listen here, old Kaiser,
Don't you think you are the wiser,
And victory with submarines is now in sight.
Uncle Sam is a great big man,
Who'll show you how the Yankees fight.
You're for aristocracy,
But we don't seem to like it,
And that is why we're coming after you.
We'll crush your hypocrisy,
Instigate democracy.
Oh, you Kaiser, then what will you do?

**REPEAT CHORUS**

# "WE'LL FOLLOW PERSHING INTO OLD BERLIN"

Lyrics: R. C. Young
Music: R. C. Young

Columbus: R. C. Young Music Co., 1917.

Our Pershing's going o'er the sea
To fight for all humanity,
And place our flag in Germany,
Where it will float on high.
So if he gives a call for volunteers,
We'll all step forward and give three cheers:

**CHORUS**
　"And we'll follow Pershing into Old Berlin,
　O'er the foes around us lying.
　With fifty thousand strong
　We'll bravely march along,
　With the Stars and Stripes a-flying,
　And right will lead us on our way,
　And the victory we'll win.
　German guns and German cursing
　Cannot stop our march with Pershing
　Into Old Berlin!"

Now ev'ryone must do his bit,
The thing for which he knows he's fit,
And none of us must idly sit,
Until the battle's won.
And when the war is over, all will be
Just one big nation of the brave and free:

**REPEAT CHORUS**

# OVER THE RHINE

Lyrics: Jack Yellen
Music: Albert Gumble
Artist: Starmer

New York and Detroit: Jerome H. Remick & Co., 1917.

104

Goodbye ev'rybody, for we're going 'cross the sea,
Going for a visit to some friends in Germany.
They don't think we're coming, but they'll find out mighty soon;
Wait until they hear us marching to a Yankee tune.

**CHORUS**
  Over the Rhine, over the Rhine,
  Over the Rhine through the German line.
  Tell Kaiser Bill that his time has come,
  We'll put his army on the bum, bum, bum.
  He'll bite the dust,
  He'll bite the dust.
  We'll get to Berlin or we'll bust!
  WE MUST!
  So come, come, come or you're goin' to miss the fun,
  For we're all going over the Rhine.

When those Germans see us, they'll have fifty-seven fits.
We'll just take the Kaiser's crown and fill it up with Schlitz.
We know lots of other things we're goin' to make him do,
And then we'll put him in a can and bring him here to you.

**REPEAT CHORUS**

# THEY'RE ON THEIR WAY TO KAN THE KAISER

Lyrics: Harry C. Pyle Jr.
Music: Louis Thomas
Artist: JH

New York: Thomas & O'Connell Music Pub. Co., 1917.

105

Our boys are going 'cross the sea, but they will soon be back.
They're going over there to get the Kaiser, the Kaiser.
They're goin' to shoot him in the rear and cut off his attack.
And then he'll be a sadder man and wiser, The Kaiser.
And then a fun'ral bell to all the world will tell
That Bill passed away and he's goin' to go to… well.

**CHORUS**
Hurray, hurray, they all are on their way;
Hurray, hurray, they're eager for the fray.
For sinking ev'ry Yankee ship you bet he'll have to pay.
They're on their way to Kan the Kaiser.

Our navy's going over there to get this German knave.
They're goin' to send his U-boats to the bottom, the bottom.
And far and near you'll hear a cheer, you'll hear the people rave:
"We went to get the Kaiser and we got him, We got him."
And in the fatherland you'll hear a German band.
They'll play for the Kaiser with a lily in his hand.

**CHORUS**
Hurray, hurray, they all are on their way.
Hurray, hurray, they're eager for the fray.
And for destroying Belgium they will make him rue the day.
They're on their way to Kan the Kaiser.

**[EXTRA CHORUSES]**
Hurray, hurray, they all are on their way.
Hurray, hurray, they're going to win the fray.
They're goin' to "Crown" the Kaiser in a different kind of way.
They're on their way to Kan the Kaiser.

Hurray, hurray, they all are on their way.
Hurray, hurray, they're feeling awful gay.
And when they get to Germany, they'll have a jamboree.
They're on their way to Kan the Kaiser.

Hurray, hurray, they all are on their way.
Hurray, hurray, you bet there's no delay.
Old Kaiser Bill can dance, but to the fiddler he must pay.
They're on their way to Kan the Kaiser.

Hurray, hurray, they all are on their way.
Hurray, hurray, they're from the U.S.A.,
For Uncle Sam will take a hand and put old Bill away.
They're on their way to Kan the Kaiser.

Hurray, hurray, they all are on their way.
Hurray, hurray, they're going to win the day.
The funeral march of Kaiser Bill our army band will play.
They're on their way to Kan the Kaiser.

Hurray, hurray, they all are on their way.
Hurray, hurray, and they are going to stay.
They're going to make old Kaiser Bill look like a country jay.
They on their way to Kan the Kaiser.

Hurray, hurray, they all are on their way.
Hurray, hurray, they're happy bright and gay.
They're goin' to do it quickly and they'll come back right away.
They're on their way to Kan the Kaiser.

# WE'LL HAVE PEACE ON EARTH AND EVEN IN BERLIN

Lyrics: Jas. A. Flanigan
Music: Thomas J. Flanagan
Artist: Starmer

Syracuse and New York: The Thomas J. Flanagan Music Co., 1917.

Hark! hear the bugle calling,
Calling for you and for me
To uphold the honor and glory
Of our homes in the land of the free.
We'll do the same as our forefathers did
A hundred years ago,
And just like the rest
We'll try and do our best
And march upon the foe.

**CHORUS**
  Just a million strong
  We're goin' to march along
  To fight for liberty.
  We'll play Yankee Doodle
  On the Kaiser's noodle
  When we reach old Germany,
  For the sons of dear Old Glory
  Have never failed to win.
  When our boys begin to shout,
  "Kaiser Wilhelm this way out!"
  We'll have peace on earth
  And even in Berlin.

And when the battle's over
And we have peace over there,
All nations then can be thankful
That our old Uncle Sam did his share.
He's there to fight for a cause that is right
And freedom thru the land.
Our cause we've attain'd,
And liberty we've gained,
We'll remember this refrain:

**CHORUS**
  Just a million strong
  We're goin' to march along
  To fight for liberty.
  We'll play Yankee Doodle
  On the Kaiser's noodle
  When we reach old Germany,
  For the sons of dear Old Glory
  Have never failed to win.
  When the German folks get wise,
  They'll take Wilson's good advice,
  And they'll drive Kaiser Wilhelm
  From Berlin.

## IT'S A LONG WAY TO BERLIN, BUT WE'LL GET THERE!

Lyrics: Arthur Fields
Music: Leon Flatow
Artist: Rosenbaum Studios

New York: Leo. Feist, Inc., 1917.

*Other featured singers with this cover design include Maurice Burkhart (twice), Francis Maguire, Neil McKinley, Ed Morton, Flora Stern, and Florence Timponi. It was also reprinted at least three times with a brown cover with a photograph of Henry Bergman, featured in* Passing Show of 1917.

Rueben Plank, a husky Yank,
Came into town one day,
And said, "I can't resist,
I really must enlist.
By heck, I'll help to get that Kaiser Bill
I hear so much about."
He passed the test, threw out his chest,
And started into shout:

**CHORUS**
  "It's a long way to Berlin, but we'll get there!
  Uncle Sam will show the way,
  Over the line, then across the Rhine,
  Shouting, 'Hip! Hip! Hooray!'
  We'll sing Yankee Doodle 'Under the Linden,'
  With some real live Yankee Pep!
  [*shout*] Hep!
  It's a long way to Berlin, but we'll get there,
  And I'm on my way by heck by heck."

Rueben Plank was in the ranks
For just a little while.
Then he soon went ahead.
He's Corp'ral Plank instead,
By heck, he gets his squad together
And at night when all is still,
They sing the chorus Rueben wrote
To Mister Kaiser Bill:

**REPEAT CHORUS**

# WHEN YANKEE DOODLE MARCHES THROUGH BERLIN THERE'LL BE A HOT TIME IN THE U.S.A.

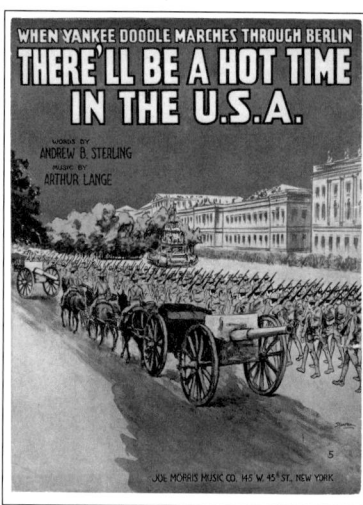

Lyrics: Andrew B. Sterling
Music: Arthur Lange
Artist: Starmer

New York: Joe Morris Music Co., 1917.

*This song was reprinted at least once.*

The whole population
Of the big French nation
Were lined up on the street one day.
Ev'ry flag was flying,
Ev'ry heart was sighing
For the Yankee boys were coming down that way;
When suddenly a Yankee voice cried out,
They could tell it was a Yankee when they heard him shout:

**CHORUS**
  "Here they come,
  Here they come,
  And the drums are beating.
  There'll be no retreating.
  They'll be there,
  They'll be there,
  For there's vict'ry in the air!
  And they'll win.
  Yes, they'll win.
  Then they'll flash the news to old Broadway.
  And when Yankee Doodle marches thro' Berlin,
  There'll be a hot time in the U.S.A."

Just picture them dashing,
When the news comes flashing,
"We've hauled the Kaiser's black flag down!"
To set bonfires burning
For the boy returning
From the trenches to his little old hometown.
"Just take a look," they heard the Yankee cry.
"Then go tell the Kaiser he can kiss himself goodbye."

**REPEAT CHORUS**

# WE'LL RAG OUR WAY THRU GERMANY, WE'LL FOX TROT OVER THE RHINE

Lyrics: E. J. Tomkins
Music: C. C. Miller

Deer Lodge, MT: Charles C. Miller, 1917.

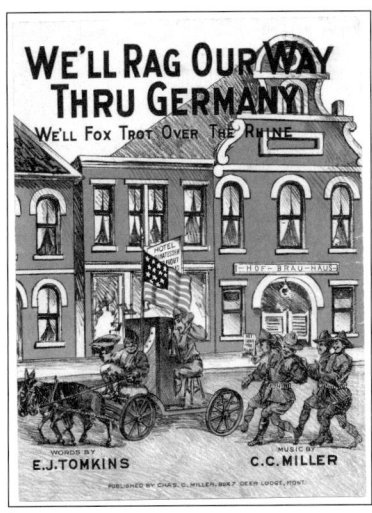

Young Sammy Jones he played piano in a cabaret,
Old Uncle Sammy called for soldiers, so he went away.
Now when he got to Europe, Sammy listened to the bands
Play French and English marches as they passed reviewing stands.
Said Sammy then, "I'm glad I came, this music's awful tame.
Some ragtime pep is what we need to liven up the game."
That night he woke up when all the lights were out;
The sentry he was startled when he heard young Sammy shout:

**CHORUS**
  "We'll rag our way thru Germany
  We will fox trot over the Rhine.
  Alsace Lorraine will be joined to France again,
  While syncopated music echoes down the line.
  Instead of soldiers we'll just leave a jazz band
  In ev'ry town we capture in that land.
  To a Yankee rag with a Yankee flag
  We will rag our way thru Germany."

All nations have their marches and their well-beloved songs,
There's just one brand of melody for which a Yankee longs.
Our Allies brave will soon be stepping with that raggy swing
And with those ragtime melodies they'll make all Europe ring.
We'll start a jitney dance in ev'ry castle on the Rhine,
A ragtime band will start to play each ev'ning prompt at nine.
We'll teach Kaiser Bill that we are here to win,
And dance to raggy music thru the streets of old Berlin.

**REPEAT CHORUS**

# WHEN THE KAISER DOES THE GOOSE-STEP TO A GOOD OLD AMERICAN RAG

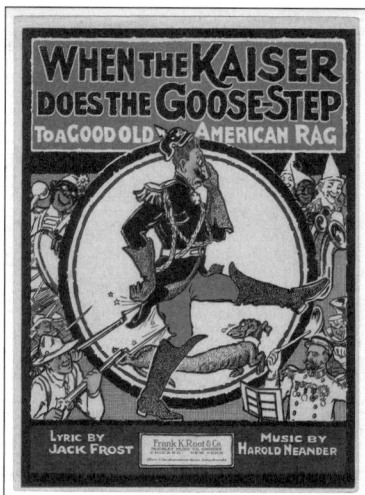

Lyrics: Jack Frost
Music: Harold Neander

Chicago and New York: Frank K. Root & Co., 1917.

There are lots of places where I'd like to be
And many, many sights that I would
  surely like to see;
But the greatest thing in all the world to give
  a man a thrill
Is surely going to happen
When the Yanks get Kaiser Bill.
They'll make him dance for fair
And I'd sure like to be there.

**CHORUS**
  When the Kaiser does the goose step to a
    good old American rag
  They'll play it jerky and make Bill "walk
    turkey" and salute our grand old flag.
  He'll be wiser when he two-steps to the
    songs of Yankee-land
  Or fox trots to a good old Dixie tune (make
    it soon, make it soon)
  There'll be a jazz band from Dixie
  And Bill won't dare say "Nixie."
  When the Yankees say, "Come, William,
    dance that drag!"
  Alexander's band from Tennessee
  Will be there to play the music for the jubilee,
  When the Kaiser does the goose step to a
    good old American rag.

Sousa's band will be right there to lead that
  dance.
"The Stars and Stripes Forever" will be play'd
  for Willie's prance.
Six Brown Brothers will fill the air with their
  big saxophones,
Imagine William's feelings
When he hears their pleading tones!
He'll dance till they get thro'
And they'll make him like it, too.

**REPEAT CHORUS**

# WE ARE OUT FOR THE SCALP OF MISTER KAISER MAN

Lyrics: Charles Summers
Music: Harry Schwartz
Artist: Will E. Livezey

Kansas City, MO: Kay-See Music Co., 1917.

There's a military autocrat in far off Germany,
Who has notified our Uncle Sam we cannot use the sea;
This Kaiser man obeys no law and uses savage means
To sink our ships and citizens with pirate submarines.

**CHORUS**
We are out for the scalp of Mister Kaiser Man,
Our hands and hearts enlisted in this Yankee plan;
So buckle on your armor and bid your girl adieu.
She will prove as faithful as our country has to you.
We will fight for humanity and true democracy,
And stand together firmly for the freedom of the sea;
So ev'ryone must do his bit for the Red, the White, and Blue,
And force this Kaiser man to bow to Yankee Doodle-Doo.

We have heroes in our army and our navy as of yore,
There's no yellow in Old Glory, we have proven that before;
Our men and women have the nerve, the brains, and coin to spend,
So hoist the flag of liberty, despotic rule must end.

**REPEAT CHORUS**

# WE ARE BOUND TO GET THE KAISER

Lyrics: William Hogan
Music: William Hogan

Flint: James Corbin, 1917.

*This song was reprinted at least twice.*

112

I hear the bugle sounding, it's calling you and me
To go and stop the Kaiser from ravaging the sea.
His method of destruction, no longer we'll endure,
So goodbye, Mister Kaiser, we are going to stop you sure.

**CHORUS**
    We're bound to get the Kaiser, just send this word along,
    We're bound to get the Kaiser, the whole world knows he's wrong,
    We're bound to get the Kaiser, and then set Belgium free,
    Peace between all nations, and freedom on the sea.

We hear the Belgians calling, to us they did appeal,
To stop those scenes appalling, on every battlefield,
Where the cruel Kaiser, when in his maddened rage,
He never showed no mercy, no virtue, youth or age.

**REPEAT CHORUS**

**CHORUS 3**
    When we cross the ocean to meet our German foes,
    We'll shake hands with the lily, the shamrock, and the rose,
    Likewise the Scottish thistle and the Russian eagle, too,
    Then all march on together 'neath the old Red, White, and Blue.

**CHORUS 4**
    When the war is over, and freedom's victory won,
    All nations then will honor the land of Washington.
    Then homeward we'll come marching, with our starry flag unfurled,
    Proclaiming human freedom throughout the Christian world.

**CHORUS 5**
   Then we'll sign a treaty to serve in future years,
   No more see homeless orphans, no more see widows' tears,
   No more such human slaughter, no more a U-boat zone,
   No more we'll see the Kaiser upon the German throne.

# GOOD-BYE, FAREWELL, RAUS MIT KAISER BILL

Lyrics: G. H. Carey
Music: C. H. Driskell

Akron: Success Music Co., 1917.

Uncle Sam is calling us to battle,
To battle for the good old U.S.A.
Put on your fighting armor and be ready.
To the tune of "Hail Columbia" march away.
Way down South in Dixie hear them calling,
Calling ev'ry man to line up with a will,
While the band plays "Marching Through
  Georgia."
Goodbye, farewell, raus mit Kaiser Bill.

### CHORUS

When the Kaiser hears the strains of Yankee
  Doodle
As the boys in khaki charge along the line,
His dream of being king of all will vanish
As he takes his farewell journey down the
  Rhine.
For "Columbia, the Gem of the Ocean,"
The Stars and Stripes will wave from ev'ry
  hill.
"Tramp, Tramp, Tramp, the Boys are
  Marching."
Goodbye, farewell, raus mit Kaiser Bill.

See! The boys in blue are marching onward,
Old Glory flies o'er evry hill and dale.
The emblem of the free proclaim the vict'ry,
For our noble boys were never known to fail.
We will fight for peace and freedom always,
Keeping it o'er ev'ry dale and ev'ry hill,
While our boys are marching to vict'ry.
Goodbye, farewell, raus mit Kaiser Bill.

**REPEAT CHORUS**

# WE'RE GOING TO HANG THE KAISER UNDER THE LINDEN TREE

Lyrics: James Kendis and James Brockman
Music: James Kendis and James Brockman
Artist: Rosenbaum Studios

New York: Kendis-Brockman Music Co. Inc., 1917.

*This song was featured in the Shubert musical comedy* Over the Top, *which starred the young Fred Astaire. The song was reprinted at least twice.*

114

Have you heard the news?
Have you heard the news?
The new that's going all around?
Chase away the blues
The weary, weary blues.
Our Yankee boys are Berlin bound.
Somebody has been fooling with the deck,
Somebody's goin' to get it in the neck.

**CHORUS**
 We're going to hang the Kaiser under the
  linden tree,
 Under the linden tree over in Germany.
 We'll take along a clever little bumble bee
 To sting him, to sting him upon the helmet,
 The helmet, the Kaiser!
 Tramp, tramp, tramp, the boys are marching
 To fight for peace and for democracy;
 We'll trim his moustache nice and neat
 And then we'll cut off his retreat
 And hang him under the linden tree.

If the rope should break,
If the rope should break,
We won't send him very far.
He will take a trip,
A lovely little trip,
Where he can play with Nick, the Czar.
Somebody has been bragging much too much.
Somebody we know surely is in Dutch.

**CHORUS**
 We're going to hang the Kaiser under the
  linden tree,
 Under the linden tree over in Germany.
 We'll take along a clever little bumble bee
 To sting him, to sting him upon the helmet,
 The helmet, the Kaiser!
 Tramp, tramp, tramp, the boys are marching
 To fight for peace and for democracy;
 We've never lost a battle yet
 And we won't lose this one, you bet.
 We'll hang him under the linden tree.

## I DON'T KNOW WHERE I'M GOING BUT I'M ON MY WAY

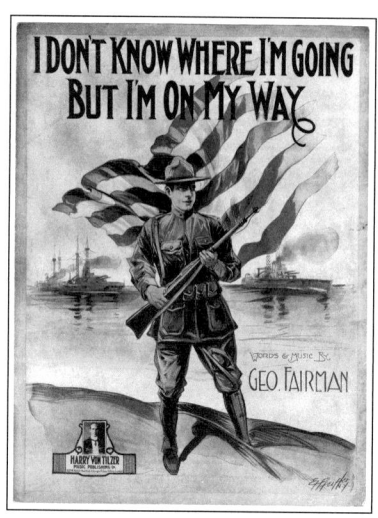

Lyrics: George Fairman
Music: George Fairman
Artist: E. H. Pfeiffer

New York: Harry Von Tilzer Music Publishing Co., 1917.

*This song was in the top 20 from September 1917 to January 1918 and reached number 9 in December. It was reprinted at least once and was recorded by both the Peerless Quartet and Henry Burr.*

Goodbye, ev'rybody, I'm off to fight the foe.
Uncle Sammy is calling me, so I must go.
Gee, I'm feeling fine,
Don't you wish that you were me?
For I'm sailing tomorrow
Over the deep blue sea.

**CHORUS**
And I don't know where I'm going,
But I'm on my way,
For I belong to the regulars
I'm proud to say.
And I'll do my duty night or day.
I don't know where I'm going,
But I'm on my way.

Take a look at me,
I'm a Yankee thro' and thro'.
I was born on July the Fourth in ninety-two,
And I'll march away with a feather in my hat,
For I'm joining the army.
What do you think of that?

**REPEAT CHORUS**

# I MAY BE GONE FOR A LONG, LONG TIME

Lyrics:  Lew Brown
Music:  Albert Von Tilzer
Artist:  André De Takacs

New York:  Broadway Music Corporation, 1917.

*This song, featured in the musical review* Hitchy-Koo, *was in the top 20 from August 1917 to February 1918 and reached number 2 in December. It was reprinted at least twice and was recorded by both the Peerless Quartet and the Shannon Four.*

116

Goodbye, dear, I'm leaving you today.
Don't cry, dear, just dry those tears away.
Duty calls and I must obey,
But I'll always hope and pray,
While I'm sailing far across the sea.
Will you always think of me?

**CHORUS**
  I may be gone for a long, long time,
  Long, long time, long, long time,
  But when I go you will know
  That I'll always pine for the day when you'll
    be mine.

  Be true to me for a long, long time,
  Rain or shine, sweetheart mine,
  And I'll be just as true to you,
  As to the Red, White, and Blue,
  Though I'm gone for a long, long time.

Someday, dear, when I come back to you,
We will build a little home for two.
Then we'll settle down, dear, for life
Far away from care and strife.
Cheer up, dear, and when I'm far away,
Don't forget to write each day.

**REPEAT CHORUS**

# OVER THE TOP

Lyrics: Alfred Bryan
Music: Pete Wendling and Jack Wells
Artist: Albert Barbelle

New York: Waterson, Berlin and Snyder Co., 1917.

*This song was reprinted at least once.*

117

See those Yankee Doodle soldiers on their way,
Down the bay,
Hip hooray!
Ev'ry gallant heart is anxious for the fray,
And they will welcome the day;
Hear those voices shout,
As the boats pull out:

**CHORUS**
 "Over the top,
 When they see us coming,
 They'll never stop;
 When we get them running,
 We'll send them back,
 Bend them back to the Rhine.
 We'll make a crack in that Hindenburg line;
 Those Yankee Doodle boys
 Will make a lot of noise,
 The old Red, White, and Blue,
 The Yankee Eagle, too;
 They'll all be there,
 Doing their share,
 When we go over the top."

Someone said those Yankee fellows couldn't fight.
Was he right?
Not tonight!
There's a half a million, count them, left to right,
And a few million in sight;
Hip hooray! they're off;
Good luck, "Mozzletoff."

**CHORUS**
 "Over the top,
 When they see us coming,
 They'll never stop;
 When we get them running,
 We'll send them back,
 Bend them back to the Rhine.
 We'll make a crack in that Hindenburg line;
 The fighting Sixty-nines,
 Will break the German lines;
 They'll hand the Kaiser, too,
 Another Waterloo;
 They'll all be there,
 Doing their share,
 When we go over the top."

# LADDIE BOY

Lyrics: Will D. Cobb
Music: Gus Edwards

New York: The Gus Edwards Music House, 1917.

*This song was in the top 20 from September to November 1918 and reached number 11 in November. It was recorded by both Nora Bayes and Albert Campbell & Henry Burr.*

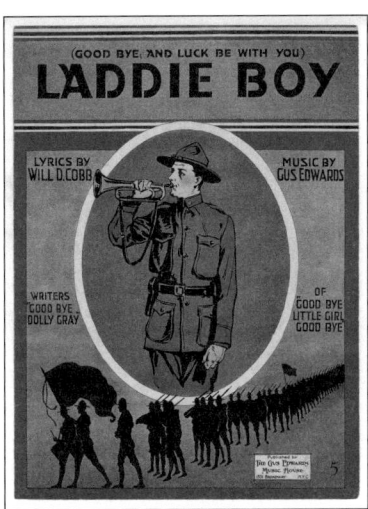

118

War in the air,
Blare, bugles, blare.
Drums beat the loud roll call.
Hark! down the street
Tramp, tramp of feet.
Up go the windows all.
North and South, East and West,
Forth they come the country's best.
Never mind that parting tear,
Let there be one parting cheer:

**CHORUS**
"Goodbye and luck be with you,
Laddie boy, Laddie boy,
Whatever your name may be.
There's a look in your eye
As you go marching by
That tells me you will dare and do and die.
And when you hear those shells begin to sing,
There'll be someone somewhere
Who cares will murmur this prayer:
'May you win your share of glory,
And come back to tell the story.'
Goodbye and good luck, Laddie boy."

Somewhere in France
There waits the chance,
One fighting chance that's all.
May you return
To hearts that yearn,
Or like a soldier fall
As in granddaddy's day,
Tho' today no blue nor gray,
Clad in khaki fine and fit
Marching on to do your bit.

**REPEAT CHORUS**

# HE SLEEPS BENEATH THE SOIL OF FRANCE

Lyrics: Tell Taylor
Music: Tell Taylor

Chicago: Tell Taylor Music Publisher, 1917.

Upon the battlefield so gray,
A wounded soldier lay.
He knew that he was going to die
There on that summer's day.
"Tell mother I'm not coming home
And tell her not to cry,
I've done the best that I knew how,
I'll meet her bye and bye."

**CHORUS**
He sleeps beneath the soil of France
So many miles away.
He left behind the one he loved
And a mother old and gray.
He fought because he knew 'twas right to fight for liberty.
And now he's sleeping over there,
Beneath the soil of France.

A crown of glory now he wears
Beyond the pearly gates.
The one he left so far away
No longer for him waits.
A smile upon her dear sweet face,
No tears bedim her eye.
She'll meet him on the other side,
A way up there on high.

**REPEAT CHORUS**

# BREAK THE NEWS TO MOTHER

Lyrics: Charles K. Harris
Music: Charles K. Harris
Artist: Starmer

New York: Chas. K. Harris, 1917.

*This song was originally published in 1897, during the Spanish-American War. It was in the top 20 from September 1917 to April 1918 and reached number 10 in November and again in February. It was reprinted at least five times, sometimes with a brown and sometimes with a green cover. It was recorded by both the Shannon Four and Henry Burr.*

120

While the shot and shell were screaming up on the battlefield
The boys in blue were fighting their noble flag to shield.
Came a cry from their brave captain,
"Look boys! Our flag is down.
Who'll volunteer to save it from disgrace?"
"I will," a young voice shouted,
"I'll bring it back or die,"
Then sprang into the thickest of the fray,
Saved the flag but gave his young life
All for his country's sake.
They brought him back and softly heard him say:

**CHORUS**
　"Just break the news to mother.
　She knows how dear I love her,
　And tell her not to wait for me,
　For I'm not coming home;
　Just say there is no other
　Can take the place of mother,
　Then kiss her dear, sweet lips for me
　And break the news to her."

From afar a noted gen'ral had witnessed this brave deed.
"Who saved our flag? Speak up, lads. 'Twas noble, brave indeed."
"There he lies, sir," said the captain,
"He's sinking very fast,"
Then slowly turned away to hide a tear.
The gen'ral in a moment
Knelt down beside the boy,
Then gave a cry that touched all hearts that day;
"It's my son! My brave young hero,
I thought you safe at home."
"Forgive me, father, for I ran away."

**REPEAT CHORUS**

# SAY A PRAYER FOR THE BOYS "OUT THERE"

Lyrics: Bernie Grossman
Music: Alex Marr
Artist: Starmer

New York: Joe Morris Music Co., 1917.

*Other featured singers with this cover design include Gertrude Cogert, Edah Delbridge Trio, Elsie Murphy, Florence Rayfield, Polly Russell, and Jeannette Yonge.*

A mighty nation hears a ringing call to arm,
A call that draws her sons from city, vale, and farm.
A nation sends the best of us across the sea,
That the rest of us forever may be free.
An' while a mighty nation's heart will yearn,
Let's pray that they soon will return.

**CHORUS**
  Won't you say a prayer for the boys out there,
  For our heroes o'er the sea,
  In that raging fray, by night and day?
  They're fighting for you and me.
  When they take their stand in no man's land,
  We know they'll do their share.
  So that we may live, their lives they give.
  Say a prayer for the boys out there.

A mighty nation's voice will reach across the sea,
And cheer the hearts of those who fight for liberty.
A nation's prayers will help the weaker ones along,
And will strengthen them when everything goes wrong.
An' while a nation's sons will do or die,
Let's call to the One up on high.

**REPEAT CHORUS**

# WHEN YANKEE DOODLE LEARNS TO "PARLEZ VOUS FRANÇAIS"

Lyrics: Will J. Hart
Music: Edward G. Nelson
Artist: Albert Barbelle

New York: A. J. Stasny Music Co., 1917.

*This song was in the top 20 from October 1917 to March 1918 and reached number 11 in November. Other featured singers with this cover design include Anna Chandler, Julia Dika, "Janet of France," and Lew Seymour. The song was recorded by Arthur Fields.*

122

When Yankee Doodle came to Paris town,
Upon his face he wore a little frown;
To those he'd meet upon the street,
He couldn't speak a word.
To find a miss that he could kiss
It seemed to be absurd.
But if this Yankee should stay there awhile,
Upon his face you're bound to see a smile.

**CHORUS**
  When Yankee Doodle learns to "Parlez
    vous Français,
  Parlez vous Français," in the proper way,
  He will call each girlie "Ma cherie."
  To every miss that wants a kiss
  He'll say, "Wee, wee, on ze Be, on ze Bou,
  On ze Boule, Boulevard."
  With a girl, with a curl,
  You can see him promenade.
  When Yankee Doodle learns to "Parlez
    vous Français,"
  "Oo la la, Sweet Papa," he will teach them
    all to say.

Soon Yankee Doodle left old Paris town,
Upon his face there was a coat of brown,
For every man of Uncle Sam
Was fighting in a trench.
Between each shell, they learned quite well
To speak a little French.
When Yankee Doodle gets back to Paree,
He'll break a million hearts, take it from me.

**REPEAT CHORUS**

# I DON'T WANT TO GET WELL

Lyrics: Howard Johnson and Harry Pease
Music: Harry Jentes
Artist: Rosenbaum Studios

New York: Leo. Feist, Inc., 1917.

*This song was in the top 20 from November 1917 to April 1918 and reached number 3 in January and February. It was reprinted at least five times and was recorded by both Arthur Fields and Van & Schenck.*

I just received an answer to a letter that I wrote,
From a pal who marched away;
He was wounded in the trenches somewhere in France,
And I worried about him night and day.
"Are you getting well?" was what I wrote;
This is what he answered in his note:

**CHORUS**
  "I don't want to get well,
  I don't want to get well,
  I'm in love with a beautiful nurse.
  Early ev'ry morning, night, and noon
  The cutest little girl comes and feeds me with the spoon.
  I don't want to get well,
  I don't want to get well.
  I'm glad they shot me on the fighting line, fine!
  The doctor says that I'm in bad condition,
  But oh, oh, oh, I've got so much ambition;
  I don't want to get well,
  I don't want to get well,
  For I'm having a wonderful time."

I showed this letter to a friend who lives next door to me
And I heard him quickly say,
"Goodbye, pal, I must be going, I'm off to war,
And I hope that I'm wounded right away;
If what's in this letter here is true,
I'll get shot and then I'll write to you:"

**CHORUS**
  "I don't want to get well,
  I don't want to get well,
  I'm in love with a beautiful nurse.
  Though the doctor's treatments show results,
  I always get a bad relapse each time she feels my pulse;
  I don't want to get well,
  I don't want to get well,
  I'm glad they shot me on the fighting line, fine!
  She holds my hand and begs me not to leave her,
  Then all at once I get so full of fever.
  I don't want to get well,
  I don't want to get well,
  For I'm having a wonderful time."

# MY RED CROSS GIRLIE

Lyrics: Harry Bewley
Music: Theodore Morse
Artist: Rosenbaum Studios

New York: Leo. Feist, Inc., 1917.

124

Ev'ry Red Cross girlie likes a soldier,
There's a feeling in her heart akin to love.
Some laddie with a gun upon his shoulder
Very often is the one she's thinking of.
Ev'ry soldier laddie has a yearning
For some noble girlie, all in white.
In his heart the light of love is always burning
For a little Red Cross girlie day and night.

**CHORUS**

"My Red Cross girlie, for you I'm calling,
Tho' you're many miles away.
My Red Cross girlie, for you I'm falling,
Longing for you night and day.
I need you, sweetheart, for I am wounded
By a cunning fellow's dart.
But don't swoon, dear,
For the wound, dear,
Is only somewhere in my heart."

Ev'ry girlie loves a soldier laddie,
And ev'ry girlie loves a boy sincere.
She loves him better sometimes than her daddy,
Proud of one who doesn't know the thing
  called fear.
A soldier goes into battle tireless,
Doesn't mind the cannon's shot and shell.
If this message he can only send by wireless
To a Red Cross girlie whom he loves so well:

**REPEAT CHORUS**

## WE'RE GOING OVER

Lyrics: Andrew B. Sterling, Bernie Grossman, and Arthur Lange
Music: Andrew B. Sterling, Bernie Grossman, and Arthur Lange
Artist: Starmer

New York: Joe Morris Music Co., 1917.

*This song reached number 20 in the top 20 in December 1917. It was reprinted at least four times.*

125

The major wrote the chorus, but he fell down on the verse.
The colonel tried to write it, but he only made it worse.
They called in Captain Cuttle, but he missed it by a mile,
So they left it to the sergeant of the file.
Said he, "We need no verse at all to this here little thing,"
So they went and taught the Sammies how to sing:

**CHORUS**
  "We're going over, we're going over;
  They want to settle up that fuss,
  And they put it up to us,
  So what do we care,
  So what do we care,
  We'll go sailing cross the foam;
  And we'll show them what the Yankee Doodle boys can do,
  Then we'll come marching home."

The boys all sang the chorus to the leader of the band;
He taught his men to play it and it sounded mighty grand.
Said he, "I'll write a part in for the fellow with the drum,
So the boys in France can hear us when we come."
The orders came next morning and they yelled, "We're on our way."
And they sang as they went sailing down the bay:

**REPEAT CHORUS**

# SOMEWHERE IN FRANCE IS THE LILY

Lyrics: Philander Johnson
Music: Joseph E. Howard
Artist: Starmer

New York, Chicago et al.: M. Witmark and Sons, 1917.

*This song was in the top 20 from December 1917 to March 1918 and reached number 11 in February. It was reprinted at least five times with the same cover design and at least twice with a new cover design featuring Joseph E. Howard. It was recorded by both Henry Burr and Charles Hart.*

One day as morning shed its glow
Across the eastern sky,
A boy and girl in accents low
In a garden said, "Goodbye!"
She said, "Remember as you stray,
When each must do his share,
The flowers blooming here today
Are emblems over there!"

**CHORUS**
　Somewhere in France is the lily,
　Close by the English rose;
　A thistle so keen,
　And a shamrock so green,
　And each loyal flow'r that grows.

Somewhere in France is a sweetheart,
Facing the battle's chance,
For the flow'r of our youth
Fights for freedom and truth
Somewhere in France.

Each morning in that garden fair,
Where sweetest perfumes dwell,
The lassie whispers low a pray'r
For the flow'rs she loves so well.
And over there as night draws near,
Amid the shot and flame,
Unto the flag he holds so dear,
A soldier breathes her name.

**REPEAT CHORUS**

# GIDDY GIDDAP! GO ON! GO ON! WE'RE ON OUR WAY TO WAR

Lyrics: Jack Frost
Music: Jack Frost

New York: Frank K. Root & Co., 1917.

*This song was reprinted at least once.*

127

You talk about your rube recruits
In overalls and jumper suits.
You ought to see the soldier boys of Pumpkinville
The day that they were call'd, by gosh!
They left their field of corn and squash
And said goodbye to all their friends in Pumpkinville.
Then Hy and Cy and Ephraham took Hezekiah's bay,
And as they rode away they sang a song that goes this way:

**CHORUS**

"Giddy Giddap! Go on! Go on!
We're on our way to war!
We're goin' to tell 'em to go to — well!
That's what we're fighting for!
We didn't want to do it, boys,
But now they've made us sore;
Giddy Giddap! Go on! Go on!
We're on our way to war!"

Miss Mandy said to Hiram Green,
"Well, you're the bravest man I've seen.
I'll be so proud when you have join'd the cavalry."

Then Hiram said, "That's right, of course,
But I ain't goin' to ride no horse.
Just let me say that I will join the infantry,
'Cause when the bugle sounds 'retreat', you bet that I'll obey.
I'll run so fast that I don't want no horses in my way."

**REPEAT CHORUS**

The boys were fighting hard one day,
And in the middle of the fray
You should have seen old Hiram Green from Pumpkinville.
He found a shell hole by his side,
He jump'd down in and tried to hide,
And wished he was back home, by gosh! in Pumpkinville.
The captain came and found him, said, "Get out where bullets burst."
Said Hy, "I beg your pardon, but I found this shell hole first."

**REPEAT CHORUS**

# LONG BOY

Lyrics: William Herschell
Music: Barclay Walker
Artist: Garth Williams

New York: Shapiro, Bernstein & Co., 1917.

*This song was in the top 20 from December 1917 to February 1918 and reached number 16 in January. It was reprinted at least five times and was recorded by both the Peerless Quartet and Steve Porter.*

128

He was just a long, lean country gink
From 'way out West where th' hop-toads wink;
He was six feet two in his stockin' feet,
An' kept gittin' thinner th' more he'd eat.
But he was as brave as he was thin,
When th' war broke out, he got right in,
Unhitch'd his plow, put th' mule away.
Then th' old folks heard him say:

**CHORUS**
"Good-by, Ma! Good-by, Pa!
Good-by, Mule, with yer old hee-haw!
I may not know what th' war's about,
But you bet, by gosh, I'll soon find out.
An', oh, my sweetheart, don't you fear,
I'll bring you a king fer a souvenir;
I'll git you a Turk an' a Kaiser, too,
An' that's about all one feller could do!"

One pair of socks was his only load
When he struck fer town by th' old dirt road.
He went right down to th' public square
An' fell in line with th' soldiers there.
Th' sergeant put him in uniform,
His gal knit mitts fer to keep him warm;
They drill'd him hard, they drill'd him long,
Then he sang his farewell song!

**REPEAT CHORUS**

# IF SAMMY SIMPSON SHOT THE CHUTES WHY SHOULDN'T HE SHOOT THE SHOTS?

129

Lyrics: Edward P. Morgan
Music: Harry Von Tilzer
Artist: E. H. Pfeiffer

New York: Harry Von Tilzer Music Publishing Co., 1917.

Down at the seashore Sammy Simpson used to shoot the chutes.
He said, "I must enlist because the navy needs recruits."
When they examined him, they saw a medal on his chest.
He pinned it there himself because he shot the chutes the best.
So Sammy posed and said, "Well, do I go?"
They gave three hearty cheers and answered, "No!"

**CHORUS**
If Simpson shot the chutes, why shouldn't he shoot the shots?
Sammy would seem so cute, dressed in a sailor's suit.
If Sammy's sister sewed some shirts for soldiers by the box,
Why shouldn't Sammy sail the sea and sew the sailors' sox?

Sammy said he surely should do something for his land.
Sitting still ashore was something Sammy couldn't stand.
Shootin' shot and shell at ships at sea would suit him lots.
If Sammy Simpson shot the chutes, why shouldn't he shoot the shots?

Now Sammy said the sergeant shouldn't say you shan't enlist,
So Sammy got so sore he slapped the sergeant on the wrist.
The sergeant said, "You shall be shot at sunrise, so beware!
Say where you will be shot," and simple Sammy told him where.
So seven sailors dressed in sailor suits
Took Sammy out and shot him in the chutes!

**REPEAT CHORUS**

# OH, SANTA CLAUS, SEND DADDY BACK TO ME.

Lyrics: Phil Ponce
Music: Sid Mitchell
Artist: Albert Barbelle

New York City: Phil Ponce Publications, 1917.

One of many mothers,
Lonesome through the war,
Watched her little children
Playing on the floor.
They seemed very happy.
She was sad because
She just read this letter
They wrote to Santa Claus:

**CHORUS**
  "I don't want a hobbyhorse for Christmas
  Or a horn that makes a lot of noise;
  Little sister doesn't want a dolly,
  We'll be glad to do without our toys.
  Mother says you'll need most of your presents
  For our soldier boys across the sea,
  So listen to my prayer
  And while you're 'over there,'
  Oh, Santa Claus, send daddy back to me."

Many times our kiddies
Show us what to do.
Here's a lesson for us,
One for me and you.
Let's make sacrifices
For our soldier's cause.
All the kids are willing.
They wrote to Santa Claus:

**REPEAT CHORUS**

# PERSHING'S CRUSADERS

## MARCH MILITAIRE

RESPECTFULLY INSCRIBED TO GEN'L JOHN J. PERSHING AND THE MEN OF THE A.E.F.

### BY E. T. PAULL

SPECIAL U.S. OFFICIAL DESIGN USED BY COURTESY OF COMMITTEE ON PUBLIC INFORMATION

PUBLISHED BY E. T. PAULL MUSIC CO. 243 WEST 42nd ST.
NEW YORK

PIANO SOLO PRICE 50¢
FOUR HAND PRICE $1.00

LONDON, ENG.
B. FELDMAN.

CHICAGO, ILL.
F. J. A. FORSTER CO.

NEW YORK
CROWN MUSIC CO.

NEW YORK
ENTERPRISE MUSIC CO.

NEW YORK
PLAZA MUSIC CO.

TORONTO, CANADA
W. R. DRAPER.

J. A. ALBERT & SON, SYDNEY, AUSTRALIA

Copyright MCMXVIII By E.T. PAULL
COPYRIGHT FOR ALL COUNTRIES

1918

# INDIANOLA

Lyrics: Frank H. Warren
Music: S. R. Henry and D. Onivas
Artist: Starmer

New York: Jos. W. Stern & Co., 1918.

*This song was in the top 20 from January to September 1918 and was number 3 in May and June. It was reprinted at least three times with the same cover design and at least twice in a slightly smaller format. It was recorded by Billy Murray, the Victor Military Band, and Prince's Band.*

Chief Bug-a-Boo was a red man who
Heard the call of war (*aw aw aw*).
Swift to the tent of his love he went.
Sighing for his little Indianola,
"Come be the bride of a chief," he cried,
"Keep me wait no more (*aw aw aw*).
Come and help me make my war paint fit.
I do my heap big bit."

**CHORUS**
  "Me hear cannon roar,
  Me help Yank win war,
  Me much like to kill,
  Scalp old Kaiser Bill;
  Me go to fight in France.
  Me do a big war dance,
  Me love a maiden so,
  Wed Chief 'fore he go."
Indianola's lover grunted twice,
  "Huh! Huh! Indianola think her chief much nice,
  Huh! Huh! Indianola ask her dad's advice."
Chief keep pleading:
  "Me hear the great big cannon roar,
  Me want to help Yank man win war,

Me like to fight and to heap much kill,
Got to go and tomahawk Kaiser Bill;
Me go along to fight in France,
Me once again do big war dance,
Me love the Indianola maiden so.
Come and marry Bug-a-Boo 'fore he go."

Then answered she to the red man's plea,
"I will be your squaw (*aw aw aw*).
Chief Bug-a-Boo, I will go with you,
Riding o'er the plain to red man's wigwam.
There will I sit and I'll knit and knit
For my warrior bold.
And when you are whooping far away,
To me you'll seem to say:"

**CHORUS**
  "Me hear cannon roar,
  Me help Yank win war,
  Me much like to kill,
  Scalp old Kaiser Bill;
  Me go to fight in France,
  Me do a big war dance,
  Me love a maiden so,
  Wed Chief 'fore he go."

Indianola's heart begins to yearn,
Indianola's cheeks begin to burn,
Indianola sighs for his return,
And his pleading:
"Me hear the great big cannon roar,
Me want to help Yank man win war;
Me like to fight and to heap much kill
Got to go and tomahawk Kaiser Bill.
Me go along to fight in France,
Me once again do big war dance,
Me love the Indianola maiden so.
Come and marry Bug-a-Boo 'fore he go."

# JUST A BABY'S PRAYER AT TWILIGHT

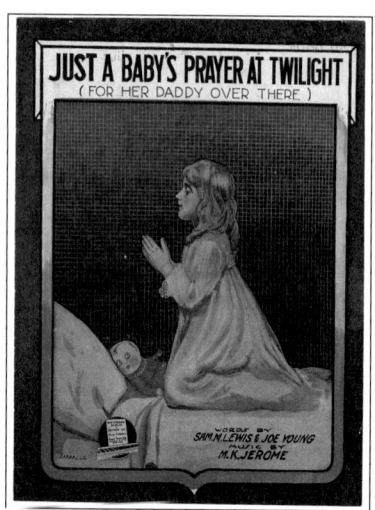

Lyrics: Sam M. Lewis and Joe Young
Music: M. K. Jerome
Artist: Albert Barbelle

New York: Waterson, Berlin, and Snyder Co., 1918.

*This song was in the top 20 from February to September 1918 and was number 1 in April and May. It was reprinted at least ten times and was also issued in Paris by Éditions Francis Salabert. It was recorded by both Prince's Orchestra and Henry Burr.*

I've heard the pray'rs of mothers,
Some of them old and gray.
I've heard the pray'rs of others,
For those who went away.
Oft times a pray'r will teach one
The meaning of goodbye.
I felt the pain of each one,
But this one made me cry:

**CHORUS**
  Just a baby's pray'r at twilight, when lights
    are low.
  Poor baby's years are filled with tears.
  There's a mother there at twilight, who's
    proud to know
  Her precious little tot
  Is dad's forget-me-not.

After saying, "Good night, Mama," she
  climbs upstairs,
Quite unawares,
And says her pray'rs:
"Oh! kindly tell my daddy that he must
  take care."
That's a baby's pray'r at twilight
For her daddy, "over there."

The gold that some folks pray for
Brings nothing but regrets.
Someday this gold won't pay for
Their many lifelong debts.
Some pray'rs may be neglected
Beyond the Golden Gates,
But when they're all collected,
Here's one that never waits:

**REPEAT CHORUS**

# JUST A BABY'S LETTER FOUND IN NO MAN'S LAND

Lyrics: Bernie Grossmann
Music: Ray Lawrence
Artist: Starmer

New York: Joe Morris Music Co., 1918.

133

Somebody wrote a letter
To someone far away.
Somebody waiting for an answer
All thro' each long, long day.
Amid the roar and rattle
There lying on the ground,
After a weary battle
That letter someone found.

**CHORUS**
  Just a baby's letter found in no man's land,
  To a soldier daddy over there,
  Filled with crosses at the ending,
  Meaning kisses baby's sending.

Just four tender words, "I love you, Daddy,"
In a simple baby hand.
That was just a baby's letter
Someone found in no man's land.

A tender little message
From one across the foam.
Four words that made each soldier laddie
Dream of his home sweet home.
They faced all kinds of danger,
Without a thought of fear,
And still that simple letter
To each eye brought a tear.

**REPEAT CHORUS**

# AMERICA, AWAKE!

Lyrics: George Clinton Baker
Music: George Clinton Baker

Santa Barbara: Liberty Publishing Co., 1918.

*Above the title inside is a special dedication to President Wilson: "To Woodrow Wilson—Our illustrious President, and intrepid Commander-in-chief; this song is faithfully dedicated." On the back of the cover is a picture of the president with the following statement by him: "I summon you, not only to sustain, but to swell the hosts that have their faces now set toward the light, their eyes lifted to the horizon where the dawn of a new age begins to brighten."*

The master Hun was walking with his marshals, wrapped in thought,
Those outlaw'd vandals stalking 'mid the ruins they had wrought!
Nor cared they for the agony of homeless, maimed, and sad!
Arch usurpers of nations free: assassins, murder mad!

**CHORUS**
We're armed sons of Lincoln; America's awake!
Defenders of freedom no Hun shall ever take!
Swing the long rifles free; let them speak for liberty!
Old Glory streaming, eagle screaming, "Yankee!"

For liberty our fathers fought, a freedom to endow:
That independence, dearly bought, shall we relinquish now?
Shall our beloved country kneel, a prey to Prussian lust?
Oh, must our children kiss the heel that ground them in the dust?

**CHORUS**
Campfires are burning; wing'd sentries sweep the air!
Our brave troops are turning the Hun hordes over there,
While our dauntless navy guards the highways of the sea.
Old Glory streaming, eagle screaming, "Yankee!"

I hear the robins singing as the roar of battle swells!
The village church bells ringing 'mid the crash of bursting shells!
I see the wheat fields gleaming in the charge of cavalry!
And in a garden dreaming, the girl who waits for me.

**REPEAT CHORUS**

# NOW'S THE TIME TO WAKE UP, AMERICA

Lyrics: Anna B. Haines
Music: Arne Emerson

Williamsport: The Melody Shop, 1918.

135

Wake up, America!
All of our struggles must be borne.
Wake up, America!
We have no time to weep or mourn.
The martrys of Tuscania now buried 'neath the sea,
The victims of the submarine cry out to you and me.

**CHORUS**
Now's the time to wake up,
Wake up, America, America, America!
Wake up and hear the call of France.
There's nothing left to time or chance.
Now's the time to wake up,
Our work has just begun.
We must show the Hun,
After that we're done.
Fight for honor,
Fight for peace and for our liberty.

Wake up, America!
And of the burden take your share.
Wake up, America!
Go join the forces over there,
Where England now is battling for the safety of the sea,
A path to make and soldiers take, to fight for you and me.

**REPEAT CHORUS**

# AMERICA'LL WIN THE WAR

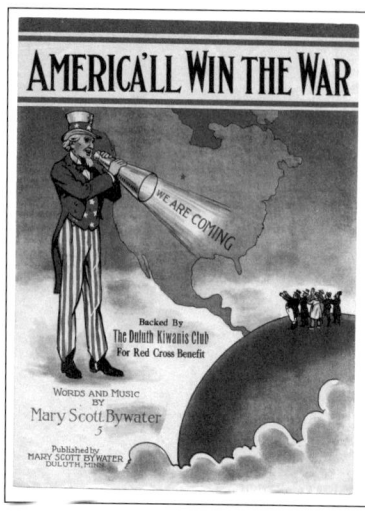

Lyrics: Mary Scott Bywater
Music: Mary Scott Bywater

Duluth: Mary Scott Bywater, 1918.

America calls her men to arms,
So be ready, my boy, to go.
We've money and guns to lick the Huns,
We hate the Kaiser so,
And this we will sing till nations ring:
"America'll win this war."
Its freedom of seas and a lasting peace,
That's what we're fighting for.

**CHORUS**
America'll win the war, boys.
America'll win the war.
America'll win the war, boys.
We've never been licked before.
We'll build us a mighty army
And fight till they want no more.
Be sure to be true to the Red, White, and Blue.
America'll win the war.

The U.S.A. is calling you
To help defend our land;
Our men they will show what we can do.
We all will take a hand,
And Kaiser Bill will want no more,
When our men get over there.
We'll rule the land and we'll rule the sea
And do it on the square.

**REPEAT CHORUS**

# OUR COUNTRY'S IN IT NOW! WE'VE GOT TO WIN IT NOW!

Lyrics: Arthur Guy Empey
Music: Charles R. McCarron and Carey Morgan

New York: Jos. W. Stern & Co., 1918.

137

Germany began this war,
Belgium had no chance,
And to help her, Italy and England joined
  with France.
They've been fighting quite a while,
Now we've joined the fray.
One and all must heed the call,
It's up to us today.

**CHORUS**
  Our country's in it now,
  We've got to win it now,
  And this is how:
  Ev'ry mother's son
  Should run and get a gun;
  We've got to punish the Hun.

  Our country's in it, men.
  Just like the minutemen,
  We're going to forge our way to victory.
  To save democracy,
  We've got to conquer Germany.

We can help by buying bonds,
Food we must conserve.
Wheatless buns help give the Huns the
  licking they deserve.
Wear an optimistic smile,
We will win the day.
Over there and over here,
Remember what I say.

**REPEAT CHORUS**

# DON'T YOU WANT TO BE A SOLDIER

Lyrics: Mr. and Mrs. Hiram B. Browning
Music: Mr. and Mrs. Hiram B. Browning

Toledo: The H. B. Browning Pub. Co., 1918.

138

The whistles blow, the folks they go
For to bid our boys goodbye.
They leave today for far away,
Far away to fight the foe.
They swing along mid cheers and songs,
And you march now by their side.
With colors bright their hearts are light
And you seem to hear them say:

**CHORUS**
  "Don't you want to be a soldier
  And fight for Uncle Sam?
  Fight for him 'neath dear Old Glory
  For your home and native land
  (So now then)

  Don't you want to be a soldier?
  He's calling now for you.
  Don't you want to be a soldier,
  Help the old Red, White, and Blue?"

The people cheer as you draw near,
They are proud of you today.
With music gay, you march away
To protect the flag you love.
A mother's prayer, a sweetheart fair
You will take across the sea.
Old Glory, too, is back of you
And is proud to hear you say:

**REPEAT CHORUS**

# ARE YOU LENDING A HAND TO YANKEE LAND?

Lyrics: J. Will Callahan
Music: Blanche M. Tice

Sioux City: Blanche M. Tice Music Pub. Co., 1918.

139

Far away across the ocean
Heroes fight for you and me,
Braving all with true devotion,
Dying for liberty;
While the flag they are defending,
Let me ask of you
If a helping hand you're lending,
And doing what you can do.

**CHORUS**
   Are you lending a hand to Yankee land,
   The country that gave you birth?
   Are you showing that you are staunch and true,
   And proving your honest worth?
   Are you standing the test, and doing your best
   Just like all the rest from East to the West?
   Are you lending a hand to Yankee land,
   The grandest of lands on earth?

Ev'rything we love and cherish,
Ev'ry blessing, great or small,
Even home itself would perish
If once the flag should fall;
Ask yourself each night and morning
When you kneel to pray,
"Have I heard my country's warning
And heeded in ev'ry way?"

**REPEAT CHORUS**

## ALL TOGETHER

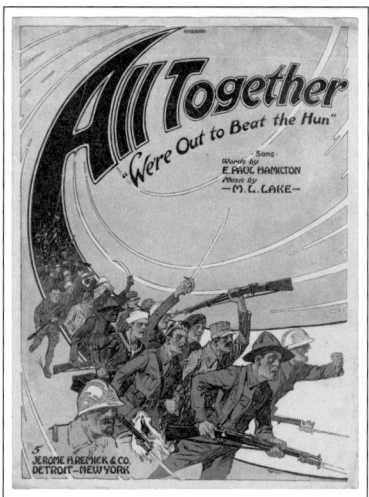

Lyrics: E. Paul Hamilton
Music: M. L. Lake
Artist: Keller

New York and Detroit: Jerome H. Remick & Co., 1918.

One night in sleep the Kaiser thought
The whole world he could rule,
And when he woke he started in
To plan, the poor old fool.
His spies he sent
On mischief bent in all lands to prepare
The fateful day without delay
When he could spring his snare.
He found a chance to hit at France thru
   Russian faith to Serb;
His robber bands in Belgian lands
The world's peace did disturb.
The Belgian braves,
The British Tars,
The mighty French Creusot
Soon proved to Bill a bitter pill; he could not
   beat the lot.

### CHORUS
   All together! Ev'ry mother's son;
   All together! We're out to beat the Hun!
   All together! We'll stick to see it thru.
   We won't give in until we win and "Win we
      must," say you.

   All together! We'll make them rue the day;
   All together! We'll make the Germans pay.
   Yes, all together! We'll stand together.
   We're right, we'll fight with all our might
      for liberty.

On women then and children, too,
The Hun waged war on seas.
Then did we try to reason why
Such horrors sure must cease.
But German ways
In our days are treach'rous and unfair.
They keep no word that German horde
And treaties they just tear.
So Uncle Sam quick told them straight, "We'll
   join the others, too."
And now we're in, we're bound to win,
We'll see the darn thing thru.
The Belgian braves,
The British Tars,
The heroes of great France,
Brave Italy, they soon will see America
   advance.

### REPEAT CHORUS

# THE FIGHT IS ON

Lyrics: J. R. Shannon
Music: Carl D. Vandersloot

Williamsport: Vandersloot Music Pub. Co., 1918.

141

Across the sea from lands so free we are going;
Our hearts are glowing,
For we are knowing that we're going over to win a fight for freedom's right from the Teuton
'Mid the shot and shell of a tyrant's hell
Now that the big fight is on.
Democracy's calling,
Autocracy's falling.
We're going to march right into old Berlin before our work is done.
Old Glory is heeding
Poor Belgium's pleading
And ev'ry American will do or die from now till the battle's won.

**CHORUS**

The fight is on:
Our blood we'll give to the drop!
We'll show our grit as we do our bit,
And the Sammies know no such word as "quit,"
For no pow'r on earth the Yankee Spirit can stop.
So shout "Hooray," for we'll win the fray
When we go over the top.

We'll sing a song of home sweet home while we're going,
For we'll be knowing
That as we're going we'll be showing deeds that will grow like seeds in history for our nation.
While we're "over there," we will do and dare
Now that the big fight is on.
The Yankees are coming
Where bullets are humming.
We're going to free again Alsace Loraine when once we take our stand
With spirit unbending
For world peace unending.
America's sons will fight with all their might till birds sing in no man's land.

**REPEAT CHORUS**

# LAFAYETTE (WE HEAR YOU CALLING)

Lyrics: Mary Earl
Music: Mary Earl
Artist: Albert Barbelle

New York: Shapiro, Bernstein & Co. Inc., 1918.

*This song was reprinted at least once.*

Out of the ages
From hist'ry's pages
There comes a silent plea.
Yet we can hear it,
Lafayette's spirit
Calling from over the sea,
For there's a debt unpaid
To France who needs our aid.

**CHORUS**
  "Lafayette, we hear you calling,
  Lafayette, 'tis not in vain
  That the tears of France are falling.
  We will help her to smile again,
  For a friend in need is a friend indeed.
  Do not think we shall ever forget.
  Lafayette, we hear you calling
  And we're coming, Lafayette."

When war clouds darkened
Our skies you hearkened,
Your sword for us was drawn.
Now we are needed,
France we have heeded.
We'll meet our debt, we have sworn,
And ev'ry mother's son
Will fight till right has won.

**REPEAT CHORUS**

# COME ACROSS, YANKEE BOY, COME ACROSS

Lyrics: Alfred Bryan
Music: Fred Fisher
Artist: André De Takacs

New York: McCarthy & Fisher Inc., 1918.

143

There's a voice I hear ringing in my ear,
It comes across the ocean, right over here.
"Hurry up," it seems to say,
"Do not waste another day,
Each gallant soldier to the war must come."
Hear the call, hear the call, ev'ryone:

**CHORUS**
"Come across, Yankee Boy, come across,
With your heart, and your sword in your hand.
Can't you see our mothers praying,
Can't you hear our brothers saying,
'You're the boss, Yankee boy, you're the boss,
And you'll help us to shoulder our cross.
If some day you'll need us, too,
We will come across for you.'
Come across, Yankee Boy, come across."

When our task is done and the victory's won,
When peace has wrapped its silence over each gun,
When the foe must pay the cost,
For the battle he has lost,
Old Kaiser Wilhelm will be sick that day.
He'll be blue through and through when they say:

**CHORUS**
"Come across, Kaiser Bill, come across,
With your sword and your crown in your hand.
Come across with Belgium's losses,
And take back your Iron Crosses.
We're the boss, Kaiser Bill, we're the boss,
And we'll see that you pay all the loss.
We have got a job for you
Cleaning out of the monkey zoo.
Come across, Yankee Boy, come across."

# SOMEWHERE IN FRANCE IS DADDY

Lyrics: Great Howard
Music: Great Howard

New York: Howard and LaVar Music Co., 1918.

*This song was reprinted at least three times, once with a somewhat different cover design.*

A little boy was sitting on his mother's knee one day,
And as he nestled close to her, these words she heard him say:
"Oh! Mama dear, please tell me why our daddy don't come home.
I miss him so and you do, too.
Why are we left alone?"
She tried hard not to cry as she answered with a sigh:

**CHORUS**
  "Somewhere in France is daddy,
  Somewhere in France is he,
  Fighting for home and country,
  Fighting, my lad, for liberty.
  I pray ev'ry night for the Allies,
  And ask God to help them win,
  For our daddy won't come back
  Till the Stars and Stripes they'll tack
  On Kaiser William's flagstaff in Berlin."

He put his arms around her neck and kissed away a tear,
And whispered to her gently, "Gee! I'm proud of daddy dear.
He's fighting for the U.S.A. to uphold Old Glory's fame
And show the world when our flag's unfurled,
We fight in freedom's name."
Then she gently gave a sigh and made him this reply:

**REPEAT CHORUS**

# WHEN THE SUN GOES DOWN IN FRANCE

Lyrics: Gilbert C. Tennant
Music: Gilbert C. Tennant
Artist: E. H. Pfeiffer

New York: Joe Morris Music Co., 1918.

*This song was reprinted at least once with the same featured singer. Other featured singers with this cover design include Marval Gunn, Barnes & Lorraine, and Frank & Rae Warner. The song was originally published in 1917 in Baltimore by Key Music Publishing Company.*

145

Many hearts were filled with pride
When our boys went off to war,
Heroes marching side by side like their
  daddies did before.
There are mothers and brothers and sisters
  and others,
Who write tender letters ev'ry day,
Letters that are cheery to make the boys feel
  glad
When they are far away.

**CHORUS**
  When the sun goes down in France,
  All our hearts are over there
  With the ones we love in France
  Fighting, we're writing.
  I know you'll do your share.

When the stars begin to shine
And all the world seems in a trance,
When our boys get in the trench,
They'll pay all we owe the French,
When the sun goes down in France.

There were cheers, a million cheers,
And a million heart beats, too;
Last goodbyes from love-lit eyes, ev'ry
  sweetheart will be true.
Though he misses the kisses, for each one he
  misses,
He'll get two or three when he returns.
Shining in each window to cheer him on his
  way
The light of vict'ry burns.

**REPEAT CHORUS**

# OVER YONDER WHERE THE LILIES GROW

Lyrics: Geoffrey O'Hara
Music: Geoffrey O'Hara
Artist: Norman Rockwell

New York: Leo Feist Inc., 1918.

*This reduced-size war edition was reprinted at least once.*

Last night I lay a-sleeping,
A vision came to me.
I saw a baby, in Flanders maybe,
Its little eyes were wet with tears.
I heard a voice so clear,
It said, "Come over here."

**CHORUS**
 "Over yonder, over yonder,
 Over yonder where the lilies grow.
 Let us wander, over yonder
 To the land of long ago,
 Where the lily of France, the fleur-de-lis
 Is calling to you and me.
 Let us wander, over yonder
 To the land where the lilies grow."

We heard a country crying,
We saw a nation's tears.
The call was heeded, when help was needed,
To try to pay a debt of years.
We send our boys away
To win the glorious day.

**REPEAT CHORUS**

# THE LILLIES OF FRANCE

Lyrics: Alan McDougall
Music: Alan McDougall

Chicago: McMullin-Ince Music Publishing Co., 1918.

Johnny Johnson of the infantry
Sailed far away o'er the sea,
Crossed the ocean in a big gray boat,
Then to his best girl he wrote,
"I have arrived in France safe at last,
Seven thousand submarines we passed.
And I'll soon be in the big advance
Fighting for the lilies of France."

**CHORUS**
Oh, you lilies of France,
Give the poor girls a chance
Waiting back in the U.S.A.
You, Marie Antoinette,
And your sister Babette
Do not take our poor rookies away.

Oh, you lilies of France,
Keep your sisters and aunts
And our boys and the moonlight apart.
They're a softhearted pack,
But we want them all back.
Oh, you lilies of France, have a heart.

Soon her answer came across the sea,
Came from the land of the free;
It was just a very short sweet note,
This was about what she wrote:
"We all were glad when your letter came,
I am well and hope that you're the same.
If with me you wish to stand some chance,
Keep away from lily of France."

**REPEAT CHORUS**

# WHEN ALEXANDER TAKES HIS RAGTIME BAND TO FRANCE

Lyrics: Alfred Bryan, Cliff Hess, and Edgar Leslie
Music: Alfred Bryan, Cliff Hess, and Edgar Leslie
Artist: Albert Barbelle

New York: Waterson, Berlin, and Snyder Co., 1918.

*This song was reprinted at least three times and was recorded by Marion Harris.*

What's that tune I hear
A-ringing in my ear?
Come on along,
Come on along,
It's a wonderful idea.
It's Alexander's band
From down in Dixieland;
He's going "over there" to do his share.

**CHORUS**
  When Alexander takes his ragtime band to France,
  He'll capture ev'ry Hun,
  And take them one by one.
  Those ragtime tunes will put the Germans in a trance;
  They'll throw their guns away,
  Hip hooray!
  And start right in to dance.
  They'll get so excited, they'll come over the top,
  Two-step back to Berlin with a skip and a hop;
  Old Hindenburg will know he has no chance,
  When Alexander takes his ragtime band to France.

There's no time to lose,
They'll put on dancing shoes;
They'll glide away,
And slide away,
When they hear those weary blues.
The goose step's on the wane,
The two-step's in again;
Like they advanced at first, they've just reversed.

**REPEAT CHORUS**

# IN FLANDERS' FIELDS

Lyrics: John McCrae
Music: Frank E. Tours

New York, Chicago et al.: M. Witmark & Sons, 1918.

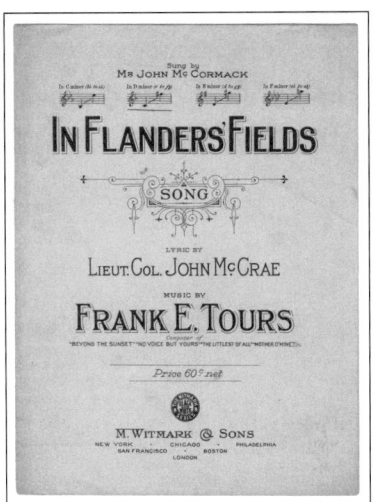
149

In Flanders' fields the poppies blow
Between the crosses, row on row,
That mark our place, and in the sky
The larks, still bravely singing, fly,
Scarce heard amid the guns below.
We are the dead.  Short days ago
We lived, felt dawn, saw sun set glow;
Loved and were loved, and now we lie
In Flanders' fields.
Take up our quarrel with the foe;
To you, from failing hands, we throw the torch.
The torch be yours to hold it high!
If ye break faith with us who die,
We shall not sleep, though poppies grow
In Flanders' fields.

# THE MEANING OF Y.M.C.A. YOU MUST COME ACROSS

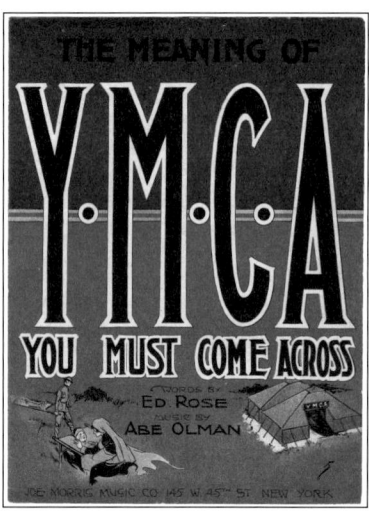

Lyrics: Ed Rose
Music: Abe Olman

New York: Joe Morris Music Co., 1918.

150

"Say, Bill, it's really wonderful," so wrote a soldier boy.
"You don't know what you're missing on the square,
The old Y.M.C.A.
Just make me proud to say,
That Yankee Doodle brain and boodle put in there.
It means a home when our day's work is thru,
But, Bill, it means a whole lot more to you."

**CHORUS**
    "Y" stands for you, young America.
    Put your gun in your soldier, my son.
    "M" is for each mother,
    So cling to one another
    Until the vict'ry's won,
    "C" is for courage to stand up and fight,
    "A" is for America, the boss.
    That spells Y.M.C.A.,
    But to the boys in the fray
    It means "You must come across."

There was a time I used to kid the old Y.M.C.A.,
But now I'm more than proud to wear the pin.
They've done their bit and more,
To help us win the war,
And like a brother to each other we have been.
And when it comes to chasing Huns, you'll find,
The "Y" is right there on the firing line.

**REPEAT CHORUS**

# ROW ON, WOODROW, ROW ON

Lyrics: M. V. B. Blood
Music: Eugene Platzmann

Kansas City, MO: Gate City Press, 1918.

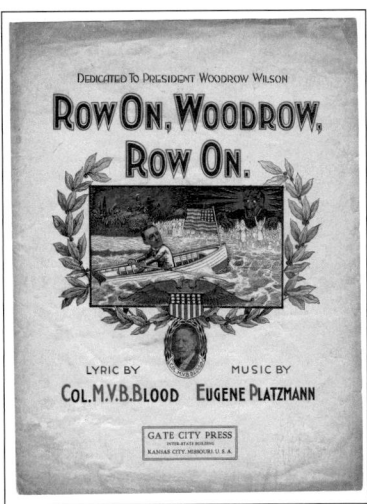

Cease rocking, your lullaby will get you soon.
Woodrow rows the boat.
Strokes are deep. Under and uppercuts they land at will,
And the rockers may rock and the knockers may knock,
Sure they'll take the count and be still.
And although the tide is high, we'll split the whitecaps oh so high.
He'll seal our fame on the apex of the sky.

**CHORUS**
So row on, Woodrow, row on.
Your strokes are mighty fine.
The rockers may rock
And the knockers may knock,
So row on, Woodrow, row on.

The course is straight but not too straight for you.
You hew to the line and in the nick of time
You'll make this Wienerwurst bunch
Feel the good old Yankee punch,
So row on, Woodrow, row on.

In vision I see outstretched arms across the sea,
Praying you hold fast,
Pulling oars for America which will them free.
And until all are free across the sea
Will Woodrow stop rowing the boat.
The undertaking is great, but not too great for him.
He'll show the cabbage heads their chance is slim.

**REPEAT CHORUS**

# THAT GRAND OLD GENTLEMAN (UNCLE SAM)

Lyrics: Will D. Cobb
Music: Gus Edwards
Artist: Dunk

New York: The Song Review Co. Inc., 1918.

152

Proud old party,
　Pale and hearty,
Hats off to him today.
Yankee, yes sir,
Home address, sir,
Washington, U.S.A.
His face is familiar to you and to me,
But you folks far across the sea:
If you forget how he looks, you're inclined,
Just paste this picture in your mind.

**CHORUS**
　He's long and lean and lanky,
　And his locks are like the snow,
　But he's just as young a Yankee
　As a hundred year ago.

　We're his ninety million nephews,
　Proud to call him Uncle Sam,
　And we'll go to the mat at the drop o' the hat,
　For that grand old gentleman.

Easy going,
No bluff throwing,
Minding his p's and q's,
Likes to fight, sir,
No not quite, sir,
Just too proud to refuse.
He's taking a trip for his health o'er the sea,
Last time I heard from him said he,
"I'm doing fine, all the family's well,
Yours truly, Uncle Sam."

**REPEAT CHORUS**

# STAND BY UNCLE SAM

Lyrics: Vernon T. Stevens
Music: Vernon T. Stevens

Battle Creek: Chas. E. Roat Music Co., 1918.

153

There's a land which is yours and mine, boys,
The home of the brave and free.
It's the land that your fathers died for
Just to keep it for you and me.
So when your land asks for your aid,
Step up, boys, don't be afraid,
For there's just one land to fight for:
It's the good old U.S.A.

**CHORUS**
There's one flag that waves above you,
It's the old Red, White, and Blue.
There's one land that you call your land
And now that land is calling you.
To one man let's all be true boys,
Let's give him a helping hand.
Come on and show your Uncle Sammy
That you're Yankee Doodle Dandy.
Stand by Uncle Sam.

Now's the time that your country needs you,
She calls for each loyal man.
Won't you stand by the land that loves you,
Just to help out old Uncle Sam?
Let ev'ry man be strong and true,
Back the land that's stood by you,
For there's just one land to die for:
It's the good old U.S.A.

**REPEAT CHORUS**

# UNCLE SAM, EVERY MAN WILL SEE YOU THROUGH

Lyrics: John C. Spray
Music: John C. Spray

Chicago: John C. Spray & Co., 1918.

154

Uncle Sam has got his sleeves rolled up,
He's knee-deep in the war.
He is striking with two million men,
He's training millions more,
And a host of Jackies wait our ships
That soon will crowd the sea.
Your Uncle Sam's just started in this fight for liberty.

**CHORUS**
But he's got to have more money now
To play the game to win,
And billions in the next loan he must see.
It takes dollars to buy guns,
And the shells that kill the Huns
Must be paid for with the coin from you and me.
Loaning Uncle Sam our money while the boys fight over there
Is the least that we at home can surely do.
So we'll rally to his call
Till the Teuton tyrants fall.
Uncle Sam, ev'ry man will see you through.

Our soldiers on the Western Front
Are smashing through the foe,
With the grit and dogged gameness
That our fighters always show.
They will conquer in the conflict;
They will set the whole world free.
Uncle Sam has only started in this war for liberty.

**REPEAT CHORUS**

# WE'RE BOUND TO WIN WITH BOYS LIKE YOU

Lyrics: James Kendis, James Brockman, and Nat Vincent
Music: James Kendis, James Brockman, and Nat Vincent
Artist: K

New York: Kendis-Brockman Music Co., Inc., 1918.

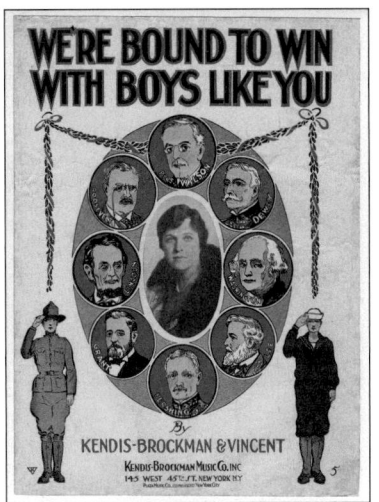

I saw a grey-haired mother kiss her soldier boy goodbye.
'Tho in her heart a sigh,
Not a teardrop dimmed her eye.
He'd just received his orders, it was time to march away,
And in that last fond moment
I heard her proudly say:

**CHORUS**
"It was boys like you at Valley Forge with Washington,
And boys like you were minutemen at Lexington.
You built up this wonderful nation and then
When Lincoln called for volunteers, you answered again.
It was boys like you, who fought with Grant and Sherman,
And with Lee way down in Dixie, too,
And this will always be a land of liberty,
For we're bound to win with boys like you."

We've read on hist'ry's pages of the deeds our sons have done,
So it's up to ev'ryone
Now to go and get the Hun.
You're in this fight for freedom, and your cause is just and right.
When you return from vict'ry,
We'll cheer with all our might:

**CHORUS**
"It was boys like you with Farragut's flotilla.
It was boys like you with Dewey at Manilla.
And with boys rough and ready you took San Juan Hill,
Whenever you were needed you have shown Yankee skill.
It was boys like you, who answered Woodrow Wilson,
And are fighting now with Pershing, too.
We've never known defeat, and hist'ry will repeat,
For we're bound to win with boys like you."

## TRENCH! TRENCH! TRENCH! OUR BOYS ARE TRENCHING

Lyrics: Wilson Dillen
Music: May Hill
Artist: Natwick

Oklahoma City: Dillen & Gormley, 1918.

Fourteen million men or more,
Fresh from freedom's happy shore,
Have gone forth to save the world's democracy;
Heedless of the word "beware,"
They've been going "Over There."
Where the fighting's thickest, they all want
  to be.
Debts we owe to the noble French,
Are repaid in ev'ry trench.

**CHORUS**
  Trench, trench, trench, our boys are trenching,
  Singing to a Yankee air;
  When their merry work is done
  And the Hun is on the run,
  There will soon be peace and quiet over there.
  With Old Glory proudly waving,
  As it always did before,
  They'll keep fighting till they free
  All the slaves in Germany,
  And they'll trench, trench, trench, till they
    win the war.

We would rather live in peace,
But their war threats did not cease,
So we had to show them what our honor meant;

Ev'ry soldier in our ranks
Breathes a carefree, happy "Thanks."
Ev'ry single mother's son is glad he went.
They will gladly do or die,
For the noble cause, that's why.

**CHORUS**
  Trench, trench, trench, our boys are trenching,
  Singing to a Yankee air;
  When their merry work is done
  And the Hun is on the run,
  There will soon be peace and quiet over there.
  With Old Glory proudly waving,
  As it always did before,
  They have guns in ev'ry trench
  That will teach the Fritzes French,
  And they'll trench, trench, trench, till they
    win the war.

**CHORUS 3**
  Trench, trench, trench, our boys are trenching,
  Singing to a Yankee air;
  When their merry work is done
  And the Hun is on the run,
  There will soon be peace and quiet over there.
  With Old Glory proudly waving,

As it always did before,
English will be spoken in
Ev'ry section of Berlin,
And they'll trench, trench, trench, till they win the war.

**(Extra Punch Lines)**
They have guns in ev'ry trench that will teach the Fritzes French.
That we practice what we preach we will prove by cannon's speech.
Tho' the Kaiser may laugh first and the U-boats do their worst.
When we free humanity, there will be a jubilee.
You will never hear of Krupp when the Kaiser is locked up.
Friends will tell the Kaiser to quit his job when we get thru.
There will be one Kaiser less when we finish up this mess.
English will be spoken in every section of Berlin.

# DO WE REMEMBER DEWEY AT MANILA?
# DO WE, DO WE, YER BET YER LIFE WE DO!

Lyrics: Mort Green
Music: Harry De Costa
Artist: K

New York, Chicago et al.: M. Witmark & Sons, 1918.

157

Our soldiers on the firing line,
Each one has done his share
Of beating back the Hun each day
On land and in the air.
But soon our sailor boys will have their chance.
It won't be long
Before they go across and then
You'll hear this little song:

**CHORUS**
"Do we remember Dewey at Manila?
Do we, do we, 'Yer bet yer life we do!'
We'll sail right up the Kiel Canal,
And after we are thro',
The Huns will all be glad to 'warble'
'Yankee Doodle,' too.
They'll learn that we remember
A certain little date.
We'll duplicate what happened back in
Eighteen Ninety-eight.
Do we remember Dewey at Manila?
Do we, do we, 'Yer bet yer life we do'!"

Each sailor lad is mighty glad
To show the world today,
Just what the U.S.A. can do
To help to win the fray.
They'll make their stand for Yankee land
Wherever they may be.
They'll get the Kaiser's goat and drive
His U-boats from the sea.

**CHORUS**
"Do we remember Dewey at Manila?
Do we, do we, 'Yer bet yer life we do!'
We'll sail right up the Kiel Canal
And after we are thro'
The Huns will all be glad to 'warble'
'Yankee Doodle,' too.
We just can't wait to get there,
We'll put them all to rout,
And in the Kaiser's palace in a chorus we will shout:
'Do we remember Dewey at Manila?
Do we, do we, 'Yer bet yer life we do'!"

# LIBERTY STATUE IS LOOKING RIGHT AT YOU

Lyrics: Arthur Guy Empey
Music: Charles R. McCarron and Carey Morgan
Artist: Starmer

New York: Jos. W. Stern, 1918.

158

Remember, soldier boy,
When you're far away,
The girl you left behind in old New York bay.
Think of Miss Liberty
Gazing across the sea.
She's waiting anxiously for victory.

**CHORUS**
　Liberty Statue is looking right at you,
　While you're fighting over there;
　Just like a mother, she's guiding each brother,
　With her light shining bright in the air.

When dark clouds lower, don't you feel blue.
Buck up and show her what you can do.
Liberty Statue says, "Here's looking at you.
You're not overlook'd over there."

Remember, soldier boy,
Wherever you are,
Her lamp of freedom shines for you like a star.
Is she downhearted? No!
She knows you'll beat the foe.
Liberty's all aglow, she loves you so.

**REPEAT CHORUS**

# I'LL MAKE YOU PROUD OF ME, MOTHER

Lyrics: Will Wood
Music: Will Wood
Artist: Henry Hutt

New York: Will Wood, 1918.

159

I know you're grieving, Mother mine,
Because I'm leaving you;
Duty is calling,
Stop your tears from falling.
I'm doing all that you want me to do;
And though it's breaking your heart,
Just remember while we're apart:

**CHORUS**
   I'll make you proud of me, Mother,
   Proud that you call me your son.
   Just as my daddy before me,
   My duty there shall be done.

   All through the rattle of battle
   Your sweet face ever I'll see.
   I'm fighting for you and Old Glory, too,
   And I'll make you proud of me.

You know I'll miss you, Mother mine,
Miss all your kisses, too;
And when I'm lonely,
I'll be thinking only
Of that great day when I come back to you;
Now dry your tears, dear, away,
For I surely know that some day:

**REPEAT CHORUS**

# KEEP A STEADY HEART (TILL THE BOYS RETURN)

Lyrics: Richard W. Pascoe
Music: Monte Carlo and Alma M. Sanders
Artist: P. W. Cronweil

Detroit: Oxford Music Publishing Co., 1918.

Soldier boys are marching
On their way to war,
Parting from you and they're parting from me
For a foreign shore.
See that little mother
Try to dry each tear.
We at home must help her
With these words of cheer.

**CHORUS**
"Keep a steady heart till the boys return,
For they need your strength
Tho' your hearts may yearn.
And when they are far, far away,
Send a letter to cheer them each day.
When their duty's done, and the war is won,
You'll know you've done your part.
Oh, American mothers, we'll bow to no others,
If you keep a steady heart."

See the sun is shining,
Dark clouds roll away,
Try not to cry when you're saying "Goodbye."
They'll come back someday.
Don't be feeling weary,
Sad of heart and blue.
If they see you're cheery,
They'll be proud of you.

**REPEAT CHORUS**

# WHAT ARE YOU GOING TO DO TO HELP THE BOYS?

Lyrics: Gus Kahn
Music: Egbert Van Alstyne
Artist: E. E. Walton

New York and Detroit: Jerome H. Remick & Co., 1918.

*This song was reprinted at least six times.*

Your Uncle Sam is calling now on ev'ry one of you.
If you're too old or young to fight there's something else to do.
If you have done a bit before, don't let the matter rest,
For Uncle Sam expects that ev'ry man will do his best.

**CHORUS**
   What are you going to do for Uncle Sam,
   What are you going to do to help the boys?
   If you mean to stay at home
   While they're fighting o'er the foam,
   The least you can do
   Is buy a Liberty bond or two.

If you're going to be a sympathetic miser,
The kind that only lends a lot of noise,
You're no better than the one who loves the Kaiser.
So what are you going to do to help the boys?

It makes no difference who you are or whence you came or how.
Your Uncle Sammy help'd you then and you must help him now.
Your brothers will be fighting for your freedom over there,
And if you love the Stars and Stripes then you must do your share.

**REPEAT CHORUS**

# SAY – YOU HAVEN'T SACRIFICED AT ALL!

Lyrics: J. Fred Lawton
Music: Will E. Dulmage

Battle Creek: United War Work Campaign 1918.

162

Lots of people think they've done their duty,
There are lots of people think they've done their bit,
So they're complaining and they're explaining
How much they sacrifice and show their grit.
But how about our heroes in the trenches,
Brave lads who fight for freedom till they fall?
If we think we've done enough, then we're not the proper stuff.
We haven't really sacrificed at all.

### CHORUS
Have you had a gun upon your good right shoulder?
Have you ever slept out in the mud?
Have you performed your duties among the rats and cooties?
Have you ever shed a drop of blood for Uncle Sammy?
Have you ever charged out there on no man's land?
Have you ever heard your captain call, "Over the top?"
Till you know how bullets sing, how they ring and how they sting,
Say you haven't sacrificed at all.

Here's a chance for you to use your money,
Here's a chance for you to use a bit of time.
Come on and use it, do not refuse it;
To loaf on Uncle Sammy is a crime.
Now get behind the men behind machine guns;
Come, do your bit and do it through and through.
When the boys come sailing home far across the briny foam,
I'll tell you what they're going to say to you.

### REPEAT CHORUS

# I'LL DO WITHOUT MEAT, I'LL DO WITHOUT WHEAT BUT I CAN'T DO WITHOUT LOVE

Lyrics: Arthur J. Lamb
Music: Frederick V. Bowers

New York: Frederick V. Bowers Inc., 1918.

Said Mary to John without any doubt,
"There's lot's of things we must do without.
To go on like this has got me vexed,
Now, what will they ask us to give up next?"

**CHORUS**
  "I can do without this, I can do without that,
  Do without sugar, do without fat,
  Do without sleep and do without light,
  Do without heat and that is all right.
  I'll keep ev'ry rule and try to keep cool,
  While the prices are soaring above.
  I'll do without meat, and I'll do without wheat,
  But I can't do without love."

Said Mary to John, "I tell all the folks
I don't eat candy, you cut out smokes;
We do without heat in our small flat,
But I won't cut out my new spring hat."

**REPEAT CHORUS**

# KEEP COOL! THE COUNTRY'S SAVING FUEL
# (I HAD TO COME HOME IN THE DARK)

Lyrics: Charles R. McCarron
Music: Charles R. McCarron
Artist: Starmer

New York: Jos. W. Stern & Co., 1918.

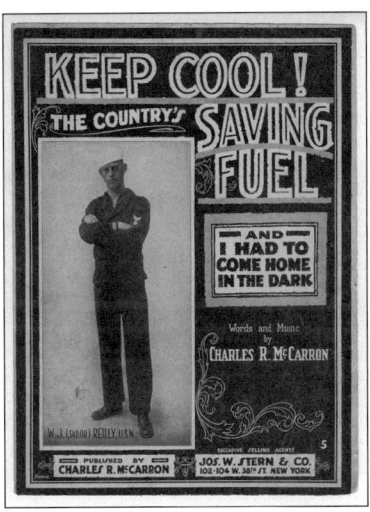

164

A married man was Pat McCann, who loved to stay out late,
And with a stout good "bawlin' out" for him his wife would wait.
No more would she accept his plea of being at the "lodge,"
And so last night he came home tight and pulled this camouflage:

**CHORUS**
"Dear, keep cool, the country's saving fuel,
And I had to come home in the dark.
Wife of mine, I started home at nine,
But the streets were all so foggy,
I walked 'round till I got groggy.
In the gloaming, I was roaming.
All the lights were out, what could I do:
I knew that you would sit up,
So, darlin', I got lit up
To find my way back home to you."

"The only lights these lightless nights that I have ever seen
Are on a sign marked 'Precinct Nine,' and both of them are green.
I know that you are mad clean through, but be a patriot.
When tempers rise, economize and never get too hot."

**CHORUS**
"Dear, keep cool, the country's saving fuel,
And I had to come home in the dark.
I was blind, my way I couldn't find.
I can swear by ten religions
All I did was look for pigeons.
You know why, dear, home they fly, dear.
In the dark a pigeon's aim is true;
So when it got too hazy,
I grabbed a squab named Daisy,
To find my way back home to you."

# IF YOU CAN'T ENLIST BUY A LIBERTY BOND (AND HELP THE U.S.A.)

Lyrics: Joseph M. Davis
Music: J. Fred Coots
Artist: André De Takacs

New York: Triangle Music Pub. Co., 1918.

165

It seems right now the talk of war is in the air,
But all this talk about the war won't bring us anywhere.
It's up to ev'ry one of us to lend a hand today
To send our men and money right into the fray;
Each one of us must do our bit, there surely is a way.
If you are wise, you'll realize
Just what I have to say:

**CHORUS**
 "If you can't enlist,
 Buy a Liberty bond
 And help the good old U.S.A.
 We don't want the Germans,
 The Heinies or Hermans
 To come and take our liberty away.

For the sake of your mother, your sister or brother,
It's up to you to fight and win the day;
So if you can't enlist,
Buy a Liberty bond and help the U.S.A.

It's up to ev'ryone to stick thru thick and thin;
We're in to beat autocracy, it's up to us to win.
The end of war depends right now what you and I can do
To bring us peace forever and with honor, too.
All that counts is men and money, it's for your sake and mine.
Make up your mind, now is the time,
And fall into the line.

**REPEAT CHORUS**

# BUY A BOND, BUY A BOND FOR LIBERTY

Lyrics: Erle Threlkeld
Music: Erle Threlkeld

Indianapolis: Seidel Music Pub., Co., Inc., 1918.

Your country calls on you today,
"Buy a bond, buy a bond, buy a bond."
She needs your aid and you can help this way:
Buy a bond, buy a bond, buy a bond.
Now a Liberty bond, it is better than gold,
It will save our great nation from suff'ring
  untold.
Buy a bond, buy a bond.
Don't delay, buy a bond today.

### CHORUS
  Buy a bond, buy a bond, buy a bond.
  Help the boys across the pond;
  They are fighting there for you,
  Yes, they're dying for you, too.
  Buy a bond, buy a bond, buy a bond.
  Help the boys across the sea,
  Far away in sunny France.
  They take a hero's chance.
  Buy a bond, buy a bond for liberty.

Your President now sounds the call:
"Hurry up, hurry up, hurry up."
To do your duty, right in line you fall.
Hurry up, hurry up, hurry up.
Buy a Liberty bond, that's the right thing to do.
Put your money at work for the Red, White,
  and Blue.
Buy a bond, buy a bond.
Don't delay, buy a bond today.

### REPEAT CHORUS

# LIBERTY LOAN MARCH

Lyrics: Leon Berg
Music: Leon Berg
Artist: Heisman

Dayton: Citizens Liberty Loan Committee, 1918.

From North to the South, from the East to the West,
From mountains and rocks to the Gulf Stream's foamy crest,
A call rings out to you, your duty now to do.
It rings so appealing and fond,
"Come Buy A Liberty Bond."
The boys at the front do their share day and night;
For freedom and right they take up their country's fight.
Thro' mighty cannon's roar, their call comes to our shore,
The call to the people at home to back the liberty loan.

Come on, young and old, bring your coin of gold,
Bring your silver, too, for we depend on you;
Ev'ry bond brings cheer to our Sammies dear,
And the foe, he will know we are there, over there.
With the bonds we buy we make the bullets fly
In the Kaiser's eye and make him sigh;
And we won't be shy till he's down to die
With a mercy cry as last goodbye.
So let's in loyalty fight for liberty,
For democracy, for victory;
Let's in unity crush old Germany
For humanity across the sea.

# IF WE HAD A MILLION LIKE HIM OVER THERE

Lyrics: Billy Baskette
Music: Billy Baskette
Artist: André De Takacs

New York: McCarthy & Fischer Inc., 1918.

168

There's a little Yankee in the U.S.A.
Proud of it I am to speak of him this day.
He's hailing from Rhode Island
And his heart is Irish true.
He'll do his best for Sammy and he'll do his best for you.
I'll bet you all the time that you've been knowin'
That I'm speaking of the Yankee Georgie Cohan.

**CHORUS**
We need a million Yankees like him on the other side,
A million like him, ev'ry Yankee true and tried.
We need that little Yankee-doodle-doodle-do or die,
When that Grand old flag is waving over you and I.
When we say, "So long, Mary," we need that Irish pep.
Ev'ry soldier man must have a fighting "rep."
We'd make a dandy showing
With the likes of Georgie Cohan,
If we had a million like him over there.

Just imagine him a general in command,
Marching 'cross the fighting line with sword in hand.
A million Yankee Doodle-boys all waiting for the time
To march right into Berlin, right across the River Rhine.
And ev'ry Irish laddie would be humming,
Devil take the Huns, the Yankee prince is coming.

**REPEAT CHORUS**

# IF I'M NOT AT THE ROLL CALL KISS MOTHER GOOD-BYE FOR ME

Lyrics: George L. Boyden
Music: George L. Boyden
Artist: E. H. Pfeiffer

Boston: Garton Brothers Music Publishers, 1918.

*This song was reprinted at least six times in New York by Leo Feist with the same cover design but in a reduced-size war edition. It was also published in Boston by George L. Boyden with a different cover design.*

'Twas just before the battle, boys,
That day I'll ne'er forget,
A lad beside me in the trench as brave as I have met.
Tho' death was near, he had no fear
'Twas very plain to see.
For just before the battle charge
He smilingly said to me:

**CHORUS**
"If I am not at the roll call
After the fighting is done,
Won't you be kind to my mother
Just for her soldier son.
Tell her I know how she loves me
And prays for me constantly.
May angels attend her,
Brave comrade, befriend her
And kiss her goodbye for me."

We all felt glad our little lad
Came thru the fight all right.
His courage in the battle gave us help to win the right.
It made his dear old mother's heart
As proud as it could be;
I wrote and told her just the words
Her brave boy had said to me.

**REPEAT CHORUS**

# I'LL BE THERE, LADDIE BOY, I'LL BE THERE

Lyrics: Jack Frost
Music: E. Clinton Keithley

Chicago and New York: Frank K. Root and Co., 1918.

Over the sea and far from me
You're sailing, my soldier lad;
But someone will yearn for your return,
One who gave all she had.
And while you are fighting,
The world's wrongs you're righting,
Remember, while over the foam,
In your dreams I'll be always near you,
When you dream of the one back home.

**CHORUS**

I'll be there when the bugle's calling,
I'll be there in the campfire's gleam;
I'll be there with a smile just to cheer you.
Ev'ryday thro' the fray I'll be near you.
When your comrades around are falling,
Then your mother will answer your pray'r;
And if fighting you fall and the Master should call,
I'll be there, laddie boy, I'll be there.

Over the sea and back to me,
In dreams you're returning home,
And still I am near to calm each fear,
No matter where you roam.
It's only a dream, dear,
But still it would seem, dear,
I'm near you by night and by day;
I'll be there thro' the long night watches,
Tho' you think I am far away.

**REPEAT CHORUS**

# (WHEN I'M GONE JUST WRITE TO MOTHER) ON A BATTLEFIELD IN FRANCE

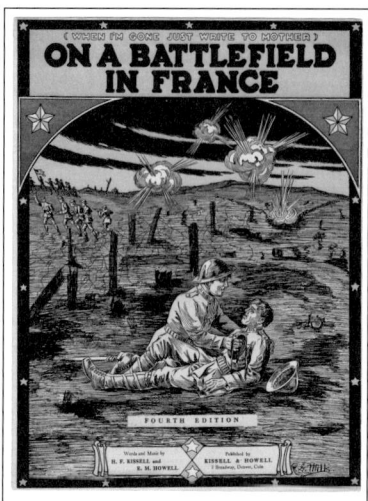

Lyrics: Henry F. Kissell and E. M. Howell
Music: Henry F. Kissell and E. M. Howell
Artist: R. G. Mills

Denver: Kissell & Howell, 1918.

*This song was reprinted at least five times, some with minor changes.*

There sleeps tonight across the sea
On a battlefield in France
A golden-haired young soldier boy,
Who led our first advance.
He died while in the battle
At the dawning of the day,
And just before he closed his eyes
His comrades heard him say:

**CHORUS**
 "When I'm gone, just write to mother.
 Tell her how I fought and fell,
 How I kept Old Glory waving
 'Mid a rain of shot and shell.

 When I'm gone, just tell my country
 That I led our first advance,
 That I died a fighting Sammy
 On a battlefield in France."

Beneath the Stars and Stripes at dawn
A hero fought and fell.
He answered to his country's call
And did his duty well.
He gave his life to save the flag,
Which marks his grave today,
And to his comrades o'er in camp
This flag still seems to say:

**REPEAT CHORUS**

# TAKE THIS MESSAGE TO MY MOTHER

Lyrics: W. H. Goodfellow
Music: C. W. MacDonald

Detroit: Universal Music Pub. Co., 1918.

172

Ev'ry brave and noble soldier has a mother
Who gives him love and strength like no other.
To know your brave lad duty he was bound,
Tho' among the missing list his name was found.

**CHORUS**
   Ev'ry thought of mother is music to my ear,
   Helps me in the battle,
   Drives away the fear.
   The one fond recollection,
   This one is most clear.
   Take this message to my mother,
   Sweetheart dear.

Ev'ry son knows he's fighting for the right.
Who on earth can take the place of mother?
The echo from France in hist'ry proud will ring,
Of that one great mother each son will sing.

**CHORUS**
   Reflections of his childhood that picture is so dear,
   Pressed close to his bosom,
   Bathed with a tear.
   For the battle won and over,
   Just tell her alone.
   Take this message to my mother,
   Home sweet home.

# THERE'S A RED BORDERED FLAG IN THE WINDOW

Lyrics: Fred Ziemer
Music: J. R. Shannon
Artist: Crit Publishing Co.

Williamsport: Vandersloot Music Pub. Co., 1918.

Why are you sad, little mother,
Why do your eyes fill with tears?
Surely some sorrow or other
Has happened to darken your years!
Is it the flag in the window,
The flag with the star of blue,
Telling a wartime story,
Breaking the heart of you?

**CHORUS**
   There's a red-bordered flag in our window,
   Hung with a tear and a prayer,
   Telling of love and devotion,
   For the boy who is now over there.

He is fighting for our Uncle Sammy,
He is safeguarding you and me;
'Tis the emblem of a mother's love
For the land of liberty.

Just dry your tears, little mother,
Think of the others like you,
Bearing some burden or other,
And serving the Red, White, and Blue;
Sometime when the war is over,
Someday when our dreams come true,
You'll share a soldier's glory,
Like mothers always do.

**REPEAT CHORUS**

# MY LITTLE SERVICE FLAG HAS SEVEN STARS

Lyrics: Stanley Murphy
Music: Harry Tierney
Artist: Starmer

New York and Detroit: Jerome H. Remick & Co., 1918.

174

When the cruel war came o'er us,
I was in the Ziegfield chorus,
With a "John" for ev'ry evening in the week.
Ev'ry night some little chappie,
Did his best to make me happy;
I was in seventh heaven, so to speak,
But then the country called her boys to war,
And all my "Johns" were true blue to the core.

**CHORUS**
   Billy's busy drillin' in the infantry,
   Artie's in the aviation corp.
   Freddy's out there with the field artillery,
   Franky's fighting on a foreign shore.
   Tommy's on a tank on the Western Front,
   Joe and Jerry both are jolly tars.
   I'm so lonesome, it's a pity,
   But I've done my little "bitty,"
   And my little service flag has seven stars.

I don't mind if days are meatless,
But the subway's always seatless,
And on John-less nights we all go home that way.
Wineless meals of cheese and crackers,
With a lot of spineless slackers
Aren't just the things to make a girlie gay.
But when the cruel war is o'er, you'll see
My generals come marching home to me.

**REPEAT CHORUS**

# IN THE GLOAMING, MOTHER DARLING, WHEN THE MESSAGE COMES TO YOU

175

Lyrics: Clinton J. Potter
Music: Floyd E. Whitmore
Artist: Chas. Hanne' Sr. Design

Scranton and New York: Whitmore Music Pub. Co., 1918.

In the gloaming, mother darling,
When the lights were dim and low,
Then I knelt down there beside you
In the golden long ago.
I can see you, dearest mother,
I can hear your voice in pray'r,
Asking Him to guide your soldier
In the trenches over there.

**CHORUS**
In the gloaming, mother darling,
When the message comes to you
Blazened in eternal glory,
Mother dear, you will be true.
He will guide you, dearest mother,
Where your dim eyes cannot see.
May He place His arms around you,
If the scroll shall honor me.

Bear up bravely, mother darling,
There must be no bitter sign.
Mother's heart must here be broken,
Mother's son must dare to die.
He is in the trench beside me,
Tho' my human eye can't see,
For I know that He is, mother,
For you said that He would be.

**CHORUS**
As you taught me how to trust Him,
Back there by the old armchair,
With your loving arms around me,
As I lisped my baby pray'r.
So, I pray you, dearest mother,
As the mother taught her son,
When the Master brings the message,
Mother, pray thy will be done.

# JUST A LETTER FOR A BOY OVER THERE FROM A GREY-HAIRED MOTHER OVER HERE

Lyrics: Andrew B. Sterling, Arthur Lange, and Alfred Solman
Music: Andrew B. Sterling, Arthur Lange, and Alfred Solman
Artist: Starmer

New York: Joe Morris Music Co., 1918.

176

There's many a smiling face that hides an aching heart,
For the mother of a soldier never cries.
There's many a mother heart will ache tonight,
There's many a trembling hand will write:

**CHORUS**
  Just a letter for a boy over there
  From a grey-haired mother over here.
  There's a kiss inside
  And words of cheer to hide
  That 'way down in her heart there's a tear.

Just a letter from a grey-haired mother.
Her heart is yearning, she says a prayer,
And there's a light burning bright
In the window tonight
Over here, for a boy over there.

There's many a mother writing to her darling boy,
But he will not answer when they call his name.
There's many a mother all in vain will wait,
There's many a letter came to late:

**REPEAT CHORUS**

# THE ANGEL GOD SENT FROM HEAVEN

Lyrics: Paul A. Smith and Robert Levenson
Music: Frank L. Levine
Artist: Dobinson Engr. Co.

Boston: Jack Mendelsohn Music Co., 1918.

177

A mother sat and wrote a note of cheer,
To one so dear,
But far from here.
She wrote, "A tear drop never dims my eye,
I never cry,
And this is why:"

**CHORUS**
  "God sent a shining angel
  To take your mother's place.
  She drives away all sorrow,
  There's sunshine in her face.
  God bless her!

That's why I never worry.
She'll keep you safe from harm,
For the angel God sent down from heaven,
Wears a red cross on her arm."

They say she's like a tender blushing rose
That comes and goes
While no one knows,
But there's no one who means so much to me.
Her face I'll see,
In days to be.

**REPEAT CHORUS**

# YOUR LIPS ARE NO MAN'S LAND BUT MINE

Lyrics: Arthur Guy Empey
Music: Charles R. McCarron and Carey Morgan

New York: Jos. W. Stern & Co., 1918.

*This song was also issued with Carl S. Graves as the featured singer as well as at least three times without any featured singer.*

178

At a dock a transport was rocking
Ev'ry chap from his cap to his stocking,
Dressed to kill,
"To kill old Kaiser Bill."
On the pier a dear little girlie,
With her tear-dimmed eyes.
Time to go,
Whistles blow,
"Au Revoir," her sweetheart cries:

**CHORUS**
  "I'm coming back someday when the fray
    is over, my darling.
  I know you'll be true, dear,
  So I'll never be blue, dear.
  Across the foam in no man's land I'll soon
    be fighting,
  But I know your lips are no man's land but
    mine."

As the boat sailed out thro' the channel,
With two flags she had made out of flannel
From the pier
She wigwagged "Goodbye, dear."
Pretty soon he wigwagged an answer,
And the code she read
From her boy,
"Ship ahoy."
This is what the wigwag said:

**REPEAT CHORUS**

# THOSE DRAFTIN' BLUES

Lyrics: Maceo Pinkard
Music: Maceo Pinkard
Artist: Natwick

New York: Jos. W. Stern & Co., 1918.

*This song was reprinted at least twice, once in a somewhat smaller format (all in blue).*

Now if you've got a lovin' man,
You'd better love him while you can.
Perhaps he'll have to go to war
To fight for dear old Uncle Sam.
They're drafting ev'ry man right now
To fight the Kaiser and his band.
Before they call your man, I say
These words you ought to understand:

**CHORUS**
"When Uncle Sam calls out your man,
Don't sigh
And cry,
Because you know he cert'nly can't refuse.
To hold him back, might make him 'slack.'
Just say, you've got those drafting blues."

You know it's gonna break your heart
To let your honey go away.
The nights will grow so long to you,
You'll soon be looking old and gray.
No matter how you love your man,
He's got to answer to his call.
I've told you in my little way
I'm sure you'll understand it all:

**CHORUS**
"When Uncle Sam, calls out your man,
Don't sigh
And cry,
Because you know he cert'nly can't refuse.
To dress in black can't bring him back.
Just say, you've got those drafting blues.

# MR. SOUSA'S YANKEE BAND

Lyrics: Gene Green and Joe Farrell
Music: Gene Green and Joe Farrell

Chicago and New York: Tell Taylor Music Publisher, 1918.

Ev'rything is hustle bustle,
Boys are goin' away to tussle
Over, over there.
Jiminy, they're glad they're goin',
Hear dem sing dat song by Cohan,
"Over, Over There."
Ev'ry step shows Yankee spirit,
Sing dat song, so they can hear it,
"Over, Over There."
Hear dat Yankee band a-comin'
Sure dey'll hear dat Yankee drummin',
"Over, Over There."

**CHORUS**
   Here comes Mister Sousa an' his Yankee band.
   Listen, Hannah, listen ain't de music grand?
   Listen to de shufflin' of de soldiers' feet,
   Music sweet and true.
   Golly, don't dat trombone sound like
     ev'rything
   Makes you want to love an' dance an' fight
     an' sing?

   Stand up, stand up, Hannah,
   An' salute de Spangled Banner.
   There's de Marseillaisey,
   Gee, but dat's a daisy
   Played by Mister Sousa's Yankee band.

Gosh, all hemlock hear dat shootin',
Dats old Uncle Sam recruitin'
Over, over here.
Sousa's band there's no resistin',
Watch 'em start de boys enlistin',
Over, over here.
Dat's de only way to win it,
Kiss me an' I'll join dis minute,
Over, over here.
While across de sea I'm flittin'
You stay home an' watch your knittin',
Over, over here.

**REPEAT CHORUS**

# I'M PROUD TO BE THE SWEETHEART OF A SOLDIER

Lyrics: Mary Earl
Music: Mary Earl
Artist: E. E. Walton

New York: Shapiro, Bernstein & Co. Inc., 1918.

There's a hero o'er the ocean,
There's another here at home,
And she makes each letter cheery
That she sends across the foam.
Tho' her little heart is aching,
Still she smiles her tears away.
The whole day long she sings love's song,
And you'll hear her fondly say:

**CHORUS**
  "I'm proud to be the sweetheart of a soldier,
  Tho' I cried when he marched away,
  For he's doing his share with the boys somewhere
  Over there, over there in the fray.

I treasure ev'ry letter that he sends me,
And they fill my heart with joy,
For he's fighting o'er the sea,
And I'm mighty proud to be
The sweetheart of a soldier boy."

When the nights seem long and dreary,
And the tears begin to start,
Then she reads his letters over,
And there's sunshine in her heart,
For she knows he's thinking of her
Just as in the long ago.
Her heart is there with him somewhere,
And she wants the world to know:

**REPEAT CHORUS**

# THERE'S SOMETHING 'BOUT A UNIFORM THAT MAKES THE LADIES FALL

Lyrics: Henry Fink
Music: Abner Silver
Artist: Starmer

New York: Shapiro, Bernstein & Co., 1918.

182

Young Willie Brown, who's been away,
Blew into town the other day,
Called upon his gal that very night excited,
So delighted.
But when he opened up the door,
He was surprised at what he saw.
There was his little sweetheart Nellie,
Making love to Sergeant Kelly,
So he couldn't help but roar:

**CHORUS**
"There's something 'bout a uniform that
  makes the ladies fall.
It's funny how a suit of clothes will
  hypnotize them all.
Some of the nicest girls I've known
Hang around old Captain Stone,
And even little Davy, who's in the Navy,
  has a harem all his own.
Soldiers here and sailors there have made
  my chances small,
But I've a scheme to fool them one and all.
I've made my mind up to enlist
And make up for the hugs and kisses that
  I've missed.
There's something 'bout a uniform that
  makes the ladies fall."

Patrolman Green is often seen
Out with a nifty little queen.
Many girls you'll find move near the Fire
  Department,
For excitement.
Around conductors girls will flock,
They have a string on ev'ry block.
But, oh! the ones who get me nervous
Are the fellows in the service,
For they work just like a clock:

**CHORUS**
"There's something 'bout a uniform that
  makes the ladies fall.
It's funny how a suit of clothes will
  hypnotize them all.
Some of the nicest girls I've known
Hang around old Captain Stone,
And even little Davy, who's in the Navy,
  has a harem all his own.
Soldiers here and sailors there have made
  my chances small
But I've a scheme to fool them one and all.
If I enlist, the girls won't dodge.
There's nothing like a little bit of camouflage.
There's something 'bout a uniform that
  makes the ladies fall.

# I'M ALL DRESSED UP TO KILL

Lyrics: Billy Gaston
Music: Billy Gaston
Artist: Billy Gaston

New York: Shapiro, Bernstein & Co. Inc., 1918.

Yankee boy has heard the call to arms,
Yankee boy has answered war's alarms.
With his gun upon his shoulder
Never was a soldier bolder.
He comes from city, villages and farms
Knowing there's a duty to be done.
This is what he says to ev'ryone:

**CHORUS**
  "I'm all dressed up to kill,
  I'm all dressed up to kill
  In my latest style grenade
  And my up-to-date trench spade.
  They say I look cute in my khaki suit and
    army boot.
  I'm all dressed up to kill
  A *boche* named Kaiser Bill.
  Oh! the things I'm dressed in will be felt,
  Especially my cartridge belt.
  I'm all dressed up to kill."

When we're in the thickest of the fray,
Mister Hun will take the count that day.
With the wallop we'll be sending
He'll see stars and stripes unending,
And he'll be glad the price of peace to pay.
Over there they put it up to us;
Now we're in, we'll settle up that fuss:

**REPEAT CHORUS**

# I'M CRAZY ABOUT MY DADDY (IN A UNIFORM)

Lyrics: Charles R. McCarron and Carey Morgan
Music: Charles R. McCarron and Carey Morgan
Artist: Starmer

New York: Jos. W. Stern & Co., 1918.

*This song was also published in red.*

I've been trav'ling 'round
With the wildest boy in town.
Folks didn't like him,
'Cause he'd always fight,
But what a difference since this war began.
He's dressed up in tan,
Now they salute my fighting man,
Some soldier.

**CHORUS**
 I'm simply crazy 'bout my daddy,
 I love him in his uniform.
 He has military eyes,
 All my feelings mobilize.
 He knows a lot about maneuvers, he puts
  me in a trance.
 When I kiss daddy, I think I'm "Somewhere
  in France."

Over there, over here
He kisses me from ear to ear.
He's some caveman when his heart is warm.
I'll tell the world it's "Good night, Germany,"
If he treats the Germans half as rough as he
 treated me.
I'm glad my daddy's in a uniform.

When he kisses me
I start to think of infantry.
Some Sunday morning,
Wedding bells will chime.
He'll get a furlough and return from war,
Medals on galore.
We'll spring drive to the parson's door.
Oh, Captain.

**REPEAT CHORUS**

## JUST LIKE WASHINGTON CROSSED THE DELAWARE, GENERAL PERSHING WILL CROSS THE RHINE

Lyrics: Howard Johnson
Music: George W. Meyer
Artist: Rosenbaum Studios

New York: Leo. Feist, Inc., 1918.

*This song was in the top 20 from May to August 1918 and reached number 6 in July. It was reprinted at least three times and was recorded by both the Peerless Quartet and Arthur Fields.*

Looking backward through the ages,
We can read on hist'ry's pages
Deeds that famous men have done.
We are told of great commanders,
Wellington and Alexanders,
And the battles they have won.
Take our own great Revolution
That began our evolution,
Washington then won his fame.
Today across the sea,
They're making history.
The Yankee spirit still remains the same.

**CHORUS**
   Just like Washington crossed the Delaware,
   So will Pershing cross the Rhine.
   As they followed after George
   At dear old Valley Forge,
   Our boys will break that line.
   It's for your land and my land
   And the sake of Auld Lang Syne.
   Just like Washington crossed the Delaware,
   Gen'ral Pershing will cross the Rhine.

There upon the roll of honor,
Ev'ryone the soul of honor,
We find heroes of the past.
Like the ones who've gone before them,
To our native land that bore them,
They were faithful to the last.
As they fought for independence,
You and I and our descendants
Must preserve democracy.
In God above we'll trust,
Our sword shall never rust,
We'll tell the world it simply has to be.

**REPEAT CHORUS**

# WHEN PERSHING'S BAND PLAYS DIXIELAND (IN BERLIN GERMANY)

Lyrics: Thomas O. Mountain
Music: Lon Sloop

Tulsa: Midwest Music Publishing Co., 1918.

There was a time in history when crowned heads ruled the world
And claimed that flags of liberty should never be unfurled.
But Washington and Lafayette destroyed that ancient pact,
And we've been free from tyranny since the Liberty Bell was cracked.
When William Third and Hindenburg declared they'd get us all,
Ten million men responded to the call.
We're going to fight for what is right, and if it is God's will,
In Berlin's gate we'll celebrate the end of Kaiser Bill.

**CHORUS**
   When Pershing's band plays Dixieland in Berlin, Germany,
   The Huns will holler "Kamerad," when they hear that melody.
   All nations then will offer thanks
   To the boys who filled the ranks.
   Mothers' tears will greet her boy,
   And sweethearts' lips will whisper joy,
   And the liberty smile will be in style.
     Goodbye artillery,
   When Pershing's band plays Dixieland in Berlin, Germany.

Let ev'ry true American contribute to the cause
To shield Old Glory from the Hun and military laws.
We'll give to ev'ry Red Cross fund, and Liberty bonds we'll buy,
For our brave boys leave home and joys and give until they die.
That Prussian pup has riled us up to the spirit of seventy-six.
We'll make them learn to like our Yankee tricks.
And when the Kaiser hands his sword to Pershing, all is o'er,
And that's the time in history when crowned heads rule no more.

**REPEAT CHORUS**

# PERSHING'S ARMY SONG

Lyrics: George G. Sherwood
Music: William Brunsvold

Valparaiso: Geo. D. Sherwood, 1918.

187

We're far away across the sea,
And fighting with old Germany.
We've got the Huns upon the run,
With hand grenades and all our guns.
Upon the border we now stand,
We're looking into German land.
We look away across the line
And see their own beloved Rhine.

**CHORUS**
Oh, liberty land, sweet liberty land!
We fight for you in foreign land.
We look away across the sea
And dream of homes where we'd love to be.

Oh, liberty land, sweet liberty land!
For thee, Old Glory, we will stand.
Where freedom reigns from shore to shore,
We'll die for you, who could do more.

We'll place the Stars and Stripes above
The palace that the Kaiser loves.
And there they'll float forevermore,
And peace proclaim from shore to shore.
Then we'll return, a loyal band,
For loved America to stand;
Sweet peace shall reign, and more and more,
We'll sing her praise from shore to shore.

**REPEAT CHORUS**

# WE'RE BUILDING A BRIDGE TO BERLIN

Lyrics: C. K. Gordon
Music: Bart. E. Grady

Boston: Oliver Ditson Company, 1918.

188

There's a land of strife and hatred o'er the Rhine;
That's where the Yanks will go
To land the knockout blow,
For democracy has bid them break the line
To civilize the country of the foe.
Berlin's their destination at the other end;
It's the city that they're driving for.
Twenty million fighters Uncle Sam can send
Beneath the Stars and Stripes to end the war.
It's the flag the Hun can't beat,
It's the flag that won't retreat.

**CHORUS**
    We're building a bridge to Berlin,
    To Berlin,
    To Berlin.
    We're going to get the Kaiser and his Potsdam crew.
    We're building a bridge to Berlin,
    To Berlin,
    To Berlin.
    There'll be Yankee Doodle doings when the boys come thro'.

We have met the Hun already in the fight,
And he begins to feel
The force of Yankee steel.
We have driven him across the Marne in flight,
And soon beyond the Rhine we'll hear him squeal,
For with the Allied armies fighting under Foch,
We are on the road to victory;
We will never stop until we beat the Boche,
And all the world is safe for liberty.
So the Yankee boys will fight
Till the Kaiser cries, "Good night!"

**REPEAT CHORUS**

# WE DON'T WANT THE BACON—
# WHAT WE WANT IS A PIECE OF THE RHINE!

Lyrics: "Kid" Howard Carr, Harry Russell, and Jimmie Havens
Music: "Kid" Howard Carr, Harry Russell, and Jimmie Havens

New York: Shapiro, Bernstein & Co., 1918.

*This song was reprinted at least twice, once in a somewhat smaller format, and was recorded by the Peerless Quartet. A note at the end of the song states: "This song has been adopted by all the Public Schools. Ask your dealer for it. LOYALTY IS THE WORD TO-DAY (Loyalty To The U.S.A.)."*

189

If you have read your hist'ry, then you're bound to know
That we have always held our own with any foe.
We've always brought the bacon home, no matter what they've done,
But we don't want the bacon now, we're out to get the Hun:

**CHORUS**
  We don't want the bacon, we don't want the bacon,
  What we want is a piece of the Rhine.
  We'll crown Bill the Kaiser with a bottle of Budweiser.
  We'll have a wonderful time.
  Old Wilhelm the Gross will shout "Vas iss Los"
  When we hit that Hindenburg Line.
  [shout:] Fine!
  We don't want the bacon, we don't want the bacon,
  What we want is a piece of the Rhine.

When first this war began, they said we had no chance.
They couldn't figure how we'd get our men to France,
But they will soon discover Uncle Sam is out to win.
We've got the Fritzies on the run, we're headed for the Berlin:

**REPEAT CHORUS**

# WHEN OLD GLORY FLOATS OVER THE RHINE

Lyrics: Leone Driscol
Music: Jean Gilbert Jones
Artist: A. D. Brown

Omaha: The Driscol-Jones Pub. Co., 1918.

Oh, can't you hear the cannons booming?
Can't you hear the dying say?
"If the folks across the waters only knew it,
They'd all be fighting for the good old U.S.A."

**CHORUS**
   Are you doing your bit for dear Old Uncle Sammie?
   Are you doing your bit for the boys across the brine?
   Don't you seem to think you hear those dear ones calling
   For volunteers to float Old Glory o'er the Rhine?

Can't you see the children weeping?
Hear those mothers cry for peace?
Don't you sit at home and wait for them to draft you.
Go and fight for the Red, White, and Blue.

**REPEAT CHORUS**

# BING! BANG! BING 'EM ON THE RHINE

Lyrics: Jack Mahoney and Allan Flynn
Music: Jack Mahoney and Allan Flynn
Artist: Starmer

New York and Detroit: Jerome H. Remick & Co., 1918.

I stood upon the corner as the boys went marching by,
I saw that "do or die" in ev'ry soldier's eye.
At first they started humming, then they burst into a song,
Each one singing, swinging right along.
They kept in step with ev'ry note and word
And as I listen'd this is what I heard:

**CHORUS**
  "We'll bing! bang! bing 'em on the Rhine, boys.
  We'll show the Kaiser, too, what a Yankee bunch can do
  When we swing, swing, swing right thru their line, boys.
  We will shake 'em and we'll make 'em yelp, 'Help!'
  When they hear those guns go bing-a-ling,
  This will be the Yankee counter sign.
  They will soon know all about it.
  Get together now and shout it:
  'Bing! Bang! Bing! Bang! Bing 'em on the Rhine'."

They sang, "We'll make the Kaiser whistle Yankee Doodle-Doo,
We'll crown the Crown Prince, too, as we have crown'd a few.
We'll make the world safe for democracy, you bet we will,
But it won't be safe for Kaiser Bill.
And when we all go swimming in the Rhine,
We'll hang our clothes on Hindenburg's old line."

**CHORUS**
  "We'll bing! bang! bing 'em on the Rhine, boys.
  We'll show the Kaiser, too, what a Yankee bunch can do
  When we swing, swing, swing right thru their line, boys.
  We will shake 'em and we'll make 'em yelp, 'Help!'
  When they hear those guns go bing-a-ling,
  This will be the Yankee counter sign.
  They won't take a drink of Pilsen;
  They'll get Haig and Haig and Wilson.
  'Bing! Bang! Bing! Bang! Bing 'em on the Rhine'."

"We'll put some Yankee pot roast on the
   Kaiser's bill of fare,
With English roast beef rare 'twill be his last
   meal there.
If he wants Russian caviar on his Vienna roll,
We will toss his Turkey for a goal,
And for dessert he'll get French pastry, then
We'll help the French to paste him once again."

**CHORUS**
   "We'll bing! bang! bing 'em on the Rhine,
      boys.
   We'll show the Kaiser, too, what a Yankee
      bunch can do
When we swing, swing, swing right thru
   their line, boys.
We will shake 'em and we'll make 'em yelp,
   'Help!'
When they hear those guns go bing-a-ling,
This will be the Yankee counter sign.
We'll hit Berlin like a rocket,
Get the watch and Rhine and hock it.
'Bing! Bang! Bing! Bang! Bing 'em on the
   Rhine'."

# WE'RE ALL GOING CALLING ON THE KAISER

Lyrics: Jack Caddigan
Music: James A. Brennan
Artist: Starmer

New York: Leo. Feist, Inc., 1918.

*This song was reprinted at least five times: once by Feist with the same cover design, once by Feist as a reduced-size war edition, and three times by Daly in Boston with the same cover design.*

192

Oh! John, pack up your kit and come along with me,
There's a party 'cross the sea,
And they need your company to grace it.
Oh! John, kiss her goodbye, you know that she'll be true.
It's very near the time to fall in line
With a million more like you.

**CHORUS**
  And we're all going calling on the Kaiser,
  For we've got to teach the Kaiser to be wiser.
  And we'll bring him something good,
  A kimono made of wood.
  We'll wish him well with shot and shell,
  The son of a gun we'll give him H__!
  We're all going calling on the Kaiser,
  The English, French, the Yanks and Irish, too.
  Don't forget what Sherman said.
  That's where he'll be when he's dead,
  For we're all going calling on the Kaiser.

Oh! boy, think of the fun in making Germans run.
They'll be running night and day,
But they'll never get away, we'll get 'em and
Oh! boy, Wilhelm the Great (?) will hear the eagle call.

We'll never stop once over the top,
Till the German pirates fall.

**CHORUS**
  And we're all going calling on the Kaiser,
  For we've got to teach the Kaiser to be wiser.
  Sure, we'll send him down below,
  Where the likes of him should go.
  We'll leave him there to rave and tear,
  And devil a one is goin' to care.
  We're all going calling on the Kaiser,
  The English, French, the Yanks and Irish, too.
  He'll be looking at his best
  With a lily on his chest,
  For we're all going calling on the Kaiser.

**CHORUS 3**
  And we're all going calling on the Kaiser,
  For we've got to teach the Kaiser to be wiser.
  When the morning glories climb,
  And it's Kaiser-picking time,
  The Kaiserine will then be seen
  Spraying a bed of myrtle green.
  We're all going calling on the Kaiser,
  The English, French, the Yanks and Irish, too.
  And an epitaph will tell
  How poor Willie went to H__!
  For we're all going calling on the Kaiser.

# WE'RE GOIN' TO KNOCK THE "HEL" OUT OF WILHELM AND IT WON'T TAKE US LONG

Lyrics: Paul Stewart
Music: Paul Stewart

Chicago and New York: Frank K. Root & Co., 1918.

*This song was reprinted at least once.*

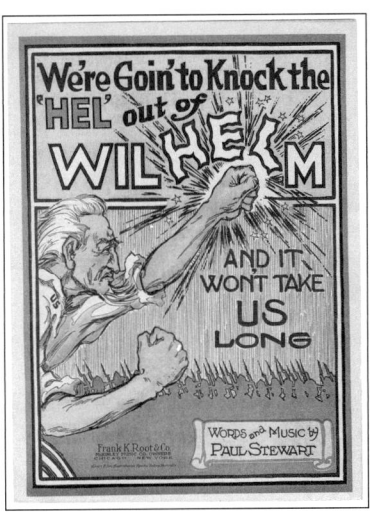

I leave today, I am on my way
Over the sea, don't you sigh for me;
There with the Belgians, the Tommies and French
I'll get some practice in rushin' a trench.
And when we land with our gun in hand,
Old Bill will shout, "Fritzies, this way out!"
Say, do you know why we're all in this war
And what we're all fightin' for?

**CHORUS**

"We're goin' to knock the 'hel' out of Wilhelm,
We're goin' to make a plain Wil'm of him;
We're thro' with Emperors, Sultans, Kaisers and such.
When it is over, they'll all be 'In Dutch.'
We're goin' to march right into old Berlin,
And that's when all of the fun will begin.
And if Wilhelm's not willin' to become just plain Bill,
He'd better be willin' to make out his last will.
We're goin' to knock the 'hel' out of Wilhelm,
And it won't take us long!"

Hip, hip, hooray! How the band will play!
All fall in line for that grand old time,
When all the Jackies, the Sammies and Tars
March into Berlin and let down the bars.
Bill will be sore that he made this war.
Over the Rhine with some friends of mine,
We're on our way to those war-ridden lands.
We've got a job on our hands.

**REPEAT CHORUS**

# THE BIGGEST THING IN A SOLDIER'S LIFE IS THE LETTER THAT COMES FROM HOME

Lyrics: Robert F. Roden
Music: Edward G. Nelson
Artist: E. E. Walton

New York: F. B. Haviland Pub. Co., 1918.

They brought him back from the firing line,
A hero wounded he lies;
He won a cross for his bravery,
But he turns with eager eyes
To a letter just from home
From his dear ones o'er the foam.

**CHORUS**
For the biggest thing in a soldier's life
Is the letter that comes from home.
Far away seem battle honors,
When he hears from the ones left alone.
In his dream he's back with mother
And his sweetheart o'er the foam,
For the biggest thing in a soldier's life,
Is the letter that comes from home.

The cross he won is forgotten now,
His thoughts are across the sea
With those he loves in his dear old home,
Those who wait so hopefully.
He forgets all thoughts of fame,
As he breathes each tender name.

**REPEAT CHORUS**

# THREE WONDERFUL LETTERS FROM HOME

Lyrics: Joe Goodwin and Ballard MacDonald
Music: James F. Hanley
Artist: Albert Barbelle

New York: Shapiro, Bernstein & Co. Inc., 1918.

*This song was in the top 20 from May to July 1918 and reached number 13 in June. It was reprinted at least four times and was recorded by both Charles Hart and Henry Burr.*

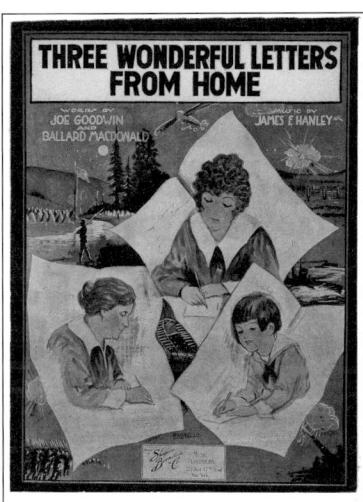

195

Three letters left a village bound for somewhere over there,
Three letters to a lonesome soldier lad.
Each one a loving story told,
Each one was worth its weight in gold.
Three messages that made his poor heart glad:

**CHORUS**
  For the first was just old-fashioned,
  And it breathed a mother's pray'r,
  While the next one started, "Darling,
  God protect you over there."

  And the third was filled with kisses,
  Sent to daddy 'cross the foam,
  From his mother, wife and baby,
  Three wonderful letters from home.

Each word was like a soft caress that soothed his aching heart,
And drove away the mis'ry and the pain.
Then joy returned to take their place
And brought a vision of each face
As o'er and o'er he read their words again:

**REPEAT CHORUS**

# HELLO CENTRAL! GIVE ME NO MAN'S LAND

Lyrics: Sam. M. Lewis and Joe Young
Music: Jean Schwartz
Artist: Albert Barbelle

New York: Waterson Berlin & Snyder Co., 1918.

*This song was in the top 20 from May to November 1918 and reached number 2 in August. Other featured singers with this cover design include Belle Baker, Frank Carter, Harry Cooper, Mignon, and William Smythe. It was recorded by both Al Jolson and Edna Brown.*

When the gray shadows creep
And the world is asleep,
In the still of the night,
Baby creeps down a flight;
First she looks all around,
Without making a sound,
Then baby toddles up to the telephone,
And whispers in a baby tone:

**CHORUS**

"Hello Central, give me no man's land,
My daddy's there, my mamma told me;
She tiptoed off to bed
After my pray'rs were said.
Don't ring when you get my number,
Or you'll disturb mamma's slumber.

I'm afraid to stand here at the 'phone,
'Cause I'm alone,
So won't you hurry;
I want to know why mamma starts to weep,
When I say, 'Now I lay me down to sleep';
Hello Central, give me no man's land."

Through the curtains of the night
Comes a beautiful light,
And the sunshine that beams,
Finds a baby in dreams.
Mamma looks in to see,
Where her darling can be;
She finds her baby still in her slumber deep,
A-whisp'ring while she's fast asleep:

**REPEAT CHORUS**

# YOU GET USED TO IT AFTER A WHILE

Lyrics: Charles A. Bayha
Music: Charles A. Bayha
Artist: Albert Barbelle

New York: Shapiro, Bernstein & Co., 1918.

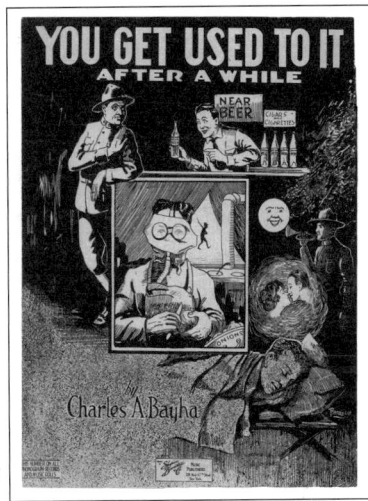

Brother Tommy joined the army when the war began.
Tommy says the army is the place for ev'ry man.
Tho' at first, the army life may strike you rather strange,
When payday rolls around, you'll find there's hardly any change.

**CHORUS**
You get used to it, after awhile,
You get used to it and learn to smile.
They wake you up each morning when the stars are shining bright,
And it's just about the time you used to kiss your girl "good night."
But you get used to it after awhile,
And you get accustomed to the army style.
The canteens sell a lot of stuff that looks the same as beer;
You buy yourself a bottle and your smiles all disappear,
And you wonder where they ever get the nerve to call it near.
But you get used to it, after awhile.

Tommy says the army is the only place to eat.
There's enough for ev'ryone and bread that's made of wheat.
Ev'ry morn, would you believe, you breakfast right in bed.
Well, if you do believe it, you can bet your brains are dead.

**CHORUS**
You get used to it, after awhile,
You get used to it and learn to smile.
You're aching for a fight; oh! how you long to meet the Hun.
Then they put you in the kitchen, where you never see a gun.
But you get used to it after awhile,
And you get accustomed to the army style.
You get a mask and then you drill for gas attacks all day,
But when you're in the kitchen, peeling onions for a stay,
Just the time you need it most they come and take the mask away.
But you get used to it, after awhile.

# K-K-K-KATY

Lyrics: Geoffrey O'Hara
Music: Geoffrey O'Hara

New York: Leo. Feist, Inc., 1918.

*This song was in the top 20 from May 1918 to January 1919 and was number 1 from July to September. It was reprinted at least once with the same cover design and at least seven times as a reduced-size war edition. It was recorded by both Billy Murray and Eugene Buckley.*

198

Jimmy was a soldier brave and bold,
Katy was a maid with hair of gold;
Like an act of fate,
Kate was standing at the gate,
Watching all the boys on dress parade.
Jimmy with the girls was just agawk,
Stuttered ev'ry time he tried to talk;
Still that night at eight,
He was there at Katy's gate,
Stuttering to her this lovesick cry:

**CHORUS**
"K-K-K-Katy, beautiful Katy,
You're the only g-g-g-girl that I adore;
When the m-m-m-moon shines,
Over the cowshed,
I'll be waiting at the k-k-k-kitchen door."

No one ever looked so nice and neat,
No one could be just as cute and sweet;
That's what Jimmy thought,
When the wedding ring he bought.
Now he's off to France the foe to meet.
Jimmy thought he'd like to take a chance,
See if he could make the Kaiser dance,
Stepping to a tune,
All about the silv'ry moon,
This is what they hear in far off France:

**REPEAT CHORUS**

# THE LITTLE GOOD FOR NOTHING'S GOOD FOR SOMETHING AFTER ALL

Lyrics: Lou Klein
Music: Harry Von Tilzer
Artist: E. H. Pfeiffer

New York, Chicago et al.: Harry Von Tilzer Music Publishing Co., 1918.

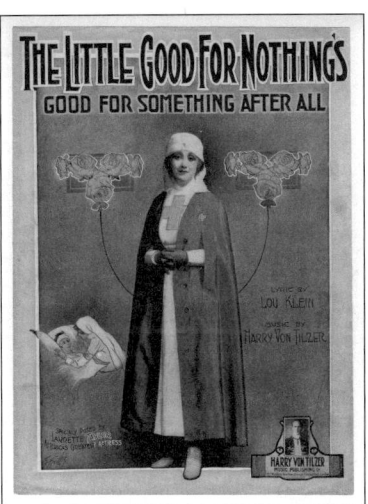
199

It's funny how a nickname clung to little Mary Brown.
They called her "good-for-nothing," a tomboy 'round the town.
As she grew up, where'er she'd go, they'd call her by that name,
But if she's good-for-nothing, angels must be just the same.

**CHORUS**
They always called her "little good-for-nothing,"
Just because like other children she was wild.
Tho' she wasn't all to blame,
Still she couldn't bear the name
That clung to her since she was but a child.
But now she's over there, she joined the Red Cross,
Giving her life at duty's call,
And the ones that used to sneer
Are the first ones now to cheer.
The little good-for-nothing's good for something after all.

In her hometown they used to frown, but now you'll hear them say,
"I knew our good-for-nothing would make us proud someday."
It may be strange but still it's true how often you will find
The ones we thought were angels turned out just the other kind.

**REPEAT CHORUS**

# THEY WERE ALL OUT OF STEP BUT JIM

Lyrics: Irving Berlin
Music: Irving Berlin
Artist: Albert Barbelle

New York: Waterson, Berlin and Snyder Co., 1918.

*This song was in the top 20 from June to October 1918 and reached number 5 in August. Other featured singers with this cover design include Miss Queenie Williams, The Dream Girls, and Mabelle Sherman & Arthur Littry. The song was recorded by both Billy Murray and Connie Farber.*

Jimmy's mother went to see her son,
Marching along on parade;
In his uniform and with his gun,
What a lovely picture he made.
She came home that ev'ning
Filled up with delight,
And to all the neighbors,
She would yell with all her might:

**CHORUS**
"Did you see my little Jimmy marching
With the soldiers up the avenue?
There was Jimmy just as stiff as starch,
Like his daddy on the seventeenth of March.
Did you notice all the lovely ladies
Casting their eyes on him?
Away he went
To live in a tent
Over in France with his regiment.
Were you there, and tell me, did you notice?
They were all out of step but Jim."

That night little Jimmy's father stood
Buying the drinks for the crowd;
You could tell that he was feeling good,
He was talking terribly loud.
Twenty times he treated.
My, but he was dry;
When his glass was empty,
He would treat again and cry:

**CHORUS**
"Did you see my little Jimmy marching,
With the soldiers up the avenue?
There was Jimmy just as stiff as starch,
Like his daddy on the seventeenth of March.
Did you notice all the lovely ladies,
Casting their eyes on him?
It made me glad
To gaze at the lad;
Lord help the Kaiser, if he's like his dad.
Were you there, and tell me, did you notice?
They were all out of step but Jim."

# GOOD MORNING, MR. ZIP-ZIP-ZIP!

Lyrics: Robert Lloyd
Music: Robert Lloyd
Artist: Henry Hutt

New York: Leo. Feist, Inc., 1918.

*This song was in the top 20 from June to November 1918 and was at number 15 in July and August. It was reprinted at least twice in a reduced-size war edition, and it was recorded by both Eugene Buckley and Arthur Fields & the Peerless Quartet.*

201

We come from ev'ry quarter,
From North, South, East, and West,
To clear the way to freedom
For the land we love the best.
We've left our occupations
And homes, so far and dear,
But when the going's rather rough
We raise this song of cheer:

**CHORUS**
  "Good morning, Mister Zip-Zip-Zip,
  With your hair cut just as short as mine.
  Good morning, Mister Zip-Zip-Zip,
  You're surely looking fine.
  Ashes to ashes, and dust to dust,
  If the Camels don't get you,
  The Fatimas must.
  Good morning, Mister Zip-Zip-Zip,
  With your hair cut just as short as,
  Your hair cut just as short as,
  Your hair cut just as short as mine."

You see them on the highway,
You meet them down the pike,
In olive drab and khaki
Are the soldiers on the hike;
And as the column passes,
The word goes down the line,
"Good morning, Mister Zip-Zip-Zip,
You're surely looking fine."

**REPEAT CHORUS**

# IF HE CAN FIGHT LIKE HE CAN LOVE, GOOD NIGHT, GERMANY!

Lyrics: Grant Clarke and Howard E. Rogers
Music: George W. Meyer
Artist: Rosenbaum Studios

New York: Leo. Feist, Inc., 1918.

*This song was in the top 20 from July to October 1918 and reached number 9 in September. Other featured singers with this cover design include Emma Carus, Flora Starr, Grace Wallace, and Rae Samuels (four times as a reduced-size war edition).*

Little Mary's beau said, "I've got to go,
I must fight for Uncle Sam."
Standing in the crowd, Mary called aloud,
"Fare thee well, my lovin' man."
All the girls said, "Ain't he nice and tall."
Mary answered, "Yes, and that's not all."

**CHORUS**
"If he can fight like he can love,
Oh, what a soldier boy he'll be!
If he's just half as good in a trench
As he was in the park on a bench,
Then ev'ry Hun had better run
And find a great big linden tree.
I know he'll be a hero 'over there'
'Cause he's a bear in any Morris chair.
And if he fights like he can love,
Why, then it's good night, Germany!"

Ev'ry single day, all the papers say,
Mary's beau is, oh, so brave.
With his little gun, chasing ev'ry Hun
He has taught them to behave.
Little Mary proudly shakes her head,
And says, "Do you remember what I said?"

**CHORUS**
"If he can fight like he can love,
Oh, what a soldier boy he'll be!
If he's just half as good in a trench
As he was in the park on a bench,
Then ev'ry Hun had better run
And find a great big linden tree.
I never saw him in a real good scrap,
But you're a goner when you're in his lap.
And if he fights like he can love,
Why, then it's good night, Germany!"

# KEEP YOUR HEAD DOWN, "FRITZIE BOY"

Lyrics: Gitz Rice
Music: Gitz Rice
Artist: Rosenbaum Studios

New York: Leo. Feist, Inc., 1918.

*This song was in the top 20 from July to October 1918 and reached number 11 in August. It was recorded by both the American Quartet and Arthur Fields. A statement above the title reads: "Inspired by a Brave Tommy and written at the Battle of Ypres 1915."*

203

Over in the trenches,
Up to their eyes in clay,
Billy and Jack and Jimmie and Joe
Are singing all the day.
When they see a German
Sticking up his snout,
They give him a chance to get out of France
When they all shout!

**CHORUS**
  "Keep your head down, Fritzie Boy.
  Keep your head down, Fritzie Boy.
  Last night in the pale moonlight,
  I saw you, I saw you.
  You were fixing your barb'd wire,
  When we open'd 'rapid fire!'
  If you want to see your 'Vater in the
    Vaterland,'
  Keep your head down, Fritzie Boy."

Soon the Boche got wiser,
Hearing this ev'ry night;
He sent us a bunch of rifle grenades
To give us all a fright,
But he couldn't stop us;
We let out a roar:
"We'll give you your fill of old Kaiser Bill
And this d— war!"

**REPEAT CHORUS**

# BIG CHIEF KILL-A-HUN

Lyrics: Alfred Bryan and Edgar Leslie
Music: Maurice Abrahams
Artist: Albert Barbelle

New York: Waterson, Berlin & Snyder Co., 1918.

204

Big Chief put his war paint on and kissed his squaw goodbye,
Threw away his pipe of peace and went to do or die.
He said, "Uncle Sammy feeds me, gives me all I get.
Now that Uncle Sammy needs me, Big Chief no forget."

**CHORUS**
Big Chief's on his way to Berlin, just to do his share;
Big Chief's goin' to make 'em squawk,
When he hits 'em with his tomahawk.
Big Chief's goin' to scalp the Kaiser, take away his gun;
Oh! oh! he have heap much fun;
Goodbye, Herman, no more German;
Big Chief Kill-a-Hun.

Pershing wants to catch the Kaiser, take him live or dead;
Big Chief says he's satisfied, if he can get his head.
There will be no more Budweiser in the Kaiser's brew,
All he's goin' to get to drink will be some Waterloo.

**REPEAT CHORUS**

# THE BEAST OF BERLIN (WE'RE GOING TO GET HIM)

Lyrics: John Clayton Calhoun
Music: John Clayton Calhoun
Artist: E. E. Walton

New York: Shapiro, Bernstein & Co., 1918.

205

Of all the animals I ever knew,
Of all the beasts within the zoo,
Of all the animals North, South, East, or West,
There's one that's truly worse than all the rest.
We're going to make a "has been" out of him,
That awful beast, the Beast of old Berlin:

**CHORUS**

  We're going to get him,
  The Beast of Berlin.
  We're going to chase him
  Until he's all in.
  We will drive him o'er the Rhine
  And we'll herd him with the swine.
  Before we're thru, the things we'll do
  Will certainly be a sin.
  We've got his number,
  We'll get him and say
  Our boys will crown him
  The American way.
  We'll trample on his dirty rag
  And force him to salute our flag
  When we get the Beast of Berlin.

We stood his camouflage and we stood too much,
But we woke up, and he's in Dutch.
We fought before and were never known to quit.
Now ev'ry mother's son will do his bit.
Oh! can't you hear the Yankee Doodle call?
We'll hunt for him until we see him fall:

**REPEAT CHORUS**

# ON TO BERLIN

Lyrics: J. C. Crisler
Music: Lee Johnson
Artist: Articue

San Francisco: Sherman, Clay & Co., 1918.

"On to Berlin" is the Allied cry,
"On to Berlin" or see freedom die.
Our fighting men will win we know,
They've got the pep and on they'll go.
We'll open up the Hindenburg Line,
We can see the Allied vict'ry sign,
And the dove of peace is bound to win.
Hosts of freedom marching in,
And their shouts will drown the din;
We'll dictate terms to Old Berlin.

**CHORUS**
   On to Berlin, boys, with your tank and plane.
   Over the top, boys, and we'll at them again.
   Over the trenches and over the Rhine,
   Nobody home on the Hindenburger Line.
   We'll hang a sign up on the Kaiser's tent,
   To point out the way that old Bill went.
   Then we'll oust the Kaiser and his kin,
   We can see his finish, he's almost in,
   And we'll dictate the terms to old Berlin.

On to Berlin and the world's release,
On to Berlin and a lasting peace;
The stars of freedom brightly shine,
As over the top and over the Rhine,
We'll over the sea and over the Alps,
And our boys will get the Kaiser's scalp.
There'll be doings in old Fritzy's town.
With a jobless German crown,
He must pay for nameless sin;
We'll make our terms in Old Berlin.

**REPEAT CHORUS**

# BE SURE TO GET THE KAISER TOO!

Lyrics: Joe Fried and Arthur C. Wilson
Music: Arther C. Wilson
Artist: Klinge

Montgomery: Fried & Wilson Publishers, 1918.

Militarism must go, our Uncle Sam has said so;
Old Wilhelm better take a tip.
Prussia we have to crush you,
And Bill we're going to get you.
That's why our boys are going to make this trip.
Your country needs no kingdom,
What it wants is its freedom;
You can bet we'll get it with a zip.

**CHORUS**
  Oh, you grand old Sammie boys,
  We're proud of you, "Hooray!"
  When you're marching into Berlin to fight for U.S.A.,
  Just remember tho' we're left behind, we're strong for you,
  And when you get over to old Berlin, boys, be sure to get the Kaiser, too.

Bill will see some whirlwind with our boys in old Berlin,
And Hindenburg will climb a tree;
While Bill is still the Kaiser
We soon will make him wiser,
When we leave home sweet home for Germany.
He'll have to quit the old gag
And then salute our great flag,
The emblem of true humanity.

**REPEAT CHORUS**

# I'LL BE OVER YOUR WAY IN THE MORNIN' BILL

Lyrics: Harry Ruby
Music: Harry Ruby
Artist: Albert Barbelle

New York: Waterson, Berlin & Snyder Co., 1918.

208

Paddy McTwist said, "I think I'll enlist,"
And he went right out and enlisted;
When they asked him later what he wished to be,
"A real aviator," said he.
After six months of training the captain said, "Pat,
Now you can fly all you will."
So Pat sat right down and wrote
This letter to old Kaiser Bill:

**CHORUS**
"I'll be over your way in the mornin', Bill,
sure and I will;
Since I'm fit to be flyin', I want to be tryin' my skill.
I can't keep still.
Sure there'll be two 'bums' fallin' before I get through.
The one that I throw and the other is you;
I'm just writin' to say I'll be over your way in the mornin', Bill."

Pat got the letter all finished and then
He just read it over and over;
He said, "Now before I send this thing away,
I'll see what the boys have to say."
"Don't be taking a chance with the mails nowadays.
It might not get there," they said,
So Pat tore the letter in two
And sent Bill this wire instead:

**CHORUS**
"I'll be over your way in the mornin', Bill,
sure and I will;
When you hear somethin' hummin', you'll know that I'm comin' to kill.
I can't keep still.
Sure I'm bringin' a present for you that is grand,
A beautiful lily to hold in your hand.
I'm just writin' to say I'll be over your way in the mornin', Bill."

# KEEP THEM DROPPING

Lyrics: George C. Cohn
Music: Walter Smith

San Francisco: Geo. C. Cohn, 1918.

Our soldier boys are over there,
Flying high up in the air,
Dropping bombs on Germany,
Just for the sake of democracy;
Soon there will be something to see
For ev'ry son of liberty;
When they start a-dropping them down,
It will be good for you and me.

**CHORUS**
   Keep them dropping,
   Keep them dropping,
   Keep them falling to the ground;
   We'll have them going,
   When we are throwing,
   And dropping them all around.

When you hit that German town
Where the Kaiser wears his crown,
Keep them dropping,
Keep them dropping,
Then the way to peace will soon be found.

Our aeroplane's up in the air,
Spreading havoc ev'rywhere;
That's the way to victory,
And that good old word called liberty.
Goodbye Kultur of Germany,
Welcome to democracy;
Then the Allies join in hand
And spread the news to ev'ry land.

**REPEAT CHORUS**

## MR. KAISER, YOU'LL BE WISER

Lyrics: Verne Hazelle
Music: John Stillwell

Hannibal: The Song Shop, 1918.

Mister Kaiser, you'll be wiser when this war our boys have won.
We're not going to stop a minute till we've got you on the run.
You're a bluffer and a duffer,
You're the one that's going to suffer
For the crimes that you've committed o'er the sea.
Put it down in black and white,
We are going to do things right
In this fight for all humanity.

**CHORUS**

   Then we'll come back; yes, we'll come back,
   There'll be a German helmet in each pack.
   No more to roam from home sweet home,
   This U. S. A. is heaven to me.
   So now let's hail, hail, the gang is here,
   Cohans, Smiths and Dooleys,
   Sure they whipped the Louies over there,
   When we got there, in our fight for liberty.

Oh, you Kaiser, you're a geyser, when it comes to bull and gas.
Take a tip from Uncle Sammie, we have had our fill of sass.
You're a piker, we don't like yer,
And some guy is going to spike yer
To a linden tree dat's growing on der Rhine.
Kaiser Bill, you've had your way,
And so now you've got to pay.
You'll be paying for a darned long time.

**REPEAT CHORUS**

Och Gott, Willie, don't be silly, can't you see that you're in wrong?
We are going to get you're nanny, we'll be there ten million strong.
You're a blighter, not a fighter,
And you're brains will be much lighter,
When the Allies' flags are flying in Berlin.
Poor old Bill, you're end is near,
You won't last throughout the year,
'Cause the Sammie boys are going to win.

**REPEAT CHORUS**

# MISTER KAISER, YOU'LL BE WISER, FOR YOU'LL DANCE TO THE TUNE OF YANKEE DOODLE DOO!

Lyrics: F. E. Mathewson
Music: F. E. Mathewson

Verona, NY: Mathewson & Mathewson, 1918.

Old Kaiser Bill,
Will get his fill,
Way over in Germany.
"Oh! Might makes right,
I'll go and fight,
I'll rule the world," said he.
So he fired his gun,
At little Belgium.
He fired it night and day.
But the boys of France
Stop'd his advance,
And to him they did say:

**CHORUS**
"Oh! Mister Kaiser!
You will be wiser,
Before this war is through!
With old England and France,
We will make you dance
To the tune of Yankee Doodle-doo.

Oh! Mister Kaiser!
You will be wiser!
This world wasn't made for you.
You may rule one nation,
But not all of God's creation,
For it's too big a job for you."

Now Uncle Sam,
The grand old man,
Look'd out across the sea.
"Oh! Right makes might;
By Jove! I'll fight,
I'll take a hand," said he.
"I will fire my gun,
At the little German;
I'll plunge into the fray.
I'll fight for right
With all my might,
For home and liberty."

**REPEAT CHORUS**

# UNCLE SAM AND HIS BATTERING RAM

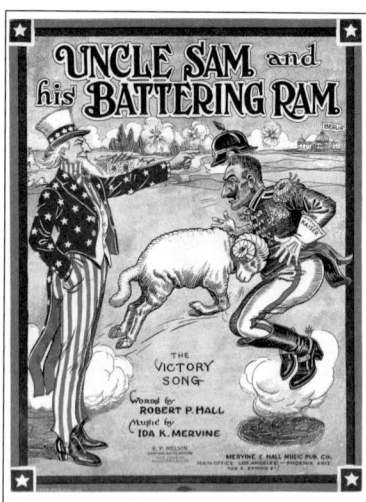

Lyrics: Robert P. Hall
Music: Ida K. Mervine
Artist: Ladd-Noon, Eng.

Los Angeles: R. P. Hall & Ida K. Marvine, 1918.

Our Uncle Sam on a mission goes;
What all he will do God only knows,
But when he gets entirely thru
And justice decrees the deed will do,
Then justice and truth and liberty
Will rule the world by democracy.

**CHORUS**
    The world now knows that Uncle Sam
    Is owner of a big-horned ram.
    If you violate his liberty,
    Then he'll go battering away.
    He will batter and battle and hammer away
      until the judgment day.
    Hurrah, hurrah, for Uncle Sam and his
      bat'ring ram.

He'll batter down all the bribers' thrones.
Then our boys will come rejoicing home.
In all the lands in ev'ry clime
A restoration for all crime;
The nations will have a righteous peace
And back it up with a world police.

**REPEAT CHORUS**

Come holy day of millennium dawn,
When truth will have bound the demon's
    throne.
When liars lay low in humble life,
Then we hear no more of war and strife.
The sunlight of truth, we all shall see;
The world will be safe for democracy.

**REPEAT CHORUS**

# THE U.S.A. WILL LAY THE KAISER AWAY

Lyrics: Jacob Dettling and Charles Roy Cox
Music: Jacob Dettling and Charles Roy Cox
Artist: Terry Engraving Co.

Columbus: Buckeye Music Pub. Co., 1918.

The Kaiser had a big idea that he could lick the world
And be a mighty ruler over all.
Some forty years preparing never did the Kaiser dream
That someday he would take a mighty fall.
He struck at Belgium, England, Russia, France and Italy,
And forced into the war the U.S.A.
Now America will use her mighty strength across the sea.
I know that you are with me when I say:

**CHORUS**
"Old Kaiser Bill will have to swallow some pill
And bury with him autocracy.
It's up to Yankee Doodle, so they say,
To make the world safe for democracy.
Kaiser Bill has gone just a little too far.
That's all Uncle Sam has to say,
For the U.S.A. is in the war to stay,
Till the Kaiser is laid away."

The great U.S. conscription and the Liberty loan bond
Was one almighty blow to Kaiser Bill.
And when he heard about the Red Cross millions for defense,
He got right busy making out his will.
He sees his monarchy is getting weaker every day;
The handwriting he reads upon the wall.
And he knows unless he gives himself up to the U.S.A.
He'll have to take his medicine, that's all.

**CHORUS**
"Our guns will roar and our great airplanes will soar.
We'll march into Berlin in the spring.
We'll win our way and you'll soon see the day
When everlasting peace of earth we'll bring.
We will take the germ out of old Germany.
Old Glory will soon lead the way,
For the U.S.A. is in the war to stay
Till the Kaiser is laid away."

# THE KAISER'S DINNER

Lyrics: C. Guy Wakefield
Music: H. B. Murtagh

Portland: Wakefield Music Co., 1918.

We're taking a dinner to Kaiser Bill,
We'll serve it to him in Berlin.
He says he's hungry and wants a feed,
Here's shrapnel salad and cannon seed.
A camel can go seven days on a drink,
This dinner will last him for life, we think.
Be patient, William, no need to fret,
We'll bring it to you on a bayonet.

**CHORUS**
  Here's a submarine sinker, and a chaser, too,
  Liquid fire for your coffee, mustard gas in your stew,
  And some bullet preserves, Bill, we prepared as a treat.
  We will forcibly feed you, old boy, you're going to eat.

The Crown Prince hurried to Paris so fast
He met himself running back home.
He found on reaching that place in the sun
There was no room there for a dirty Hun.
The Yankees have brought the whole bunch to bay
And taught Ludendorff not to get so gay.
Go tell your papa while yet there's time
To select his shock troops to defend the Rhine.

**CHORUS**
  Liberty motors by thousands and a million tanks.
  You found you started something when you riled the Yanks.
  You did not look for Samuel to start so swift a gait.
  You have no chance at all, Bill, we'll get you sure as fate.

# I'D LIKE TO SEE THE KAISER WITH A LILY IN HIS HAND

Lyrics: Henry Lewis, Howard Johnson, and Billy Frisch
Music: Henry Lewis, Howard Johnson, and Billy Frisch

New York: Leo. Feist, Inc., 1918.

*This song was reprinted at least once.*

Scene is in a schoolroom and the lessons are begun,
Teacher says to children in the class:
"If you behave today and try to do you your lessons well,
I'll grant you any wish you may ask."
And just then a little curly head
Raised his hand and stood right up and said:

**CHORUS**
  "I'd like to see all mothers free from sorrow,
  I'd like to see poor Belgium free from pain;
  I'd like to see this cruel conflict ended,
  I'd like to see my daddy once again.
  I'd like to see Yankees win this battle,
  I'd like to see France get back her promised land;
  I'd like to see this whole big world united,
  And I'd like to see the Kaiser with a lily in his hand!"

Teacher said, "Now, curly head, I think that's very nice,
I agree with ev'rything you say.
I'm going to have you teach the other children of the class,
So they can tell their ma and pa today.
I now want each child to stand in line.
Curly head will teach you all this rhyme."

**REPEAT CHORUS**

# ON THE SIDEWALKS OF BERLIN

Lyrics: E. Clinton Keithley
Music: E. Clinton Keithley
Artist: H

Chicago and New York: Frank K. Root & Co., 1918.

216

Now we all know the Kaiser each day is getting wiser,
That someday soon he'll lose his little crown,
For he's hikin' to the border to get his crew in order
To keep the Yankees out of Berlin town.
But he'll get all that's coming some fine day,
For this is what I heard a soldier say:

**CHORUS**
"We're drivin' 'em back, boys, we're drivin' 'em back.
We're gettin' nearer ev'ryday.
We're goin' to *smash* that Hindenburg line,
And then we'll cross the River Rhine.
And when we are done, boys, then we'll have some fun.
We're goin' to tan the Kaiser's skin,
And we'll sing 'Hail! Hail! the Gang's all Here!'
On the sidewalks of Berlin."

There'll come a time when Willie will see how awf'ly silly
That he was when he tried to rule the world,
For altho' he whipped the Russians, what a diff'rence when his Prussians
Against the men of Uncle Sam were hurled!
There'll be a change in Germany someday.
You feel it when you hear the soldiers say:

**REPEAT CHORUS**

# WHEN I SEND YOU A PICTURE OF BERLIN, YOU'LL KNOW IT'S OVER, "OVER THERE." I'M COMING HOME.

Lyrics: Frank Fay, Ben Ryan, and Dave Dreyer
Music: Frank Fay, Ben Ryan, and Dave Dreyer
Artist: E. H. Pfeiffer

New York: Harry Von Tilzer Music Publishing Co., 1918.

*This song was reprinted at least once and was recorded by Arthur Fields & the Peerless Quartet.*

217

Johnny Johnson feeling fit,
Uniform and army kit.
Johnny was a cam'ra fiend,
Of that trip had often dreamed.
Sweetheart crying at the pier,
Said, "I'm proud of you, my dear.
Now you'll realize your dreams,
Taking pictures of those scenes."
Said John, "That's what I'll do,
And I'll send them home to you."

**CHORUS**
  "When I send you a picture of London,
  Then you'll know I've landed safely 'Over There.'
  When I send you a snapshot of Paris,
  You'll know I'm ready to do and dare.
  (I'll do my share.)
  You'll know I'm thinking about you,
  When I send you my photo all alone.
  But when I send you a picture of Berlin,
  You'll know it's over, 'Over There.'
  I'm coming home. "

Sweetheart waving at the pier,
Saw the transport disappear,
Dried her tears and heaved a sigh,
Said, "He'll come back 'bye and bye.'
There are millions more like him
Full of vim in fighting trim,
Smiling when they sail away.
Our debt to France they're glad to pay.
We'll miss them all at home,
But there's truth in Johnny's poem."

**REPEAT CHORUS**

# THERE'LL BE A HOT TIME FOR THE OLD MEN WHILE THE YOUNG MEN ARE AWAY

218

Lyrics: Grant Clarke
Music: George W. Meyer
Artist: Rosenbaum Studios

New York: Leo. Feist, Inc., 1918.

*Other featured singers with this cover design include Bailey & Cowan and Maurice Burkhart.*

All the girls are grieving
'Cause the boys are leaving,
Gone to face the foe.
But the men of fifty,
They feel mighty nifty,
They don't have to go.
Young men they are sailing ev'ryday.
Who will love the girls while they're away?

**CHORUS**
There'll be a hot time for the old men
While the young men are away.
When the young men go to France,
Oh, won't the old men have a wonderful chance
To raise the dickens with all the chickens.
They'll have ev'rything their way.
Now that the young men have all disappeared
Ev'ry young girl grabs a man with a beard;
There'll be a hot time for the old men
While the young men are away.

While the young men stayed here,
They had ev'ry maid here.
Things have changed somehow,
And the real old fellow
Never was as mellow
As he is right now.
It's not very hard to figure them,
All the old men who think they're young again.

**CHORUS**
There'll be a hot time for the old men
While the young men are away.
When the young men go to France,
Oh, won't the old men have a wonderful chance
To raise the dickens with all the chickens.
They'll have ev'rything their way.
All the old men read the papers and laughed
When all the young men were caught in the draft.
There'll be a hot time for the old men
While the young men are away.

# WE'LL MAKE THE GERMANS ALL SING YANKEE DOODLE DOO

Lyrics: David M. Kinnear
Music: Gerrit B. Fisher

Albany: Capital City Music Bureau, 1918.

Now then go forward, boys, so strong and brave and true,
And we are sure you'll win the fight,
For you are in the fray and France and England say
That they both know that you're alright;
So march along, heads high and shoulder arms so proud,
And do your bit with all your might.
Just give the Kaiser Bill a good old lively time
And show him how the Yankees fight.

**CHORUS**
We're going over there, we're going thru the air,
We're going to fight for the Red, White, and Blue.
We'll make that bloomin' Kaiser pack up and run,
And we will teach a Yank song to ev'ry Hun,
For when we reach Berlin and Old Bill let's us in
And all the Teutons stand in line,
They've got to learn it, they've got to sing it too.
We'll make the Germans all sing "Yankee Doodle Doo."

We know there's just one thing that you will surely do,
When on Old Bill you get the drop;
You'll make that Butcher Hun pick up his tools and run,
For you will chase him o'er the top;
Go right on to Berlin, you're surely going to win
And make the Kaiser hock his crown.
And when you come back home, your welcome will be great
In ev'ry good old U.S. town.

**REPEAT CHORUS**

# WE'LL ALL MAKE BILLY PAY THE BILL HE OWES

Lyrics: Walt J. Jansen
Music: Will P. Jansen

Chicago: Unity Music Publishers, 1918.

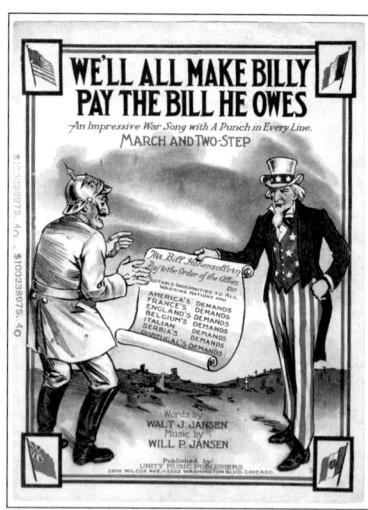

The time has come when we all have a chance to do our share,
For liberty is now at stake, so let us have a care;
The Kaiser wants to rule the earth, he thought he had a chance,
Until the Yankees landed on the battlefields of France.

**CHORUS**
We'll all make Billy pay the bill he owes.
He needs a mauling, goodness only knows.
He owes the world a debt, we never will forget,
We'll make him,
Yes, make him,
We'll make him pay it yet;
We'll tame him and it won't take very long.
The Yanks are on the way
Five million strong;
There's more than one good way to make the Kaiser pay.
We'll all make Billy pay the bill he owes.

Our cause is grand because we stand for liberty and right,
It's up to all to sacrifice, to help and give or fight,
And when we win the war, then we'll all roar a billion cheers.
We'll make the Kaiser pay for what he's plann'd for many years.

**REPEAT CHORUS**

## BELGIUM, DRY YOUR TEARS

Lyrics: Arthur Freed
Music: Al Piantadosi
Artist: Starmer

New York: Al. Piantadosi & Co. Inc., 1918.

*This song was reprinted at least once with the same cover design. It was also issued in a slightly smaller size with a brown cover design by Sachs.*

221

Belgium, we can hear you calling,
Belgium dear, your tears are falling;
Still you've kept a brave heart true blue.
We are filled with love for you.
Clouds of fear soon pass away,
Love's golden sun will come to stay:

**CHORUS**
   Belgium, Belgium, dry your tears,
   We will be at your side.
   Into our hearts with a message you came,
   Every American loves your dear name.
   Mothers, sweethearts, brothers of war,
   It's you we're fighting for,
   And we'll never stop,
   Till we're "over the top."
   Belgium, dry your tears.

Belgium, though you're worn and tired,
You have left us all inspired,
For you have shown us grit and bravery,
Spurred us on to victory.
Land of hero's staunch and true,
We'll soon be marching side of you:

**REPEAT CHORUS**

# BRING BACK A BELGIAN BABY TO ME

Lyrics: Ben Black
Music: Ben Black
Artist: W. R. De Lappe

San Francisco: Sherman, Clay & Co., 1918.

It's very dif'rent, Daddy, since you went away,
Mother seems so lonely and I get so tired of play.
But now the war is over, why it makes me feel so glad,
For there is something that I want, and, gee, I want it bad!
Please do this favor, Daddy dear, for me,
When you come back from across the sea:

### CHORUS
"Bring back a Belgian baby to me,
I think they're just as sweet as can be;
One who's lost a father or mother,
A sister or brother.
I'm sure that we could love each other.
They don't know what the war was about,
They're just as innocent as they can be.
So bring back, bring back a Belgian baby to me."

You must have been quite busy, Daddy, fighting day and night.
Mother says 'twas awfully hard to teach the Hun what's right.
She says that there are lots of babes who have no place to sleep.
And ev'ry time I think of it, why I just want to weep.
Now, Daddy, we have lots of room to spare,
And ev'rything I've got I'll gladly share.

### REPEAT CHORUS

# MY BELGIAN ROSE

Lyrics: George Benoit, Robert Levenson, and Ted Garton
Music: George Benoit, Robert Levenson, and Ted Garton

New York: Leo. Feist, Inc., 1918.

*This song was in the top 20 from July to December 1918 and reached number 4 in September. Other featured singers with this cover design include Louisa Glaum (no. 364) and Yvette of Yvette & Saranoff. It was also reprinted at least four times as a reduced-size war edition. It was recorded by both Charles Elliot & Elliot Shaw and Albert Campbell & Henry Burr.*

Rose of Belgium, drooping so low,
Lift up your head, for we love you so.
Robbed of your sunshine, you're fading away,
But you'll live to bloom on a happier day.
America is calling to you,
Speaking in words divine:
"My home shall be thy home,
And all my treasures thine."

### CHORUS

Belgian Rose, my drooping Belgian Rose,
For ev'ry hour of sorrow you've had,
You'll have a year in which to be glad.
You were not born in vain, for you will bloom again.
And tho' they've taken all your sunshine and dew,
We'll make an American beauty of you,
And you will find repose over here, my Belgian Rose.

Once your rosebuds bloom'd thru the land,
Then came the tyrant with sword in hand.
Crushed 'neath his footsteps, you fell to the ground,
But still in your heart there is a life to be found.
America will bring back your bloom.
Holding you to her breast,
No harm shall befall you,
And you'll find peace and rest.

### REPEAT CHORUS

# I'M GONNA PIN A MEDAL ON THE GIRL I LEFT BEHIND

Lyrics: Irving Berlin
Music: Irving Berlin
Artist: Albert Barbelle

New York: Waterson, Berlin & Snyder Co., 1918.

*This song, originally featured in* Ziegfield Follies of 1918, *was in the top 20 in August and September 1918 and reached number 14 in September. It was recorded by the Peerless Quartet.*

"Over there" in France,
In a big advance,
Little Johnny stood the test;
Johnny held his ground,
Now he struts around
With a medal on his chest.
There's a happy look in his eyes,
And ev'ry now and then he cries:

**CHORUS**
"I'm gonna pin my medal on the girl I left behind,
She deserves it more than I
For the way she said, 'Goodbye.'
You should have seen her try to keep away the tears that blind,
A braver hero, would be hard to find.
She puts a smile in ev'ry letter that she signs,
But I can read what's in her heart between the lines;
And when I get back,
Yes, when I get back,
I'm gonna pin my medal on the girl I left behind."

When the boys come home,
From across the foam,
To the girls they love the best,
There'll be more than one
Little Yankee son,
With a medal on his chest.
When the drive is over this spring,
A lot of soldier boys will sing:

**REPEAT CHORUS**

# WHEN YOU COME BACK AND YOU WILL COME BACK, THERE'S THE WHOLE WORLD WAITING FOR YOU

Lyrics: George M. Cohan
Music: George M. Cohan
Artist: K

New York, Chicago et al.: M. Witmark and Sons, 1918.

*This song, first featured in* Cohan Review of 1918, *was in the top 20 from August to December 1918 and reached number 5 in October. It was reprinted at least three times and was recorded by John McCormack and the Orpheus Quartet. The original title of the song was somewhat less sanguine: "When You Come Back (If You Do Come Back, There's a Whole World Waiting for You)."*

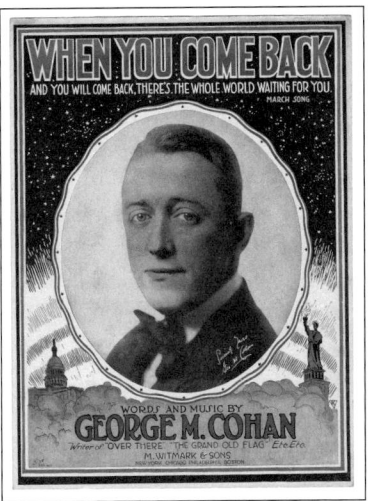

225

From Frisco Bay to old Broadway,
Today all over the U.S.A.,
We know we're fighting the foe.
So we all stand steady and ready to go,
We know no fear, we know no tear,
And all we hear is the Yankee cheer.
I heard a girlie say to her boy as he marched away:

**CHORUS**
"When you come back, yes, when you come back,
You'll hear the Yankee cry, 'Atta boy, Jack!'
And when you return, remember to bring
Some little thing that you get from the king.
And drop me a line from Germany,
Do, Yankee Doodle, do;
When you come back,
And you will come back,
There's the whole world waiting for you."

It's rum, tum, tum, the fife and drum,
So march in time, for the time has come
To smash right thru with a bang,
With the same old spirit when liberty rang.
To win, begin to rush right in,
And fly our flag over old Berlin.
Let's let our message be to the Yankee across the sea:

**REPEAT CHORUS**

## OH! FRENCHY

Lyrics: Sam Ehrlich
Music: Con Conrad
Artist: E. E. Walton

New York: Broadway Music Corporation, 1918.

*This song was in the top 20 from September 1918 to March 1919 and was number 2 in October and December and again in February. It was reprinted at least seven times with the same cover design and at least twice in a slightly smaller format with the same cover design in both red and brown.*

Rosie Green was a village queen, who enlisted as a nurse.
She waited for a chance
And left for France with an ambulance.
Rosie Green met a chap named Jean, a soldier from Paree,
When he said, "Parlevous, my pet,"
She said, "I will, but not just yet."
When he'd speak in French to her, she'd answer lovingly:

**CHORUS**
 "Oh! Frenchy, oh, Frenchy, Frenchy,
 Although your language is so new to me,
 When you say, "Oui oui, la la,"
 "We" means you and me, la la.
 Oh! Frenchy, oh, Frenchy, Frenchy,
 You've won my love with your bravery.
 March on, march on, with any girl you see,
 But when you la la la la la,
 Oh, Frenchy save your la la la's for me."

Rosie Green married soldier Jean when his furlough time arrived.
She said, "Go pack your grip.
We'll take a trip on a big steam ship."
Rosie Green took her soldier Jean down home somewhere in Maine.
They say her rural pa and ma,
Refused to do that oo la la,
But when she's alone with him, you'll hear this same refrain:

**REPEAT CHORUS**

# COME ON, PAPA

Lyrics: Edgar Leslie and Harry Ruby
Music: Edgar Leslie and Harry Ruby
Artist: Albert Barbelle

New York: Waterson, Berlin, and Snyder Co., 1918.

*This song, which was part of* Ziegfield Follies of 1918, *was in the top 20 from March to June 1919 and reached number 7 in April. Another featured singer was Wellington Cross (at least four separate printings in a larger format). The song was recorded by Joseph C. Smith's Orchestra.*

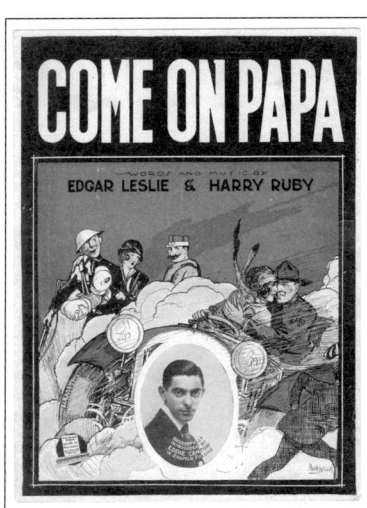

227

Sweet Marie, in gay Paree,
Had a motor car;
It filled her heart with joy,
To drive a Yankee boy;
On the sly, she'd wink her eye.
If one came her way,
She'd stop her motor car,
And then she'd say:

**CHORUS**
  "Come on, Papa,
  Hop in ze motor car,
  Sit by mamma,
  And hold ze hand;
  You start to raise for me,
  What zay call ze deuce;
  I'll be so sweet to you,
  Like ze Charlotte Russe;
  Come on, Papa,
  Beneath the shining star,

  Bounce your babee,
  Upon ze knee;
  I'll give you ze kiss like ze mam'selles do.
  Each time you ask for one, I'll give you two,
  Comme ci comme ça,
  And when you're in ze car,
  You love mama, oo-la-la! oo-la-la!
  Come on, Papa! Come on, Papa."

Yankee boys make lots of noise,
When they're in Paree;
They like to promenade,
Up on ze Boulevard;
They all know Marie and so,
Anytime she's near,
They knock each other down,
Each time they hear:

**REPEAT CHORUS**

# WEE, WEE, MARIE, WILL YOU DO ZIS FOR ME

Lyrics: Alfred Bryan and Joe McCarthy
Music: Fred Fisher
Artist: André De Takacs

New York: McCarthy & Fisher Inc., 1918.

*This song was in the top 20 from September 1918 to February 1919 and reached number 10 in December. It was reprinted at least three times, once with a similar cover design but a new title: "Oui Oui Marie." It was recorded by Arthur Fields, Irving Kaufman, and Rachel Grant & Billy Murray.*

Poor Johnny's heart went pitty, pitty pat
Somewhere in sunny France.
He met a girl by chance with ze naughty, naughty glance.
She looked just like a kitty, kitty cat,
She loved to dance and play.
Tho' he learned no French when he left the trench,
He knew well enough to say:

**CHORUS**
"Oui oui, Marie, will you do zis for me?
Oui oui, Marie, then I'll do zat for you.
I love your eyes that make me feel so spoony,
You'll drive me loony, you're teasing me.
Why can't we parley-vous like other sweethearts do?
I want a kiss or two from ma cherie.
Oui oui, Marie, if you'll do zis for me,
Then I'll do zat for you.
Oui oui, Marie,
Oui oui, Marie."

They walked along the boule boulevard,
He whispered, "You for me,
Someday in gay Paree I will make you marry me."
Just then a bunch of bully bully boys
Threw kisses on the sly.
Marie got wise when they rolled their eyes,
They sang as they passed her by:

**REPEAT CHORUS**

# YOU'LL HAVE TO PUT HIM TO SLEEP WITH THE MARSEILLAISE AND WAKE HIM UP WITH A OO-LA-LA

Lyrics: Andrew B. Sterling
Music: Harry Von Tilzer
Artist: E. H. Pfeiffer

New York, Chicago et al.: Harry Von Tilzer Music Publishing Co., 1918.

*This song was reprinted at least twice.*

Girls, have you heard the very latest news?
Girls, when you do, you'll surely get the blues.
You had better learn to parlez vous,
When your soldier boy comes back to you.
Girls, he has learned a lot of things in France;
Girls, when you marry him, you'll get your chance.
You'll have to do your talking in French,
When he comes back from the trench.

**CHORUS**
You'll have to do your little parlez vous.
You'll have to coo just like the French girls do.
You'll have to tease in French, you'll have to squeeze in French.
You'll have to la la la la all in French.
You'll have to learn to say "comme ci comme ca,"
And when you sing for your papa,
It's up to you to sing ze French songs too,
Because when you get through, with Yankee Doodle-doo,
You'll have to put him to sleep with the Marseillaise
And wake him up with a "oo la la."

Girls, you have heard about ze French coquette.
Girls, she has never overlooked a bet.
Picture one now sitting on a bench,
Teaching your boy how to spoon in French.
Girls, "over there" they have such loving ways.
Girls, "over there" they have no loveless days,
And ev'ry kiss is chockfull of pep.
When he comes back, watch your step.

**REPEAT CHORUS**

# UNCLE SAM, DON'T TAKE MY MAN AWAY

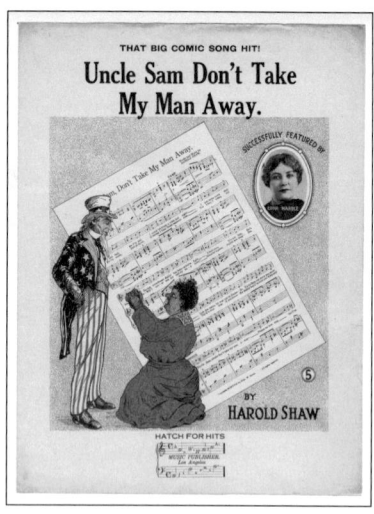

Lyrics: Harold Shaw
Music: Harold Shaw

Los Angeles: Chas. W. Hatch, 1918.

I feel bad, awf'ly sad,
I couldn't sleep a wink last night.
I got some news that made me blue.
Saving sweetheart daddy has been called to fight.
I don't care, it's not fair,
He's been at war with me now just a year.
Just the same, he was not to blame,
So, Uncle Sam, my story you must hear:

**CHORUS**
"Oh, Uncle Sam, please don't take my man away.
Please let him stay, for I've learned to love him
More and more each day
He's been away.
He could never learn to fight,
All he knows is pinch and bite,
Yet when it comes to lovin', he's alright,
Ev'ry night.
So when that bugle tells the boys to fall in line,
Please think of me and leave my daddy boy behind.
He has seen more stars and stripes
Than all the armies in this fight,
So, Uncle Sam, don't take my man away."

Ev'ry morn, just at dawn
It seems I hear those cannons roar,
Yet when I wake, my heart most breaks.
Will I never see my daddy anymore?
Since he's gone, nights are long.
His little bed seems like a lonely grave,
Yet it's true that if you knew
My daddy boy, I'm sure you'd try and save.

**REPEAT CHORUS**

# MAMMY'S CHOCOLATE SOLDIER

Lyrics: Sidney Mitchell
Music: Archie Gottler

New York: Waterson, Berlin & Snyder Co., 1918.

*This song was in the top 20 from October to December 1918 and reached number 13 in November. It was recorded by both Marion Harris and Nora Bayes.*

Pickaninny, cute in his khaki suit,
Wanted to join the kiddies playing soldier, as a new recruit;
Because his skin was brown
The white kids turned him down,
So he ran home crying to his mammy, saddest little kid in town.
Mammy drove his tears away, when he heard her say:

**CHORUS**
"Come and lay your kinky head on mammy's shoulder,
Don't you cry, you're mammy's little choc'late soldier;
And a soldier can't be crying, even though he thinks he's dying,
So stop those tears from running down
Your little cheeks of choc'late brown.
Come and let these loving arms of mammy hold you,
Try to be a soldier like your mammy told you;
Though your skin is dark as night,
I know your little pickaninny heart is white,
And you'll always be your mammy's choc'late soldier."

Years have passed away, mammy old and gray
Stands in the crowd to watch the soldiers as they bravely marched away;
And her heart fills with joy,
For when she sees her boy,
He is really mammy's choc'late soldier, and his gun is not a toy.
Mammy thinks of long ago, and sings soft and low:

**REPEAT CHORUS**

# WHEN THE GOOD LORD MAKES A RECORD OF A HERO'S DEED HE DRAWS NO COLOR LINE

Lyrics: Val Trainor
Music: Harry De Costa
Artist: K

New York, Chicago et al.: M. Witmark & Sons, 1918.

Dear old colored mammy
Talking to her boy,
Knows he's going over,
Bids farewell to joy.
She says, "I'll be lonesome
When you march away,
But Uncle Sammy needs you
And I'm proud of you today."

**CHORUS**
"Your granddad did his duty in the Civil War,
He fell by his master's side.
Your daddy bravely did his bit at San Juan Hill,
You know that's where he died.
So I know that you will do your duty, too,
And remember, son of mine,
When the good Lord makes a record of a hero's deed,
He draws no color line."

Where the shells are bursting
Over there in France,
Driving Huns before them,
Colored troops advance.
Underneath Old Glory,
Fight with pride and joy,
For each one knows the story
Dear old mammy told her boy:

**REPEAT CHORUS**

# THEY'LL BE MIGHTY PROUD IN DIXIE OF THEIR OLD BLACK JOE

Lyrics: Harry Carroll
Music: Harry Carroll
Artist: Starmer

New York: Shapiro, Bernstein and Co., 1918.

The other day I chanced to roam
Beside an old log cabin home.
I saw an aged darky dressed in khaki
'Bout to 'cross the foam.
I said, "Old man, why must you go,
Your head of hair is white as snow?"
He said: "I'm not obliged to, sonny,
But I want this world to know:"

**CHORUS**
  "I'm a comin', I'm a comin',
  And I'm mighty proud to go,
  'Cause I seem to hear the bugles callin',
  'Come on, Old Black Joe.'
  I've got the same old happy banjo,
  And the same old trusty gun,
  And they're the same old weapons that I used
  In the days of sixty-one.

  I'll swim across the old Rhine River,
  And when I get there, I won't leave no rind
    I know.
  I'll give the whole world liberty,
  Just like Lincoln did for me;
  Then they'll be doggone proud in Dixie
  Of their Old Black Joe."

I proudly took him by the hand,
I said: "Your sentiment is grand,
But don't you think the folks will kind o' miss
Old Joe from Dixieland?
I saw a teardrop in his eye,
And as he waved a fond goodbye
He said: "My Uncle Sammy's callin',
And for him I'll live or die."

**REPEAT CHORUS**

## OH! HOW I HATE TO GET UP IN THE MORNING

Lyrics: Irving Berlin
Music: Irving Berlin
Artist: Albert Barbelle

New York: Waterson, Berlin and Snyder Co., 1918.

*This song, which was featured in* Ziegfield Follies of 1918 *as well as in the show* Yip, Yip, Yaphank, *was in the top 20 from September 1918 to January 1919 and reached number 3 in November. Other featured singers with this cover design include The Dream Girls, Bob Hall, Florence Timponi, and Horace Wright & Rene Dietrich. It was also issued in a smaller version featuring Eddie Cantor. The song was recorded by Arthur Fields.*

234

The other day I chanced to meet a soldier friend of mine;
He'd been in camp for sev'ral weeks and he was looking fine;
His muscles had developed and his cheeks were rosy red;
I asked him how he liked the life, and this is what he said:

**CHORUS**
"Oh! how I hate to get up in the morning,
Oh! how I'd love to remain in bed,
For the hardest blow of all is to hear the bugler call:
'You've got to get up, you've got to get up,
You've got to get up this morning!'
Someday I'm going to murder the bugler,
Someday they're going to find him dead;
I'll amputate his reveille, and step upon it heavily,
And spend the rest of my life in bed."

A bugler in the army is the luckiest man of men,
He wakes the boys at five and then goes back to bed again;
He doesn't have to blow again until the afternoon;
If ev'rything goes well with me, I'll be a bugler soon.

**CHORUS**
"Oh! how I hate to get up in the morning,
Oh! how I'd love to remain in bed;
For the hardest blow of all, is to hear the bugler call:
'You've got to get up, you've got to get up,
You've got to get up this morning!'
Oh boy! The minute the battle is over,
Oh boy! The minute the foes is dead;
I'll put my uniform away and move to Philadelphia,
And spend the rest of my life in bed."

# THE RUSSIANS WERE RUSHIN'
# THE YANKS STARTED YANKIN'

Lyrics: Charles McCarron and Carey Morgan
Music: Charles McCarron and Carey Morgan
Artist: E. E. Walton

New York: Broadway Music Corporation, 1918.

*This song was reprinted at least twice and was recorded by Arthur Fields.*

I dreamed of a scene in an old soldier's home,
The year was nineteen fifty-three.
With medals galore that he'd won in this war,
He sat smoking peacefully.
"Tell me of the war of nineteen seventeen,"
Said the grandson who stood by his side.
"How did they fix up that terrible mix-up?"
And proudly the old man replied:

**CHORUS**
   "The Russians were rushin' the Prussians,
   The Prussians were crushin' the Russians.
   The Balkans were balkin' and Turkey was
      squawkin',
   Rasputin disputin' and Italy scootin'.
   The Boches all bulled Bolshevikis,
   The British were skittish at sea.
   But the good Lord I'm thankin',
   The Yanks started yankin'
   And yanked Kaiser Bill up a tree."

My dream quickly changed to a schoolroom
   that day,
The lesson was geography.
A child raised her hand, said, "I don't
   understand;
This map looks all wrong to me.
What is this strange place that is marked
   Germany?"
And the teacher replied with a roar,
"Why, that's an old map, dear; since we had
   that scrap, dear,
There's no such place any more.

**CHORUS**
   The Russians were rushin' the Prussians,
   The Prussians were crushin' the Russians.
   The good old Italians were hurling battalions.
   Canadians raidin' and Frenchmen invadin',
   The Bulgars were bulgin' the Belgians,
   But Yanks started yankin' you see.
   And when peace was conceded,
   Some new maps were needed.
   They ruined geography.

# OH! HOW I WISH I COULD SLEEP UNTIL MY DADDY COMES HOME.

236

Lyrics: Sam M. Lewis and Joe Young
Music: Peter Wendling
Artist: Albert Barbelle

New York: Waterson, Berlin and Snyder Co., 1918.

*This song was in the top 20 from October 1918 to February 1919 and was number 3 in November and December. It was reprinted at least once and was recorded by Henry Burr.*

"Early to bed, early to rise,"
I heard a mother say to her angel eyes;
"Dream of your dad, my little lad,
Don't wake until the sun appears in the skies."
"I hate the sunshine," he said,
"It makes me get out of bed.

**CHORUS**

"Oh! how I wish I could sleep, until my daddy comes home;
Oh! Mamma, why must we always be all alone?
I miss him more ev'ryday,
How can you ask me to play?
You're always sighing and crying, since he went away.

Last night I heard daddy call,
But I was dreaming, that's all;
He kissed me, and he said,
'Go to bed, my own.'
Oh! Mamma, that's when I thought,
God made the nighttime too short;
Oh! how I wish I could sleep, until my daddy comes home."

Two little eyes, dotted with tears,
They tell a story full of darkness and fears;
Two shoulders bear sorrow and care,
A weight too great for just a baby in years.
"Mamma," the laddie explains,
"Sunshine brings nothing but pains."

**REPEAT CHORUS**

# I MISS DADDY'S GOOD-NIGHT KISS

Lyrics: James Kendis and James Brockman
Music: James Kendis and James Brockman
Artist: Rosenbaum Studios

New York: Kendis-Brockman Music Pub. Co. Inc., 1918.

Shades of night are falling,
Hear a mother calling,
"Sweet baby, come to bed
And rest your sleepy head.
Service flag is flying, your daddy had to go.
He'll come back maybe;" then little baby
  whispered soft and low:

**CHORUS**
  "Oh, how I miss daddy's good-night kiss,"
  Sweet baby sighs, little tear-dimmed eyes.
  She can't forget, he said, "Soon I'll be
    returning."
  She's daddy's pet and her little heart is
    yearning.

In mother's arms, see her baby's charms,
She held her tight, kissed her good night.
Behind her smiles there was a tear,
While baby whispered, Mama dear,
"Oh, how I miss daddy's good-night kiss."

Mother tells a story,
Fills her heart with glory,
And soon in slumber deep,
She's fallen fast asleep.
Just another picture that brings tears to your
  eyes,
She sighs in sorrow, "He'll come tomorrow."
  Baby wakes and cries:

**REPEAT CHORUS**

# WOULD YOU RATHER BE A COLONEL WITH AN EAGLE ON YOUR SHOULDER, OR A PRIVATE WITH A CHICKEN ON YOUR KNEE?

Lyrics: Sidney D. Mitchell
Music: Archie Gottler
Artist: Rosenbaum Studios

New York: Leo. Feist Inc., 1918.

*This song, which was featured in* Ziegfield Follies of 1918, *was in the top 20 from December 1918 to March 1919 and reached number 16 in January. It was recorded by both Eugene Buckley and Arthur Fields.*

Once I heard a father ask his soldier son,
"Why can't you advance like other boys have done?
You've been a private mighty long.
Won't you tell me what is wrong?"
And then the soldier lad
Said, "Listen to me, Dad:"

**CHORUS**
  "I'd rather be a private than a colonel in the army.
  A private has more fun,
  When his day's work is done;
  And when he goes on hikes,
  In ev'ry town he strikes,
  Girls discover him, and just smother him with things he likes;
  But girlies act so shy when colonel passes by,
  He holds his head so high with dignity;
  So would you rather be a colonel with an eagle on your shoulder,
  Or a private with a chicken on your knee?

"Ev'ry night you find some private in the park,
Spooning on a bench where it is nice and dark.
He's just as happy as can be,
With his girlie on his knee,
But colonel never dares
To mix in such affairs."

**CHORUS**
  "I'd rather be a private than a colonel in the army.
  A colonel out in France
  Can never take a chance,
  For tho' his job is great,
  He dare not make a date;
  All that he can do is just 'parley-voo' then hesitate,
  But privates meet the ma and then they treat the pa,
  And then they 'oo-la-la' with 'wee Marie'.
  So would you rather be a colonel with an eagle on your shoulder,
  Or a private with a chicken on your knee?"

# THAT'S THE IRISH IN ME

Lyrics: George Graff
Music: Bert Grant
Artist: Albert Barbelle

New York: Waterson, Berlin & Snyder Co.., 1918.

"Mother mine," said Pat O'Brien, "I'm going over there,
You ought to know I have to go and do me bit and share.
Me father was a fighting man,
An Irish man and so;
You know, little mother mine, I just have to go.

**CHORUS**
 I've kissed all of me sweethearts goodbye,
 I've whispered I'll be back bye and bye;
 Of all the fights the Irish were at,
 Here's the biggest scrap of all;
 We couldn't miss that.

That's why I'll sail across the blue sea,
And leave you me own Machree;
And though me heart will break at parting,
I'm crazy to be starting,
But that's the Irish in me.

We can't let the Germans put the English on the shelf,
For that's a job we've always been a-saving for ourself.
We'll help them win their battles and sure when the truth is known:
'Twill be practisin' for us when we start our own."

**REPEAT CHORUS**

# THE ROSE OF NO MAN'S LAND

Lyrics: Jack Caddigan
Music: James A. Brennan

Boston: Jack Mendelsohn Music Co., 1918.

*This song was in the top 20 from December 1918 to April 1919 and reached number 1 in January. It was reprinted at least seven times in New York by Leo Feist as a reduced-size war edition. It was recorded by Hugh Donovan, Henry Burr, and Charles Hart & Elliot Shaw.*

I've seen some beautiful flowers
Grow in life's garden fair.
I've spent some wonderful hours
Lost in their fragrance rare;
But I have found another,
Wondrous beyond compare.

**CHORUS**

   There's a rose that grows on no man's land,
   And it's wonderful to see.
   Tho' it's sprayed with tears,
   It will live for years
   In my garden of memory.

It's the one red rose the soldier knows,
It's the work of the Master's hand.
'Mid the war's great curse
Stands the Red Cross nurse.
She's the rose of no man's land.

Out of the heavenly splendor,
Down to the trail of woe,
God in His mercy has sent her,
Cheering the world below;
We call her "Rose of Heaven,"
We've learned to love her so.

**REPEAT CHORUS**

# WHEN THE FLOWERS BLOOM ON NO MAN'S LAND WHAT A WONDERFUL DAY THAT WILL BE

Lyrics: Howard E. Rogers
Music: Archie Gottler
Artist: Albert Barbelle

New York: Kalmar, Puck & Abrahams Consolidated, Inc., 1918.

*This song was also published with Dorothy Jarrett as the featured singer.*

241

There's a vision always haunts me
Of a day I long to see,
When hearts that are sad all will be glad
On this wonderful day to be;
When joys take the place of fears
And smiles take the place of tears.

**CHORUS**
When the flowers bloom on no man's land,
Bringing a message of peace and love,
And the cannon's roar is heard no more,
What a blessing from above.
When the sun shines through the clouds of war,
When peace covers all of the earth and sea,
And when each mother's son has laid down his gun,
What a wonderful day that will be.

Ev'rywhere a heart is longing,
Praying that the day is done
When far from alarms, safe from all harms
Ev'ry mother will hold her son;
When goodwill to ev'ry man
Will be ev'ry nation's plan.

**REPEAT CHORUS**

# IT'S ALL OVER NOW

Lyrics: George Fairman
Music: George Fairman
Artist: Rosenbaum Studios

New York: George Fairman, 1918.

*This song was reprinted at least once.*

242

The world war is over and roses are blooming
Over the lands of the brave and the free.
Love birds are singing,
Joy bells are ringing,
Ringing for you and for me.

**CHORUS**
  It's all over now, it's all over now.
  Darkness has turned into sunshine.
  It seems like a dream somehow.
  There's joy eve'rywhere,
  The world's free from care;
  There'll be no more fears,
  No more heartaches and tears,
  For it's all over now.

Don't think of the past, try and dream of tomorrow.
Forget your troubles and be of good cheer.
Loved ones returning,
For you they're yearning.
Sorrow will soon disappear.

**REPEAT CHORUS**

# NOW ALL THE WORLD'S AT PEACE

Lyrics: Fleta Jan Brown
Music: Peter de Rose

New York: F. B. Haviland Pub. Co., 1918.

Now that the fighting is over,
Now that the war is done,
Thru' all the fears and the heartaches and tears
There's been a vict'ry won.
The cannons have ceased loudly booming
Over the right or wrong.
Now love rules the world with its banners unfurled
We will give a cheer and song:

**CHORUS**
"Skies are now bluer,
Sunshine more bright.
Hearts will be truer
In the new dawn's light.
Homes will be brighter
Now that battles cease.
Tears turn to smiles
Now all the world's at peace."

Over the mountain of trouble
There lies a valley green.
High up above is the kingdom of love
So peaceful and serene.
And deep in each heart is a longing
For liberty and right,
And out of the gloom of the great cannon's boom
Has come happiness and light:

**REPEAT CHORUS**

# ALL ABOARD FOR HOME SWEET HOME

Lyrics: Addison Burkhart
Music: Al Piantadosi and Jack Glogau
Artist: Starmer

New York: Al Piantadosi & Co. Inc., 1918.

*Other featured singers with this cover design include the Courtney Sisters and Mel Klee. The song was also printed with a similar cover design but without any featured singer as well as with a smaller brown cover featuring Elsie White.*

244

Cheer up, mothers, dry your tears.
He's coming back to you.
Sweethearts, you'll soon hear the cheers
For your hero true.
Battles' roar he'll hear no more.
Soon he'll sail from France's shore.
When he's paid the debt
He owes to Lafayette,
He will say goodbye and cry:

**CHORUS**
  "All aboard for home sweet home;
  Again to the girl I left behind
  I'll go sailing 'cross the foam.
  Again what a welcome there I'll find,
  And the day that I return to her
  I will make that girl my own.
  Hello, dear hometown, I'm homeward bound.
  All aboard for home sweet home."

When our boys sail up the bay,
A great day that will be;
They'll be more than proud to say,
"Hello, Liberty."
With joy our hearts will be filled,
Soon our France we will rebuild,
For you've been true blue.
So now we say to you,
"Au Revoir" but not "Goodbye."

**REPEAT CHORUS**

# MY DADDY'S COMING HOME

Lyrics: David W. Cooper
Music: David W. Cooper

Boston: D. W. Cooper Music Co., 1918.

*This song was also issued without an illustrated cover.*

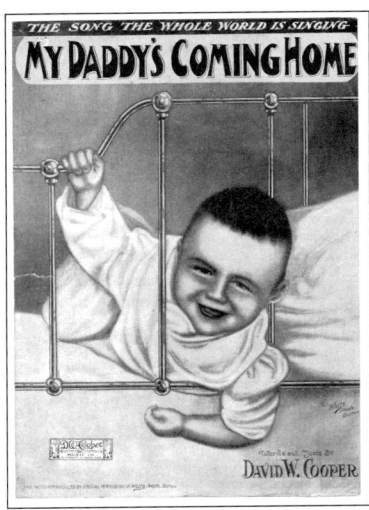

245

Hear the bells all ringing,
Hear the whistles blow.
Gee! but we're glad;
No one is sad,
This is the greatest we've ever had.
See the love-light shining
In my mother's eyes.
Now listen while I tell you
Just why she's in paradise.

**CHORUS**
   My daddy's coming home!
   My daddy's coming home!
   Oh! I'm jumping for joy, just like each girl
     and boy
   Who's got someone over the foam.
   We've kept the home fires burning bright,
   And in the window there's a light.
   All our worries are o'er,
   Mother will cry no more,
   'Cause my daddy's coming home.

Oh! how long we've waited
For this day to come.
They're on their way
Back home to stay,
Marching along to a tune of fife and drum.
When I see my daddy,
I will climb his knee,
And we'll make up what we've missed
Since he went away from me.

**REPEAT CHORUS**

# WELCOME HOME, LADDIE BOY, WELCOME HOME

Lyrics: Will D. Cobb
Music: Gus Edwards
Artist: Dunk

New York, Chicago et al.: M. Witmark & Sons, 1918.

What's that noise?
That's our boys
A-marching up the street.
Grab your bonnet, Kate.
Hurry, don't be late.
You must be there your boys to greet.
"Oh, goodbye and luck be with you, laddie
  boy."
That's what we sang as they marched away,
But now they've won their share of glory,
And come back to tell the story.
Let this be our song today:

**CHORUS**
  "Welcome home, laddie boy, welcome home,
  To the arms you left for arms across the foam,
  To the one you loved the strongest on that
    parting day,
  To the one you kissed the longest when you
    marched away.

  But now you're home again, home again,
  Never more to roam again.
  Here's the way I feel about it,
  From the roof I want to shout it,
  Welcome home, laddie boy, welcome home!"

How's it feel
When your heel
Hits your own hometown street?
Kinda good, I guess.
Well, I should say yes;
It's Uncle Sammy's turn to treat.
And the best he's got, he'll give you, laddie boy,
But that's not any too good for you,
For you've upheld his starry banner
In the well-known Yankee manner.
You've shown all the world who's who!

**REPEAT CHORUS**

# MOTHERS OF AMERICA, YOU HAVE DONE YOUR SHARE!

Lyrics: Harry Ellis
Music: Lew Porter

New York, Chicago, and London: Jos. W. Stern & Co., 1918.

*This song was also published with Eva Tanguay as the featured singer.*

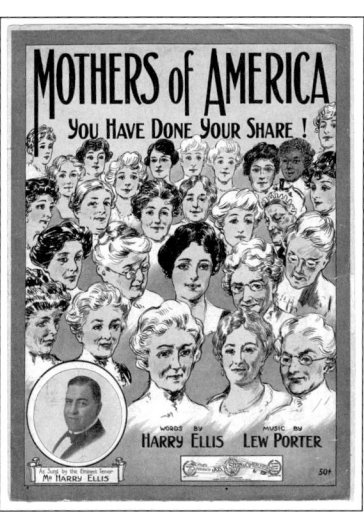

When all is said and done,
When ev'rything is won,
Who paid the price to win the war?
Who sacrificed her all,
And answered to the call?
M-O-T-H-E-R.

**CHORUS**
  Mothers of America, you have done your share.
  You have given ev'ry son,
  So our battles could be won.
  And with a smile you sent them over there;
  When he wins upon the battlefield of glory,
  For his safe return you say a prayer.
  You have given to the strife
  Your heart, your soul, your life.
  Mothers of America, you have done your share.

Then when the boys return
Each mother's heart will yearn
To meet their loved ones from afar,
While standing by her side,
Another smiles in pride.
F-A-T-H-E-R.

**REPEAT CHORUS**

# TILL WE MEET AGAIN

Lyrics: Raymond B. Egan
Music: Richard A. Whiting
Artist: F. S. M.

Detroit and New York: Jerome H. Remick and Co., 1918.

*This song was in the top 20 from November 1918 to September 1919 and remained at number 1 from February to April 1919. It was reprinted at least six times, sometimes in a slightly larger format. It was also recorded by Albert Campbell & Henry Burr, Charles Hart & Lewis James, Gitz Rice & Vernon Dalhart, and Nicholas Orlando's Orchestra.*

There's a song in the land of the lily
Each sweetheart has heard with a sigh;
Over high garden walls
This sweet echo falls
As a soldier boy whispers goodbye.

**CHORUS**
"Smile the while you kiss me sad adieu,
When the clouds roll by I'll come to you.
Then the skies will seem more blue.
Down in lovers' lane, my dearie,
Wedding bells will ring so merrily.
Ev'ry tear will be a memory,
So wait and pray each night for me,
Till we meet again."

Tho' goodbye means the birth of a teardrop,
Hello means the birth of a smile.
And the smile will erase
The tear-blighting trace
When we meet in the after-a-while.

**REPEAT CHORUS**

# DEAR OLD PAL OF MINE

Lyrics: Harold Robe
Music: Gitz Rice

New York: G. Ricordi & Co., Inc., 1918.

*This song was in the top 20 from January to March 1919 and reached number 10 in February. It was recorded by John McCormack, Oscar Seagle, and Joseph C. Smith's Orchestra.*

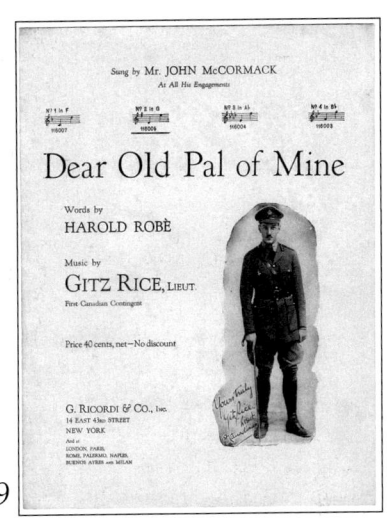

All my life is empty,
Since I went away;
Skies don't seem to be so clear.
May some angel sentry
Guard you while I stray,
And fate be kind to join us some sweet day.

**CHORUS**
  Oh, how I want you,
  Dear old pal of mine;
  Each night and day I pray you're always mine.
  Sweetheart, may God bless you.
  Angel hands caress you,
  While sweet dreams rest you,
  Dear old pal of mine.

Dearie, I'm so lonely,
How I miss your smile,
And your tender loving way.
I just want you only,
Want you all the while.
May God decree I have you back someday.

**REPEAT CHORUS**

# 1919

# AMERICAN CRUSADERS

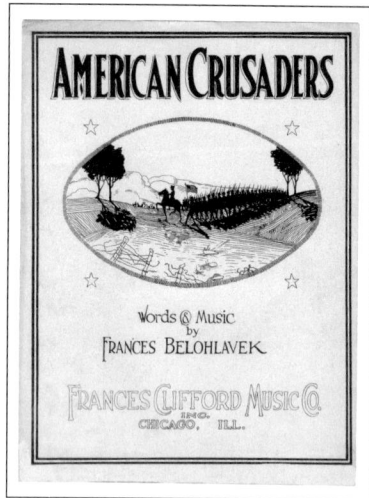

Lyrics: Frances Belohlavek
Music: Frances Belohlavek

Chicago: Frances Clifford Music Co. Inc., 1919.

250

The world was all in turmoil,
The fire of battle raged;
The "Song of Hate" was on men's lips,
And "Right of Might" was praised.
The call of "Truth" was sounded
By all the Allies bold.
The call of "Truth" was heeded,
This tyrant to withhold.

**CHORUS**
American Crusaders,
From freedom's land they came.
The love of God was in their hearts.
They could not strive in vain.

They came, they saw, the conquer'd,
That nations might be free.
American Crusaders,
Brave sons of liberty.

The battle has subsided,
The world is calm again.
"Peace on Earth," "Goodwill t'ward Men,"
And "Might of Right" now reign.
American Crusaders
With their brave allies bold
Have raised on high the standard,
Like crusaders of old.

**REPEAT CHORUS**

# WE ARE PROUD OF YOU!

Lyrics: George B. F. Chaffee
Music: George B. F. Chaffee

Ruthven, IA: George B. F. Chaffee, 1919.

251

We have heard the wondrous story
Of our brave boys in khaki,
How they fought beneath Old Glory
In that land so far away,
How they nobly took their stand,
In that shell-plowed no man's land,
Midst the shriek of shot and shell
In that carnage of hell,
At the battle of the Marne,
And of Chateau Theirry, too.
Say our brave soldier boys,
"We are proud of you."

On the battlefields so gory,
Where you charged them with a cheer,
Winning thus undying glory
Tho' the price you paid was dear,
But you got behind the Hun
And you kept him on the run,
Till he reached the river Rhine.
There the Boche begun to whine,
Knowing that he must surrender,
And to hated Yankees, too.
Say our brave soldier boys,
"We are proud of you."

You have wallowed in the trenches,
In the filth and the mire,
Been where sleet and cold rain drenches
Without water, food or fire.
You have seen brave comrades fall,
Heard, for aid their pleading call,
Off'ring up their lives, that we
Might be happy, might be free.
You are welcome to our fireside,
Of our best we'll offer, too.
Say our brave soldier boys,
"We are proud of you."

# NOW THAT THE WAR IS OVER

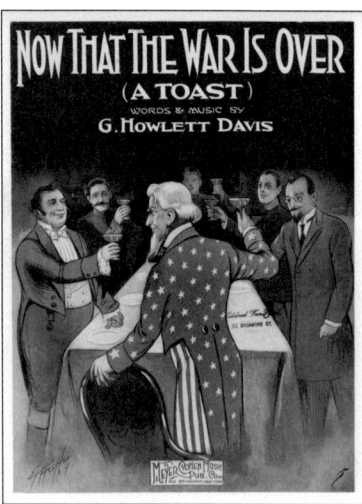

Lyrics: G. Howlett Davis
Music: G. Howlett Davis
Artist: E. H. Pfeiffer

New York: Meyer Cohen Music Pub. Co. Inc., 1919.

252

Now that the war is over
And the guns are silent once more,
Let's give a toast to our soldier boys,
Who have fought and won the war.

**CHORUS**
So here's good cheer to the living,
And a blessing to those who are dead.
For mothers, wives, and sweethearts,
We order rejoicing instead.

Let's help all nations who suffered
Through a tyrant's ambition and lust,
Prove the emblem on our coinage
In justice and God we trust.

**REPEAT CHORUS**

# FLEUR-DE-LYS, FLOW'R OF FRANCE, BLOOM AGAIN

Lyrics: Robert Levenson
Music: Robert Levenson
Artist: V. C. Plunkett

Boston: D. W. Cooper Music Co., 1919.

*A French version by Henri Herigault Pelletier is printed above the English version.*

Flower of France, with your petals all gone.
Flower of France, come see it is dawn!
The sunshine that you've missed for so long
Is coming back to make you so strong.
Your long night is thru', can't you see?
You must now bloom, a new Fleur-de-lys.

**CHORUS**

Fleur-de-lys, Fleur-de-lys,
Flow'r of France, bloom again for me.
Clouds that made you wither away
All are gone, and I know you will now live for aye.
Our happy smile will be your sunshine.
Tears we've shed will be your rain.
Come show the world what France can do!
Fleur-de-lys, flow'r of France, bloom again.
Fleur-de-lys, flow'r of France, bloom again.

I can recall when you bloom'd ev'rywhere,
Shining so fair, and scenting the air.
The spreading fields that once were so white
Have changed to red somehow in the night,
But you'll make them white once again.
You have weathered the storm not in vain.

**REPEAT CHORUS**

# OUR WILSON IS THE GREATEST MAN THIS WORLD HAS EVER KNOWN

Lyrics: Adelbert Reynolds
Music: Carl Demangate

Glens Falls: Harrington & Reynolds Publishers, 1919.

When Huns got out their guns and started their great war
On Belgium, France and England, and sev'ral nations more,
Then Allies were all certain that they could whip the Hun,
But had to call on Wilson before the trick was done.

**CHORUS**
   Our Wilson is the greatest man this world has ever known;
   He is the only president to leave his native home
   And sail away to foreign lands, the guest of foreign kings,
   To teach them that democracy forever peace will bring.

Then Wilson took command and called his Yankees out;
Three million strong he sent on to help the Allies out.
Then o'er the top our boys went and victory was won;
Then Wilson tho't he'd better go settle with the Hun.

**REPEAT CHORUS**

On ship *George Washington* then Wilson sailed away
To see all nations righted and that the Huns must pay.
By plans of this great leader for peace and love and right,
All nations in the future will arbitrate, not fight.

**REPEAT CHORUS**

# GOOD-BYE, SHOT AND SHELL!

Lyrics: Lou Spero
Music: Gerald Peck
Artist: Starmer

New York: Jos. W. Stern & Co., 1919.

Peace, peace, welcome sound,
Flash the news the whole world 'round.
Run tell mother, sister, brother,
Daddy's on his way.
Peace, peace, Yankee crowned,
Old Flag never touched the ground.
Colors fling, no more sighing,
Celebrate the day.

**CHORUS**
Good-bye shot, good-bye shell,
Good-bye suffering, good-bye hell!
Good-bye slavery of nations,
Good-bye beans for daily rations,
Good-bye Czar, and King and Kaiser,
Now we trust you all are wiser.
"War times, war times, come again no more,"
For it's good-bye, good-bye,
Good-bye, shot and shell.

Peace, peace, welcome word,
Best in many years we've heard.
Run tell mother, sister, brother,
Decorate with flow'rs.

Peace, peace, Lafayette,
Uncle Sammy's paid his debt.
Yankee Doodle's off his noodle,
For the Huns are ours.

**CHORUS**
Good-bye shot, good-bye shell,
Good-bye suffering, good-bye hell!
Good-bye slavery of nations,
Good-bye beans for daily rations,
Good-bye cooties, rats and stenches,
No more muddy, bloody trenches.
"War times, war times, come again no more,"
For it's good-bye, good-bye,
Good-bye shot and shell.

*Alternate lines in the middle of the chorus*
Good-bye gas bombs, torture filling,
No more Zepp'lins baby killing.

Good-bye battlefields' sad meaning,
Hindenburg and submarining.

# HADN'T BILL FORGOTTEN TO RECKON WITH UNCLE SAM

Lyrics: Charlotte Ratcliff
Music: J. C. Halls

Chillicothe: Charlotte Ratcliff, 1919.

256

Old Kaiser Bill once said to the Von Hindenburg and Krupp,
"Let Germany get busy, and blow all nations up.
Then I, Emperor William, will be ruler of the world.
Across the sea, old Germany shall have her flag unfurled."

**CHORUS**
But Bill had forgotten to reckon with Uncle Sam.
He tho't he had all Europe whipp'd, when biff, bang, bam:
Sam blew up all Bill's submarines, and landed on the shore.
Now "Gott mit uns" und Kaiser Bill, he's nixie anymore.

Bill started out for Paris, so he filled up all his tanks,
Was moving right along until halted by the Yanks.
Bill gazed upon the solid line of Uncle Sammie's lads,
His knees begin to quiver and he hollered, "Kamerad."

**REPEAT CHORUS**

"Down on your marrow bones," cried out Uncle Sammie's lads.
"We do not trust you or your old plea of 'Kamerad.'
You sneered at 'our America,' but tell us if you can,
If you had not forgotten first to think of Uncle Sam."

**REPEAT CHORUS**

# YANKEE DOODLE IN BERLIN

Lyrics: Harry Williams
Music: Charles N. Daniels

San Francisco: Daniels & Wilson, Inc., 1919.

*On the back cover is a full-page advertisement for* Yankee Doodle in Berlin, *Mack Sennett's "latest comedy in five acts."*

257

Yankee Doodle rode upon a bony pony;
He was just a clown, but still he got to town.
Hindenburg, although his heart was stony, phony,
Never got to see
Dear old Paree,

**CHORUS**
But Yankee Doodle always goes to town,
And Yankee Doodle's in Berlin.
Each tearful German who calls it a "cheek"
Tells it to Herman, then he "bawls a week"
  (*cry baby*).
Yankee Doodle made a German thin,
He's even lost his double chin.
All the linden trees shake a "shimmie" in the breeze,
For lanky Yankee Doodle's in Berlin.

What about the Kaiser's Paris dinner?
Sinner! was it very much? He only got in Dutch,
And though Yankee Doodle is a thinner, winner
He'll go anywhere
And on the square,

**CHORUS**
For Yankee Doodle always goes to town,
And Yankee Doodle's in Berlin.
Each tearful German who calls it a "cheek"
Tells it to Herman, then he "bawls a week"
  (*cry baby*).
Yankee Doodle made a German thin
He's even lost his double chin.
All the merry Dutch don't amount to very much,
For lanky Yankee Doodle's in Berlin.

# THTOP YOUR THTUTTERING, JIMMY

Lyrics: Hal Blake Cowles
Music: Hal Blake Cowles
Artist: Lionel S. Reiss

New York: Leo. Feist Inc., 1919.

*This song was also published in a larger format with a different cover design.*

Jimmy was a soldier, who stuttered like a gawk,
But no one ever told us how Katy used to talk.
Tho' she'd always listen to ev'ry word he'd say,
She could never figure out, just what it was all about.
When she found she was in doubt, she'd lisp to him this way:

**CHORUS**
"Thtop your thtuttering, Jimmy; goodneth, can't you thee,
You alwayth thtart to thtutter, when you make love to me?
Put your armth around me, thqueethe me nithe and fine,
But thtop your thtuttering Jimmy, cauthe you're only waithting time."

Jimmy didn't stutter much after he left Kate,
But seemed to lose the habit, as he left the garden gate.
But when he would see her, he'd talk the same old way.
Was it something in her eye? Was it something in her sigh?
I think it was just because he loved to hear her say:

**CHORUS**
"Thtop your thtuttering, Jimmy; goodneth, can't you thee,
You alwayth thtart to thtutter, when you make love to me?
Put your armth around me, thqueethe me nithe and tight,
But thtop your thtuttering Jimmy, cauthe I can't thtay here all night."

# THE COOTIE TICKLE

Lyrics: Jack Yellen
Music: Abe Olman
Artist: Rosenbaum Studios

New York: Leo. Feist, Inc., 1919.

259

You've heard of the shimmie dance,
But do you know it started back in France?
I learn'd from a soldier man
How this funny little dance began.
At a ragtime jubilee
The soldiers gave one night in gay Paree,
A "cullud gent" by accident
Introduced this novelty:

**CHORUS**
    Mose began to "Ball-the-Jack,"
    Just then up and down his back
    He felt a cute little cootie, wigglin', wigglin', in its track.
    That's what made him shake and twist;
    He did something just like this.
    And ev'ryone began to wiggle with 'im,
    Their shoulders movin' to the raggy rhythm;
    It's the "Cootie Tickle" back in France,
    Over here it's the shimmie dance.

Now in ev'ry cabaret
The minute that the band begins to play
Ev'rybody on the floor
Dances like they never did before;
It's done in so many ways,
And when I see it, I just sit and gaze,
And all the while I have to smile,
Thinking of what caused this craze.

**REPEAT CHORUS**

# SALVATION LASSIE OF MINE

Lyrics: Jack Caddigan and Chick Story
Music: Jack Caddigan and Chick Story

New York: Leo. Feist, Inc., 1919.

*This song was in the top 20 in March and April 1919 and reached number 18 in April. It was reprinted several times—sometimes in a smaller format—and was recorded by both Charles Harrison and Charles Hart & Lewis James.*

They say it's in heaven that all angels dwell,
But I've come to learn that they're on earth just as well;
And how would I know that the like could be so,
If I hadn't found one down here below:

**CHORUS**
A sweet little angel that went o'er the sea,
With the emblem of God in her hand,
A wonderful angel who brought there to me,
The sweet of a war-furrowed land.
The crown on her head was a ribbon of red,
A symbol of all that's divine.
Tho' she called each a brother, she's more like a mother,
Salvation Lassie of mine.

Perhaps in the future I'll meet her again
In that world where no one knows sorrow or pain;
And when that time comes and the last word is said,
Then place on my bosom, her band of red:

**REPEAT CHORUS**

# HOW 'YA GONNA KEEP 'EM DOWN ON THE FARM (AFTER THEY'VE SEEN PAREE)?

Lyrics: Sam M. Lewis and Joe Young
Music: Walter Donaldson
Artist: Albert Barbelle

New York: Waterson, Berlin and Snyder, Co., 1919.

*This song was in the top 20 from March to August 1919 and reached number 2 in May. It was reprinted at least three times: twice in blue (and slightly larger) and once in brown (also slightly larger). The song was recorded by Nora Bayes, Byron G. Harlan, and Arthur Fields.*

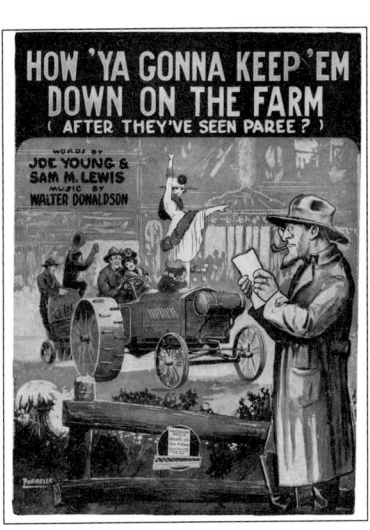

261

"Reuben, Reuben, I've been thinking,"
Said his wifey dear;
"Now that all is peaceful and calm,
The boys will soon be back on the farm."
Mister Reuben started winking,
And slowly rubbed his chin;
He pulled his chair up close to mother,
And he asked her with a grin:

**CHORUS**
"How 'ya gonna keep 'em, down on the
   farm,
After they've seen Paree?
How 'ya gonna keep 'em away from
   Broadway,
Jazzin' aroun',
And paintin' the town?
How 'ya gonna keep 'em away from harm?
That's a mystery;
They'll never want to see a rake or plow,
And who the deuce can parley-vous a cow?
How 'ya gonna keep 'em down on the
   farm,
After they've seen Paree?

"Reuben, Reuben, you're mistaken,"
Said his wifey dear;
"Once a farmer, always a jay,
And farmers always stick to the hay."
"Mother Reuben, I'm not fakin',
Tho' you many think it strange,
But wine and women can play the mischief,
With a boy who's loose with change:"

**CHORUS**
"How 'ya gonna keep 'em, down on the
   farm,
After they've seen Paree?
How 'ya gonna keep 'em away from
   Broadway,
Jazzin' aroun',
And paintin' the town?
How 'ya gonna keep 'em away from harm?
That's a mystery;
Imagine Reuben when he meets his pa,
He'll kiss his cheek and holler, 'Oo-la-la!'
How 'ya gonna keep 'em down on the
   farm,
After they've seen Paree?"

# DON'T CRY, FRENCHY

Lyrics: Sam M. Lewis and Joe Young
Music: Walter Donaldson
Artist: Albert Barbelle

New York: Waterson, Berlin, and Snyder Co., 1919.

*In the top 20 in May and June 1919 this song was number 19. Another printing is slightly smaller and has a different cover design. The song was recorded by both Lewis James and Charles Hart & Elliot Shaw.*

They met while clouds were hanging over Flanders,
A soldier's glance, a war romance;
But now he's leaving her alone in Flanders,
And he softly whispers to his maid of France:

### CHORUS
"Don't cry, Frenchy, don't cry,
When you kiss me goodbye;
I will always keep the fleur-de-lis, dear,
You gave to me, dear, so dry your eye.
Sometime, Frenchy, sometime,
We'll hear wedding bells chime.
Oh! Please don't cry, Frenchy, don't cry, don't cry;
Until we meet again, goodbye, goodbye."

"The peaceful stars will heal the scars of Flanders,
One tiny spark will light the dark;
For it will bring a message back to Flanders,
Just a word of love to you, my Joan of Arc:"

### REPEAT CHORUS

# LITTLE FRENCH MOTHER, GOOD-BYE!

Lyrics: Jack Caddigan and Chick Story
Music: Jack Caddigan and Chick Story
Artist: Norman Rockwell

New York: Leo. Feist, Inc., 1919.

Where the shadows gathered on that foreign shore,
There they met to say goodbye and meet no more.
As he took her in his arms to kiss away a tear,
Softly he whispered in her ear:

**CHORUS**
"Little French mother, goodbye, goodbye,
Dry up the tear in your eye, don't cry.
I knew from the start that someday we'd part,
But down in my heart,
Oh, I wish I could stay a little longer.

Little French mother, don't sigh, don't sigh,
A million others love you just the same as I.
You did all a mother could,
You're the flow'r of womanhood,
Little French mother, goodbye!"

"In the book of life on pages bound in gold,
There they'll find the sweetest story ever told,
It will tell the world how much sweet mother love can do;
And just how much we think of you."

**REPEAT CHORUS**

# AMERICA NEVER TOOK WATER AND AMERICA NEVER WILL

Lyrics: J. Keirn Brennan, Gus Edwards, and Paul Cunningham
Words: J. Keirn Brennan, Gus Edwards, and Paul Cunningham
Artist: Dunk

New York: M. Whitmark & Sons, 1919.

264

Slowly but surely a transport of joy
Docked at her pier up the bay.
"Tell us the news, old pal, we've been away!"
That's what each boy seemed to say;
When someone said the country's going dry,
They listened, then they all began to cry:

**CHORUS**
  "Why America never took water,
  So why should she take it now?
  England gave us ale and porter,
  To drink their wines the French have taught
    us how.
  Of water in the trenches, we surely had our
    fill,
  So we can't understand why you should
    hand it to us still,
  For America never took water,
  And America never will!"

One fighting Yank said, "If such is the case,
This is no place then for me!
I'm going back again, back o'er the sea,
Where I can live happily."
His comrades said, "Before you start to go,
It seems to us it's time you ought to know."

**CHORUS**
  "That America never took water,
  So why should she take it now?
  England gave us ale and porter,
  To drink their wines the French have taught
    us how.
  Old Jack and Jill took water, that's why
    they took a spill.
  The same thing's apt to happen to this
    famous drinking bill,
  For America never took water,
  And America never will!"

# THE ALCOHOLIC BLUES

Lyrics: Edward Laska
Music: Albert Von Tilzer

New York: Broadway Music Corporation, 1919.

*This song was in the top 20 from June to August 1919 and reached number 13 in July. It was recorded by both Billy Murray and Vernon Dalhart.*

265

I love my country, 'deed I do,
But oh, that war has made me blue.
I like fightin', that's my name,
But fightin' is the least about the fightin' game.
When Mister Hoover said to cut my dinner down,
I never even hesitate, I never frown;
I cut my sugar, I cut my coal,
But now they dug deep in my soul.

**CHORUS**
   I've got the blues, I've got the blues,
   I've got the alcoholic blues.
   No more beer my heart to cheer;
   Goodbye, whiskey, you used to make me frisky.
   So long, highball, so long, gin.

Oh, tell me when you comin' back agin?
Blues, I've got the blues
Since they amputated my booze.
Lordy, Lordy, war is well,
You know, I don't have to tell.
Oh, I've got the alcoholic blues.

Prohibition that's the name,
Prohibition drives me insane.
I'm so thirsty, soon I'll die,
I'm simply goin' to 'vaporate, I'm just that dry.
I wouldn't mind to live forever in a trench,
Just if my daily thirst they only let me quench.
And not with bevo or ginger ale;
I want real stuff by the pail.

**REPEAT CHORUS**

# HE'S HAD NO LOVIN' FOR A LONG LONG TIME

Lyrics: William Tracey
Music: Maceo Pinkard
Artist: E. E. Walton

New York: Broadway Music Corporation, 1919.

Now that it's over and peace is declared,
Our nation is wild with joy.
Ev'ry young girlie is getting prepared
To welcome her soldier boy.
Listen, girls, he's been true blue.
Now the rest is up to you.

**CHORUS**
  Oh, you know he's had no lovin' for a long, long time.
  He's got to have a lot of it now.
  Just hide away the service flag you waved for him,
  And give him all the kisses that you've saved for him.
  Since he went away
  He's been busy each day.
  His medals will tell you just how.
  And just to make up for the fun he's been missin'
  Your boy's entitled to some huggin' and kissin'.
  He's had no loving for a long, long time,
  And he's got to have a lot of it now.

Fix up the parlor, get ev'rything set,
And put on his fav'rite gown.
Give him the welcome a hero should get
The day he arrives in town.
He's been gone a long, long while.
Meet him with a great big smile.

**CHORUS**
  Oh, you know he's had no loving for a long, long time.
  He's got to have a lot of it now.
  To thank you for the many nights you prayed for him
  He even wore those awful socks you made for him.
  He's traveling miles
  Just for one of your smiles
  For he has been true to his vow.
  There're pretty girls in France but you needn't worry,
  You know that he'll forget them all in a hurry.
  He's had no lovin' for a long, long time,
  And he's got to have a lot of it now.

# MY BARNEY LIES OVER THE OCEAN
# (JUST THE WAY HE LIED TO ME)

Lyrics: Joe Young and Sam M. Lewis
Music: Bert Grant
Artist: Albert Barbelle

New York: Waterson, Berlin and Snyder Co., 1919.

*In the top 20 in June and July 1919 this song was number 19 and then number 18. It was reprinted at least once and was recorded by both Nora Bayes and Billy Murray.*

267

Barney Carney promised he'd be true to Molly O.
The day he went away to war about a year ago;
In ev'ry note that Barney wrote, he called her "Ma Cherie."
She read the name and said with shame, "This isn't meant for me."
All the neighbors noticed there were teardrops in her eye,
And when they asked her how was Barney, she'd begin to cry:

## CHORUS

"My Barney lies over the ocean,
My Barney lies over the sea;
Sure he said he went to war to help the women,
And I think he's helped himself to two or three;
Now he's got a little girl in Belgium, and one in Paree,
And I know the little things he tells 'em, when they're on his knee,
Sure my Barney lies over the ocean,
Just the way he lied to me."

Barney wrote a letter home the day the war was through.
He started off with "Molly, dear, I'm coming home to you."
He didn't say what week or day, nor did he say what year,
And Molly O. said, "Wurrawoe, it's all a joke, I fear."
People said he'd have to wait until the ships come back,
And Molly said, "Why wait for them, why don't he take a hack?"

## REPEAT CHORUS

# AND HE'D SAY "OO-LA-LA! WEE-WEE"

Lyrics: Harry Ruby and George Jessel
Music: Harry Ruby and George Jessel
Artist: Albert Barbelle

New York: Waterson, Berlin, and Snyder, Co., 1919.

*This song was in the top 20 from October 1919 to January 1920 and reached number 9 in November. It was reprinted at least twice with a different cover design and was recorded by Billy Murray.*

Willie Earl met a sweet young girl one day in France.
Her naughty little glance
Put Willie in a trance;
Willie Earl couldn't understand her talk, you see.
He only knew two words in French
That he learned in the trench.
They were "oo-la la!" and "wee-wee."
They would spoon beneath the moon above;
It was fun to hear them making love.

**CHORUS**
   She'd say, "Compronay voo, papa?"
   And he'd say, "Oo-la la! Wee-wee."
   She'd smile and whisper, "Mercy bacoo."
   He'd answer, "I don't mind if I do."
   She'd say, "If you be my papa,
   Then I will be your ma cherie."
   She'd pinch his cheek and say, "You keskasay."
   He'd say, "Not now, dear, but later I may."
   Then she'd say, "Compronay voo, papa?"
   And he'd say, "Oo-la la! Wee-wee."

Willie Earl said, "This little girl is meant for me.
No more I'll cross the sea,
I'll stay in Gay Paree."
Ev'ryday you would hear him say to his babee,
"Your talk I do not know but I,
Will manage to get by
With my "oo-la la!" and "wee-wee."
Ev'ry ev'ning Willie would rehearse;
Instead of getting better, he got worse.

**CHORUS**
   She'd say, "Compronay voo, papa?"
   And he'd say, "Oo-la la! Wee-wee,"
   She'd say, "Come see," and then roll her eyes.
   He'd answer, "Baby, you'd be surprised."
   Each ev'ning they would promenade
   Up on ze boulevarde, you see;
   One day at lunch, she said, "Café voola."
   He said, "My dear, don't forget where you are;"
   Then she'd say, "Compronay voo, papa?"
   And he'd say, "Oo-la la! Wee-wee."

# I WONDER WHAT'S ZE MATTER WIZ MY OO-LA-LA?
# (COME WHAT MAY, I CAN'T SAY, OO-ZE-OO-LA-LA-LA-LA)

Lyrics: Jack Frost
Music: F. Henri Klickmann
Artist: H.

Chicago, New York et al.: Frank K. Root and Co., 1919.

I just received a letter from a soldier 'cross the foam;
He's got it in his dome that he's not coming home.
He says he's had a dandy visit since he left the trench
In wining 'bout and dining out and learning to talk French.
The Frenchy girls are going to his head.
Just tell me what you think; here's what he said:

**CHORUS**
   "Now I wonder what's ze matter wiz my 'Oo-la-la?'
   Ze French baby she say maybe she teach you 'Papa.'
   I can say, 'Come-see, come-sa.'
   I've got ze sweet 'Mama,'
   And when we start 'parlayvooing,'
   How I love ze little squeeze again.
   I say, 'Parisienne, my heart is yearning and I'm learning,
   But I wonder what's ze matter wiz my 'Oo-la-la?'
   Come what may, I can't say, 'Oo-ze-oo-la-la-la-la'."

He says he knows we're waiting, but we'll have to wait in vain;
He's going to remain somewhere near old Champagne.
Ze "Oo-la-la", ze "Oo-la-la" has got him in a trance;
There's always something doing, "parlayvooing" there in France.
Sometimes I think he's hazy in the head,
And only since these crazy words I've read:

**REPEAT CHORUS**

# DON'T FORGET THE BOYS (WHO FOUGHT FOR YOU AND ME)

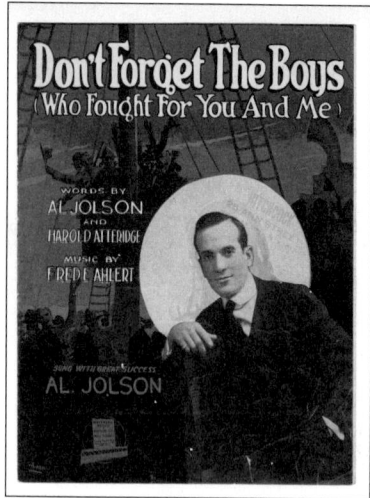

Lyrics: Al Jolson and Harold Atteridge
Music: Fred E. Ahlert
Artist: Albert Barbelle

New York: Waterson, Berlin & Snyder Co., 1919.

270

America, the war is through, you did your job real well,
You kicked the Crown Prince off his perch, and gave the Kaiser hell;
We're sitting back, we're satisfied, but li'ble to forget,
That you and you and you and I still owe the greatest debt;
The boys who fought with all they had to give
Demand that gift of God, the right to live.

**CHORUS**
  Don't forget the boys, who fought for you and me.
  From that fight at Chateau Thierry,
  They are bruised and worn and weary
  For the sake of liberty.
  Don't forget the boys, now that the world is free;
  Give them back the chance they had before,
  When they marched away to win the war;
  So don't forget the boys, who fought for you and me.

We never knew the day would come we'd have to lick the Hun,
That you and you and you or I might have to get a gun.
From East and West, and North and South they answered to the roll,
And ev'ry mother's son of them was there to give his soul.
For those who died our blessings ne'er will cease;
They left in honor, for the cause of peace.

**CHORUS**
  Don't forget the boys, who fought for you and me;
  Let America be mother,
  To each tired little brother;
  That is true democracy.
  Don't forget the boys, now that the world is free;
  We shall be a nation proud and strong,
  If you help your soldier boys along;
  So don't forget the boys, who fought for you and me.

# I'VE GOT MY CAPTAIN WORKING FOR ME NOW

Lyrics: Irving Berlin
Music: Irving Berlin

New York: Irving Berlin, Inc., 1919.

*This song was in the top 20 from October 1919 to January 1920 and reached number 6 in November and December 1919. It was recorded by Al Jolson, Eddie Cantor, and Billy Murray.*

Johnny Jones was a first class private
In the army last year.
Now he's back to bus'ness in his father's place.
Sunday night I saw him with a smiling face.
When I asked why he felt so happy
Johnny chuckled with glee.
He winked his eye and made this reply:
"Something wonderful has happened to me."

**CHORUS**
"I've got the guy who used to be my
  captain working for me.
He wanted work, so I made him a clerk in
  my father's factory,
And bye and bye I'm gonna have him
  wrapped in work up to his brow.
I make him open the office ev'ry morning at
  eight;
I come around about four hours late.
Ev'rything comes to those who wait.
I've got my captain working for me now.

"He's not worth what I have to pay him,
But I'll never complain.
I've agreed to give him fifty dollars per;
It's worth twice as much to hear him call me
  'Sir.'
While I sit in my cozy office,
He's outside working hard
Out in the hall at my beck and call
With a feather duster standing on guard."

**CHORUS**
"I've got the guy who used to be my
  captain working for me.
He wanted work so I made him a clerk in
  my father's factory,
And bye and bye I'm gonna have him
  wrapped in work up to his brow.
When I come into the office he gets up on
  his feet,
Stands at attention and gives me his seat.
Who was it said, 'Revenge is sweet.'
I've got my captain working for me now."

# MY CHOC'LATE SOLDIER SAMMY BOY

Lyrics: Egbert Van Alstyne
Music: Egbert Van Alstyne
Artist: Starmer

Detroit and New York: Jerome H. Remick & Co., 1919.

272

Just hear that band a-playin' down the street.
Just hear the sound of drums and marchin' feet.
That's Colonel Jackson and his colored brigade
Just back from Over There and out on parade.
Just see the crowd a-swayin' to and fro.
The p'rade is startin'; Honey, come let's go
See that chile of mine,
Watch him markin' time
Waiting for that bugle blow.

**CHORUS**
　See him marchin' along.
　Hear him hummin' a song.
　Watch that baby throw out his chest.
　See them medals pinn'd on his breast.
　Lord, love him, I'm so happy and proud,
　Feel like shoutin' out loud.
　My Honey, come, come, come to your mammy.
　My Choc'late Soldier Sammy Boy.

This afternoon there'll be a barbecue,
A thousand chickens and a possum stew.
Old Parson Jones is goin' to make the address
While Alexander's Band is taking a rest.
There's goin' to be some dancin' in the park.
I'll bet there'll be some spoonin' after dark.
My boy Sammy
Will take his mammy.
Oh! Lordy, won't we have a lark.

**REPEAT CHORUS**

# PLEASE DON'T TAKE MY HAREM AWAY

Lyrics: Will E. Skidmore and Marshall Walker
Music: Will E. Skidmore and Marshall Walker
Artist: Rosenbaum Studios

New York: Leo. Feist Inc., 1919.

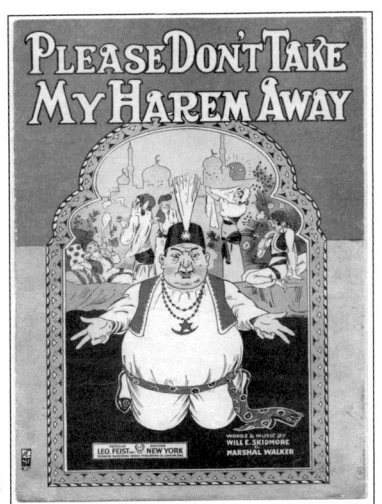

The Sultan sent the Allies a note,
And this is what the "Old Codger" wrote:
"I am glad that peace has come at last,
But there's one favor that I'd like to ask.
You can have the land that I own,
You can have what's left of my throne,
Take my army any day you choose.
There's only one thing that I hate to lose:"

**CHORUS**
"Please don't take my harem away.
Let me keep my oriental bombashay.
Woodrow's Fourteen Points I've read from
  end to beginnin',
But he don't even mention takin' my wild
  wimmin'.
That's the reason I stuck to 'Bill,'
'Cause he swore he'd keep my harem filled.
With my wives all gone,
You can have me shot at dawn,
So please don't take my harem away."

"I was a bitter foe I confess,
But won't you grant me this one request?
I don't care to be a Sultan Grand.
I ask this favor just as man to man;
Habit is a hard thing to break,
And a lifelong habit's at stake.
I will do most anything you say,
If you will only let me have my way:"

**CHORUS**
"Please don't take my harem away.
Let me keep my oriental bombashay.
When you queer'd "Old Brigham Young,"
  you sure played the dickens,
But you ain't got the right to take my
  'Turkish chickens.'
That's the reason I stuck to 'Bill,'
'Cause he wore he'd keep my harem filled.
When I hear that tune,
I go crazy as a loon,
So please don't take my harem away."

1920

# ALL HAIL! TO FOCH! SALUT! A FOCH!

Lyrics: Francis C. Chantereau
Music: Francis C. Chantereau

Boston: Franco-American Music Publishing Co., 1920.

*French lyrics are printed below the English lyrics.*

From ev'rywhere in this day of splendor
We hear the sound of thousands of clamors.
It is for Marshal Foch! Master of all,
With the Allies he forced the Huns to fall.
It was for our right, and our liberty,
That he and they fought for humanity.

**CHORUS**

All hail! to Foch! man of the hour,
Of his name we all can be proud.
He has stop'd the Huns with the Yanks
And chased them all the way out of France.

He had them kneeled crying to stop
Before his men could reach the top.
So let's all sing in unity,
"Yes, he has saved he saved humanity."

When all the guns around Chateau Thierry
Were throwing death in terrible fury,
Calling on his leaders all brave and bright,
He said, "My soldiers march on to the fight."
It was from this day that our gallant sons
Fought on while saying death to all the Huns.

**REPEAT CHORUS**

# GET UP AND GET OUT

Lyrics: Gordon Johnstone
Music: Geoffrey O'Hara
Artist: L. S. R.

New York: Leo. Feist Inc., 1920.

275

Don't you think that people in this land have talk'd enough?
Don't you think the time has come to call their little bluff?
Ask them what's the matter,
Make them "can" their chatter,
And then proceed to make the party rough.
Tell them they're a menace to the land,
Tell them in a way they'll understand.

**CHORUS**
Get up and get out,
If you've got any doubt
About this U.S.A.
If you don't like it here,
Why the ocean is clear,
There's a boat going home ev'ryday.

Now we don't want to brag,
But there's only one flag,
The flag that will never fall.
Lay your life down for that.
If you won't, here's your hat.
Just get up and get out, that's all!

This old land was good enough to accept you and me,
Good enough for Washington and Lincoln, Grant, and Lee.
When the world was shaking,
Yankee lads were making
Some hist'ry over there across the sea.
Tell the world of ev'ry creed and birth,
Here's the grandest land on God's green earth.

**REPEAT CHORUS**

# LEAGUE OF NATIONS BLUES

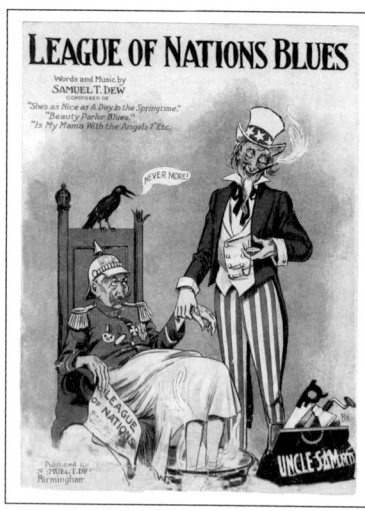

Lyrics: Samuel T. Dew
Music: Samuel T. Dew
Artist: B. N.

Birmingham: Samuel T. Dew, 1920.

Old Kaiser Bill was feeling bum, said he, "I'm feeling blue.
I ate so blamed much sauerkraut, till I don't know what to do."
So he called in all his medicine men and had them thump his chest,
Look at his tongue and feel his pulse; said they, "You need a rest.
We recommend new scenery, a change of air does good.
You had better seek another clime, annex it if you could.
Just annex France and Belgium too, and England if you choose."
'Twas then the doctors named the case the League of Nations Blues.

## CHORUS

He caught a case of League of Nations Blues.
He thought he could get anything at any time he'd choose.
One day he had a thought that told him that he ought to take a trip.
He'd like to visit Uncle Sammy, 'twas on his program that he would.

He'd rule Brittania and also rule the waves, he'd live in France and Belgium, too.
Our class of music got his goat, 'twas not the kind he'd use.
We played them all at once and called them League of Nations Blues.

The change of air helped Kaiser Bill, the change of scene the same.
It took him down a peg or two, and it also changed his name.
He is resting in a lovely home that's furnished to a T.
With plenty "you know what" to drink he's living swimmingly.
He has regained his former health and from the facts I learn
That he has lots of time to smoke and lots of time to burn.
He also hears from Germany that they cut out the booze.
They sing and dance and fight and play the League of Nations Blues.

**REPEAT CHORUS**

# Plates

# 1914

1

2

3

4

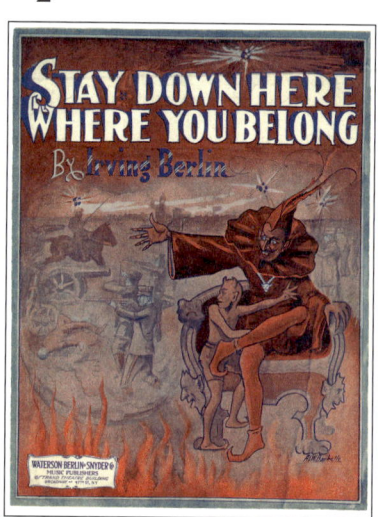

5

6

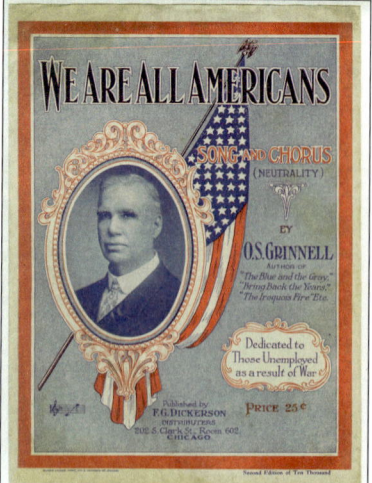

7

8

9

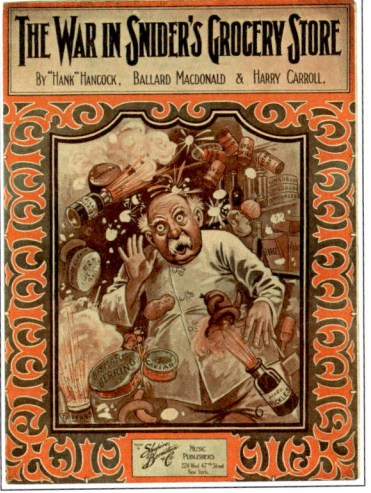
10

11

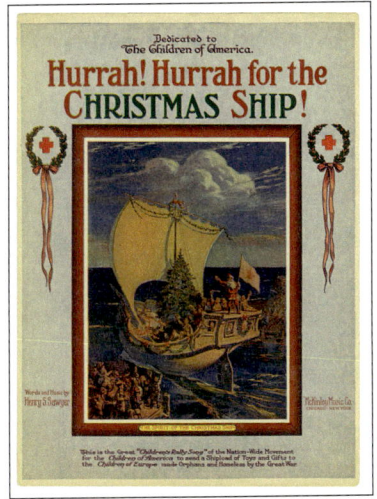
12

1915

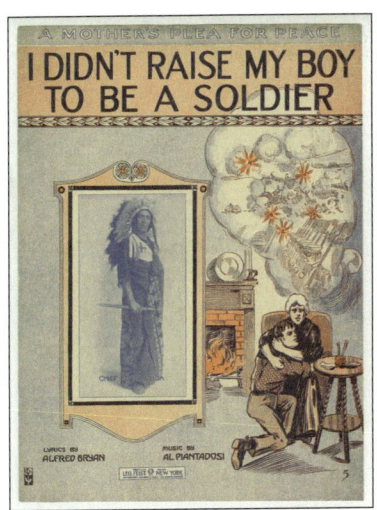
13

14

15

17

18

19

20

21

22

23

24

25

1915

26

27

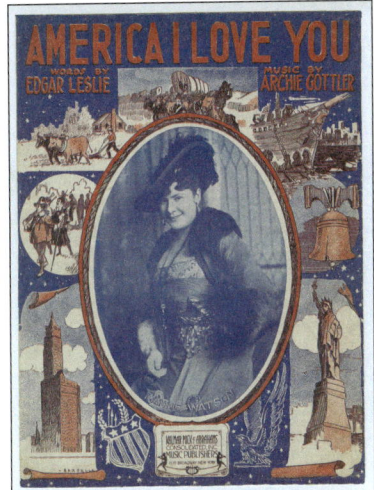
28

29

30

31

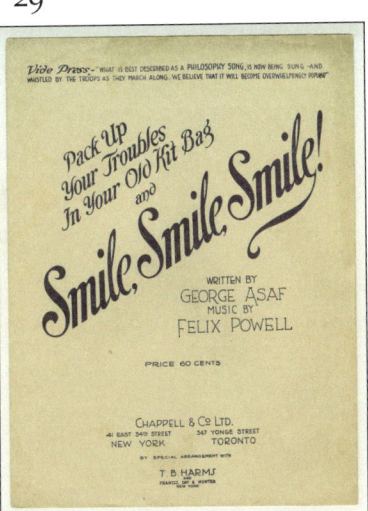
32

33

1916

34

35

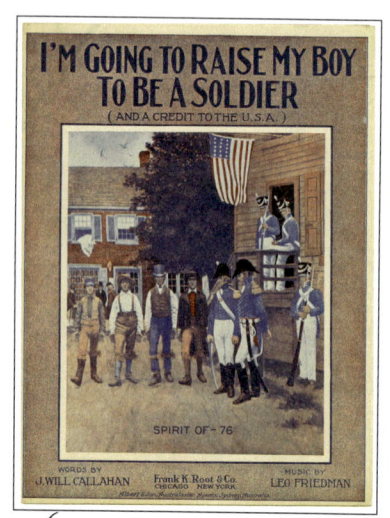
36

37

38

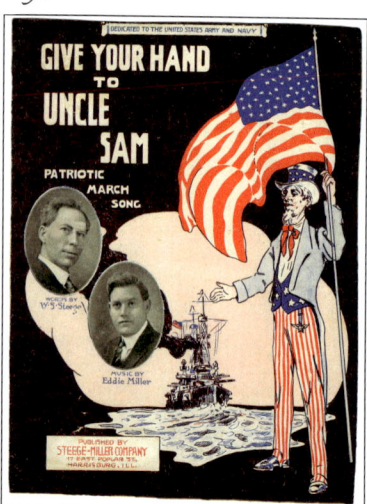
39

40

41

1917

42

43

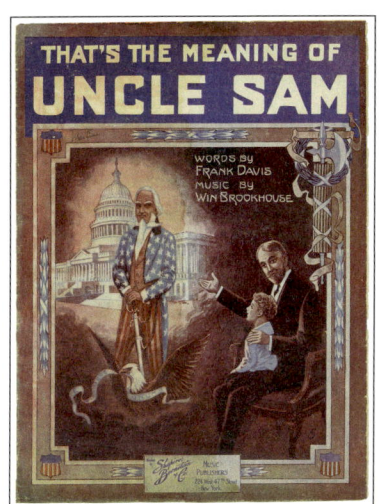
44

45

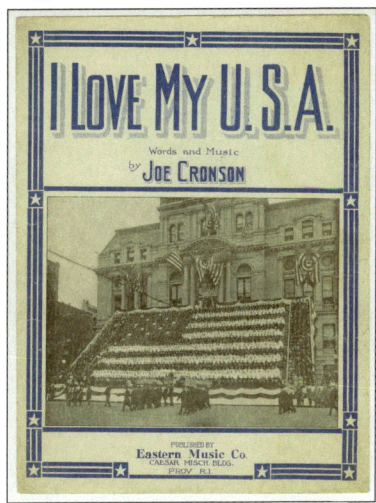
46

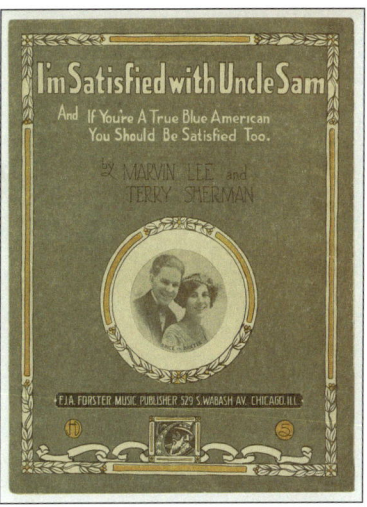
47

48

1917

49

50

51

52

53

54

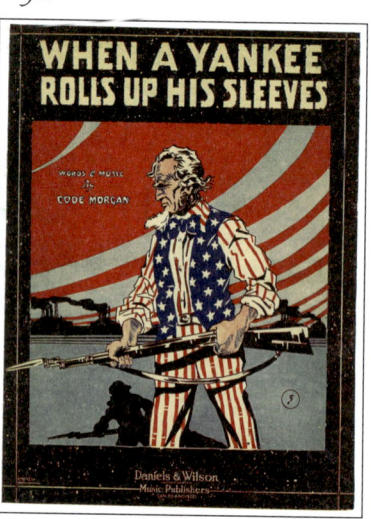
55

56

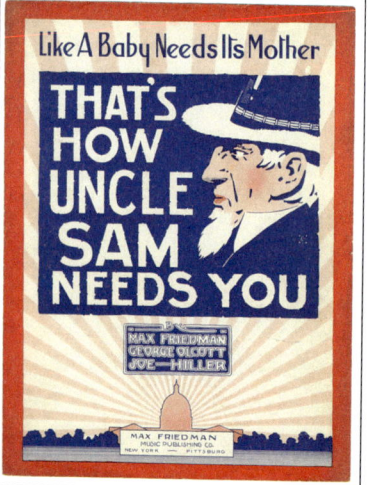
57

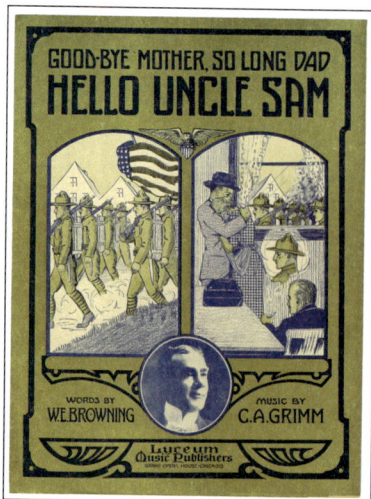
58

59

60

61

62

64

65

66

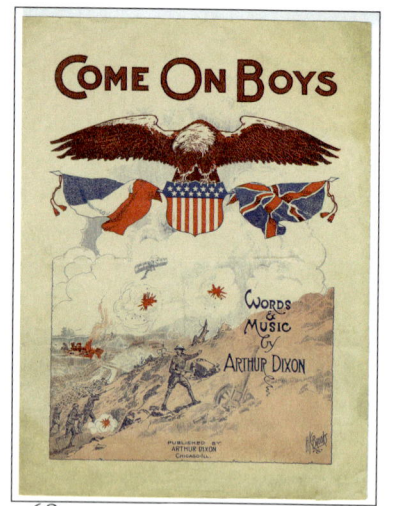
68

69

70

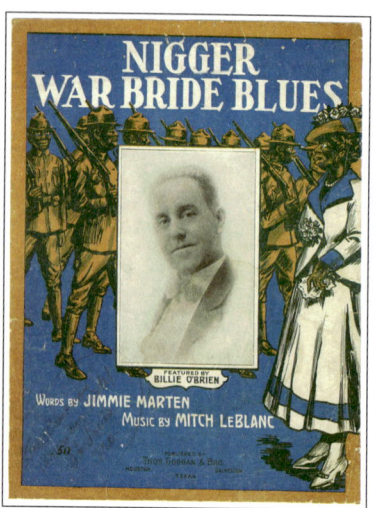
71

72

73

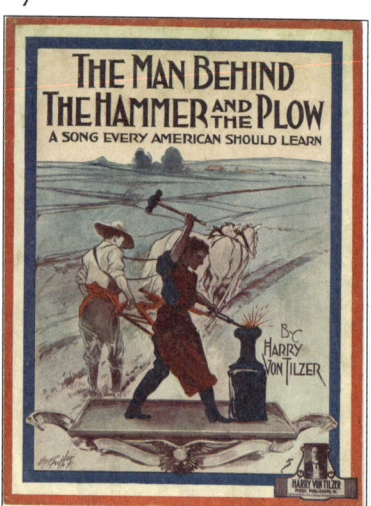
74

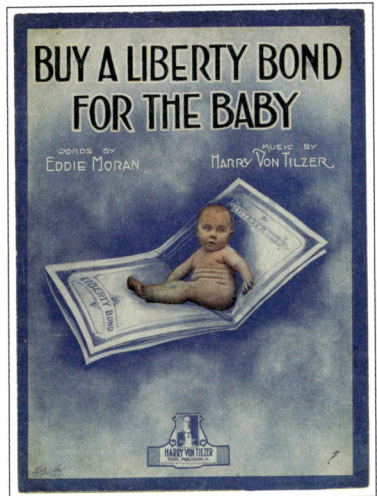
77

78

79

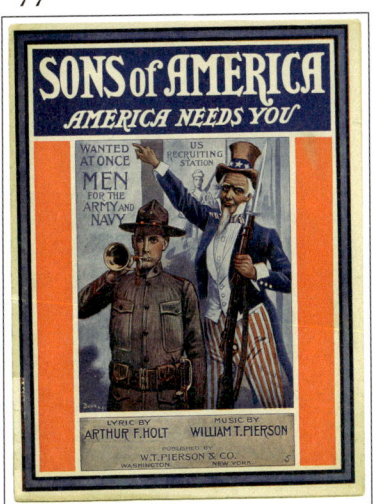
80

81

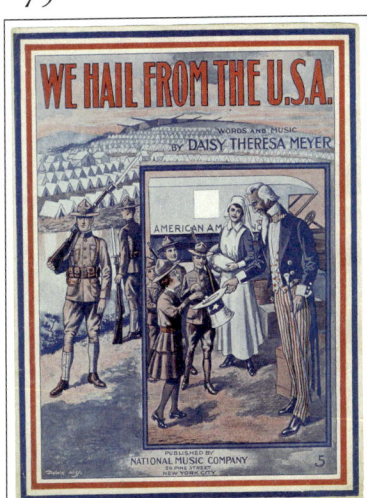
82

83

84

85

86

87

88

89

90

91

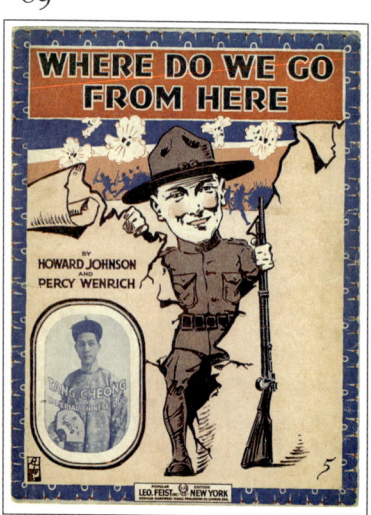
92

93

94

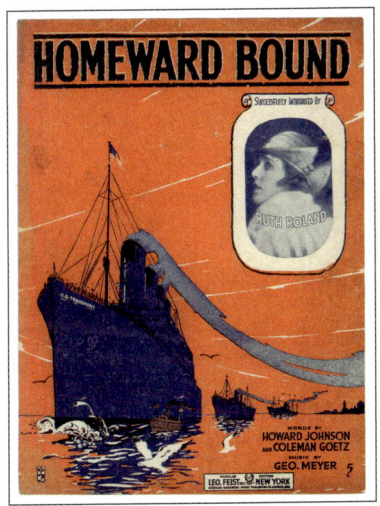
95

96

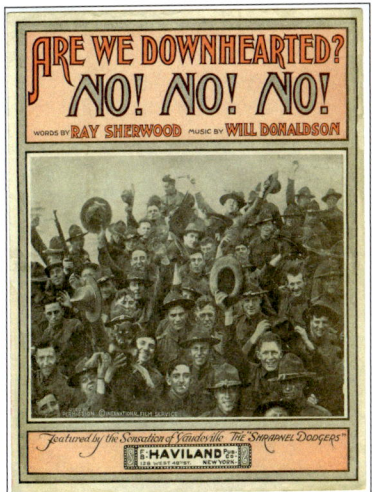
97

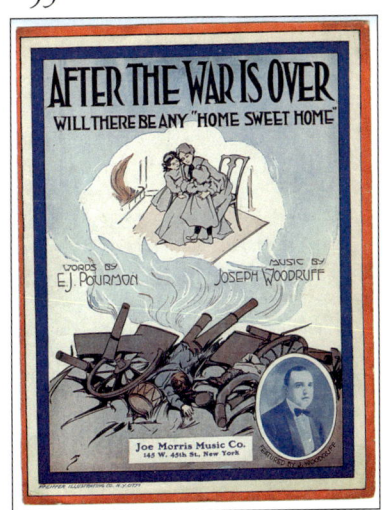
98

99

100

101

102

103

104

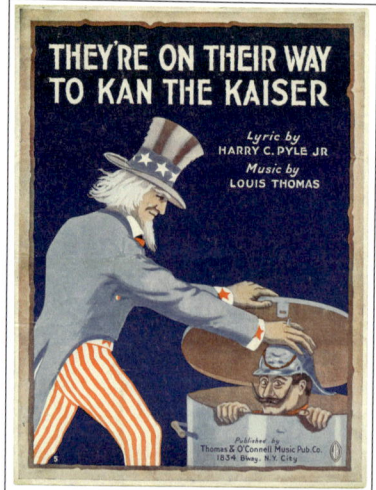
105

106

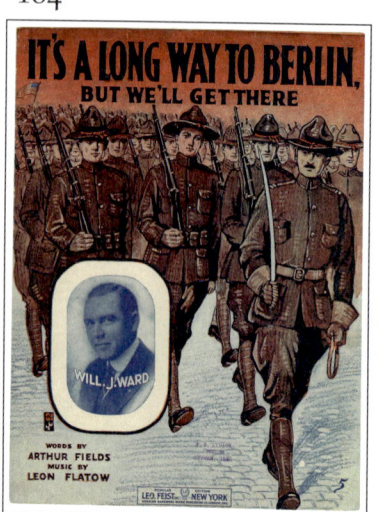
107

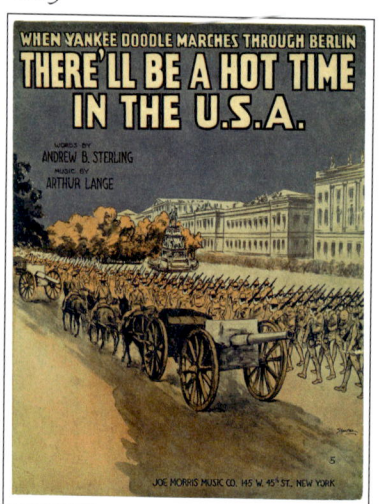
108

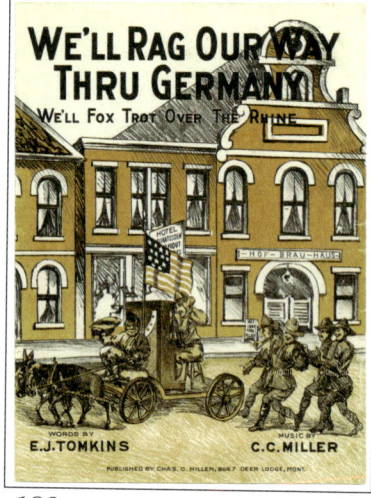
109

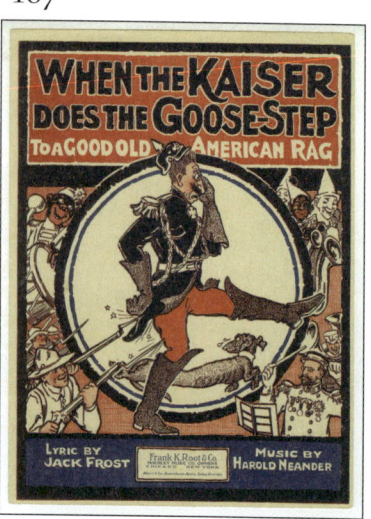
110

111

112

113

114

115

116

117

118

119

120

121

122

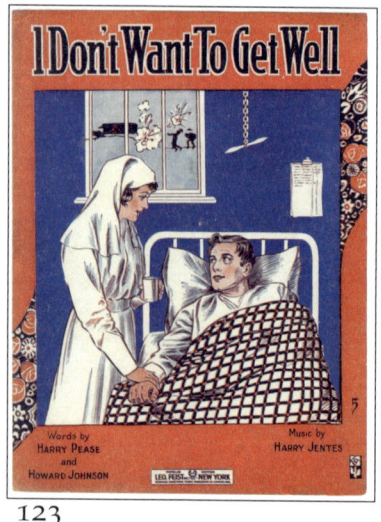
123

124

125

126

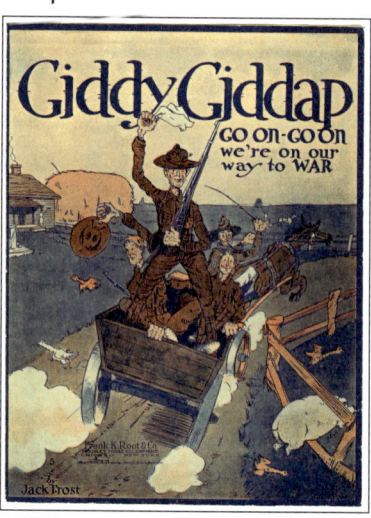
127

128

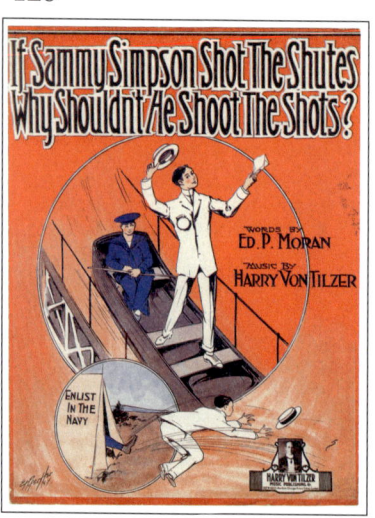
129

130

# 1918

131

132

133

134

135

136

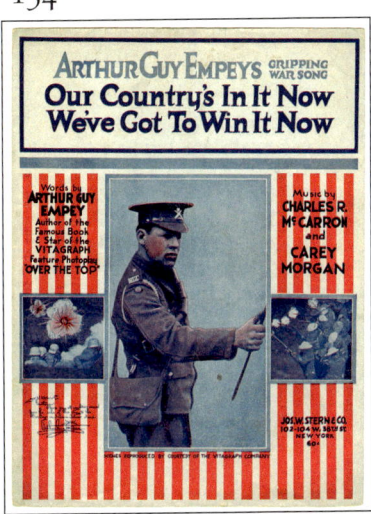

137

138

139

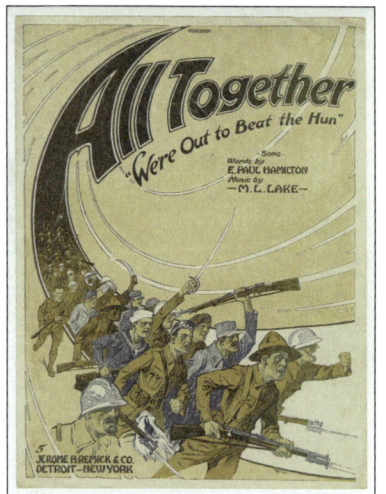
140

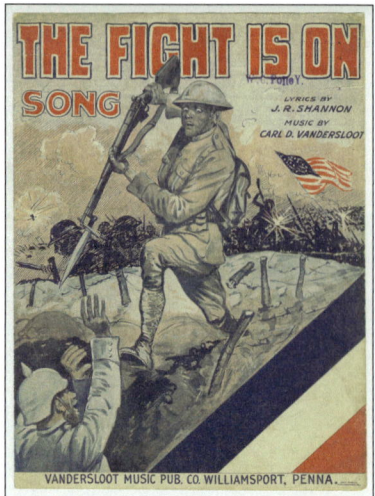
141

142

143

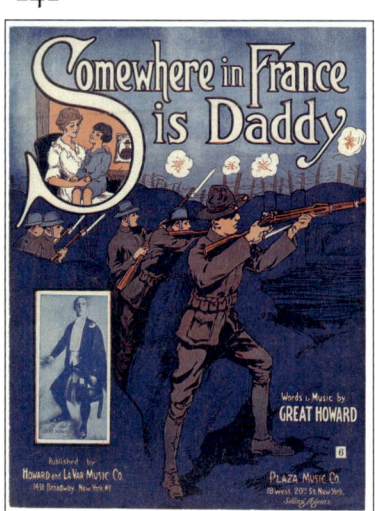
144

145

146

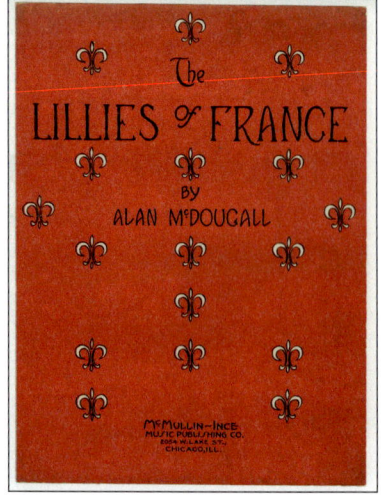
147

148

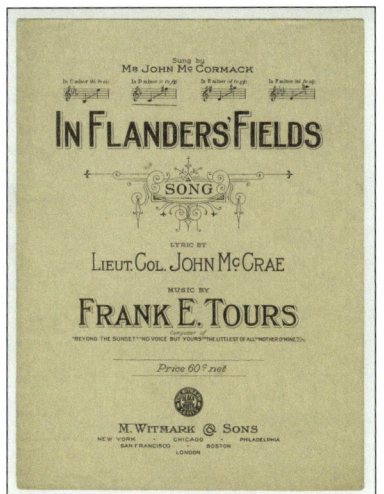
149

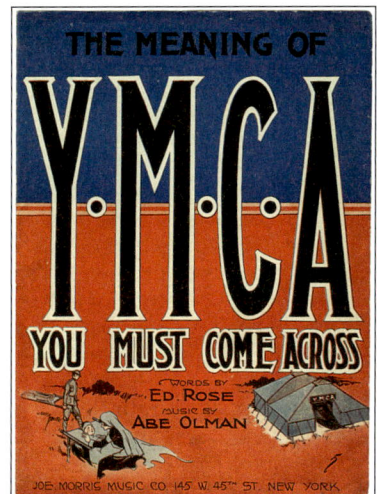
150

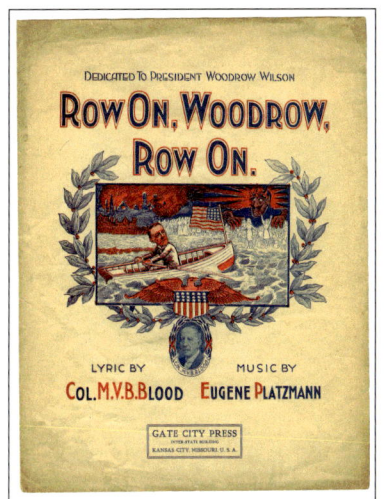
151

152

153

154

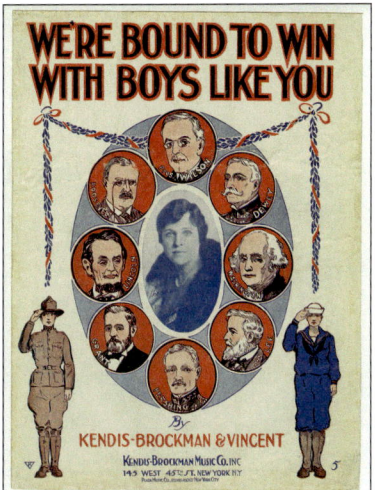
155

156

157

158

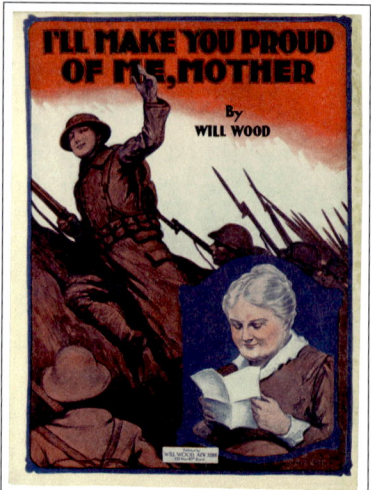
159

160

161

162

163

164

165

166

167

168

169

171

172

173

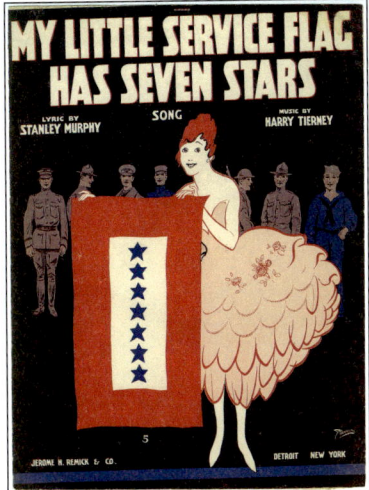
174

175

176

177

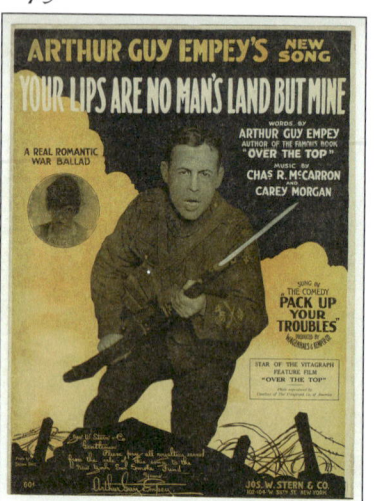
178

179

180

181

182

183

1918

184

185

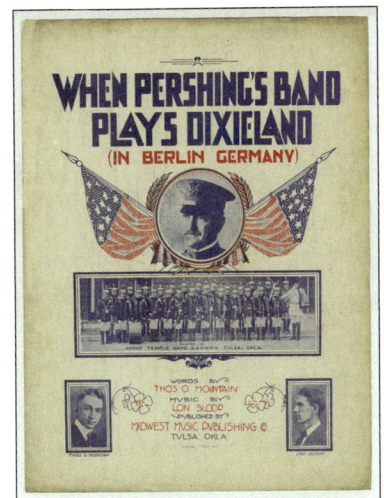

186

187

188

189

190

191

192

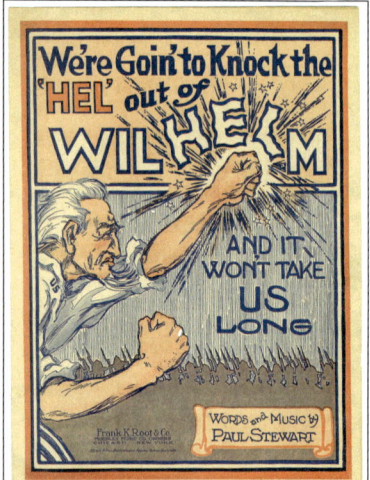
193

194

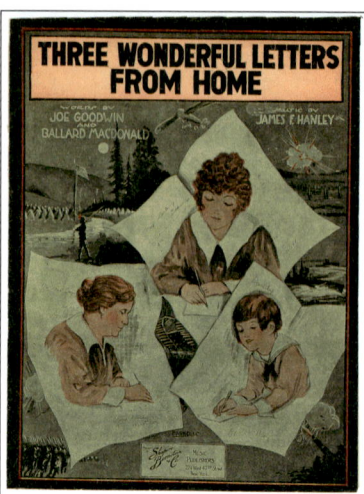
195

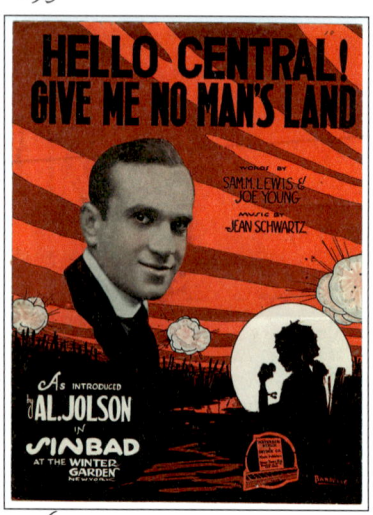
196

197

198

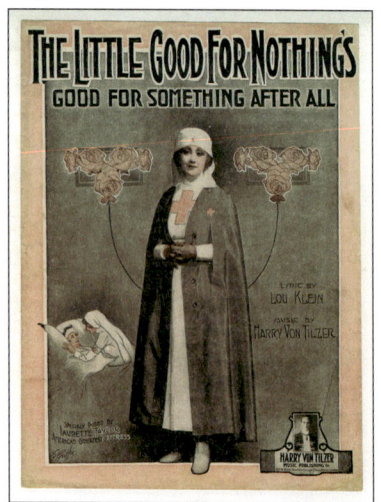
199

200

201

202

203

204

205

206

207

208

209

210

211

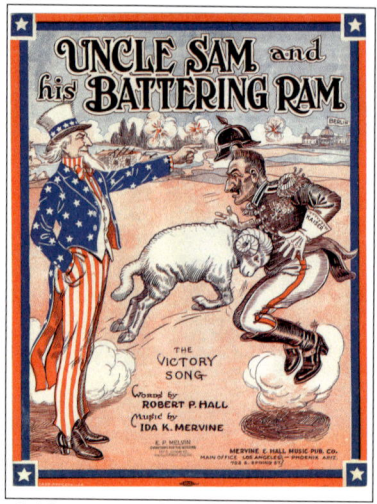
212

213

214

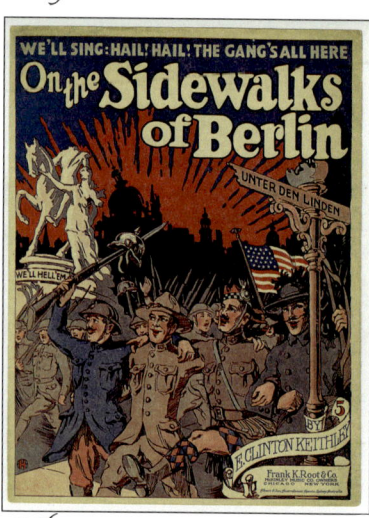
216

217

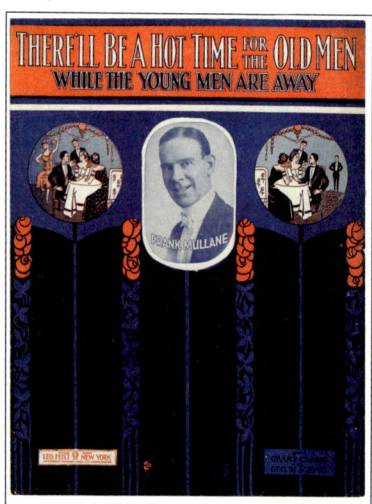
218

220

221

222

223

224

225

226

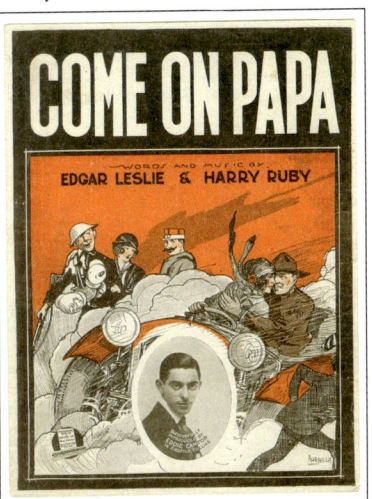
227

228

229

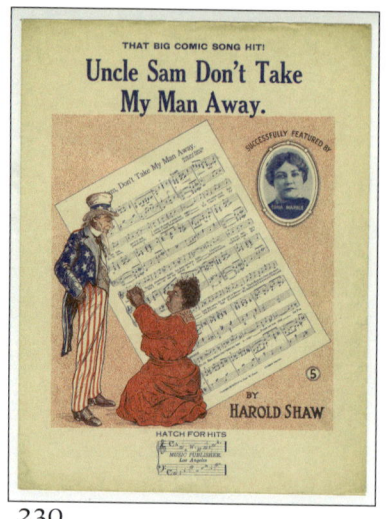

230

231

232

233

234

235

236

237

238

239

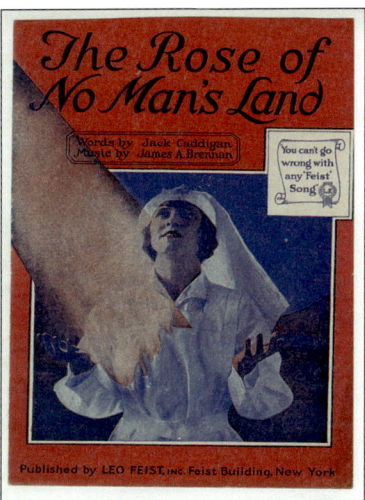
240

241

243

244

247

248

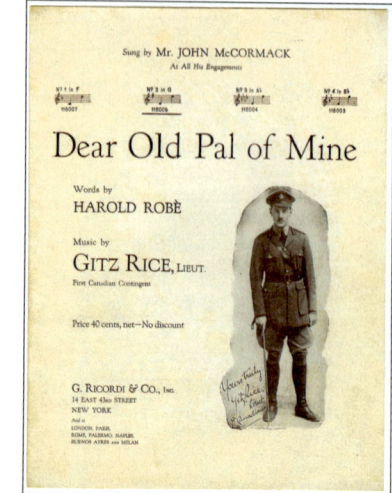
249

# 1919

250

251

252

253

254

255

256

257

258

259

260

261

262

263

264

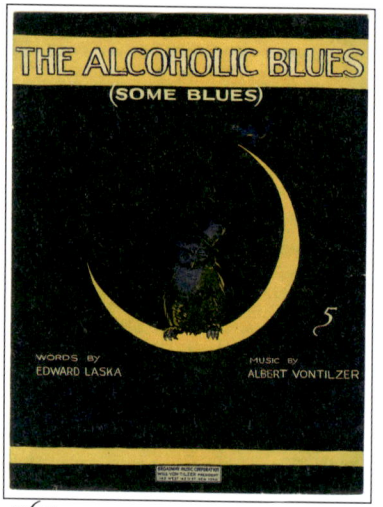
265

266

267

268

269

270

271

272

1920

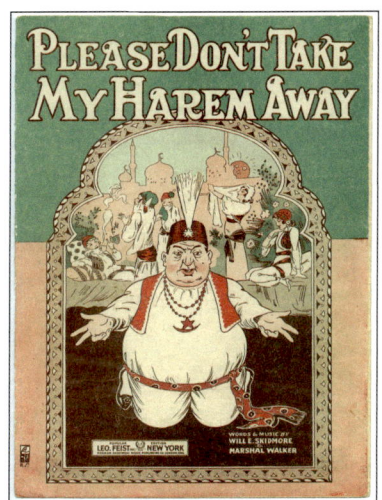

273

274

275

276

# Additional Covers

## 1914

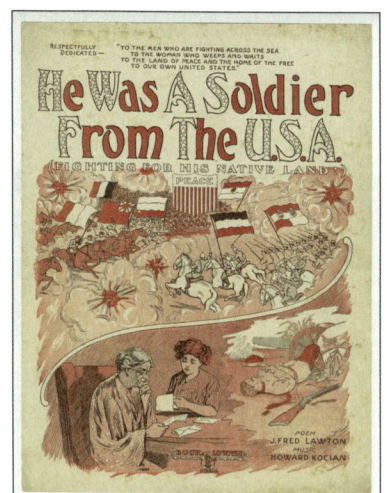
277

278

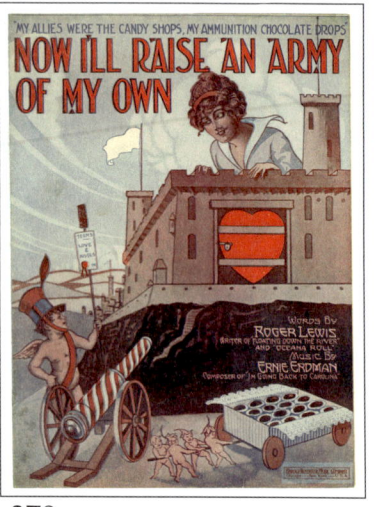
279

280

281

282

284

Additional Covers

1915

285

286

287

288

289

290

291

292

# 1916

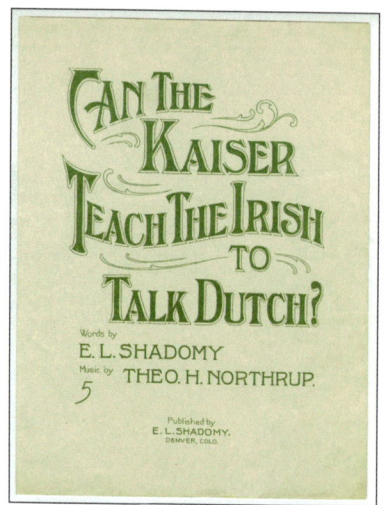
293

294

295

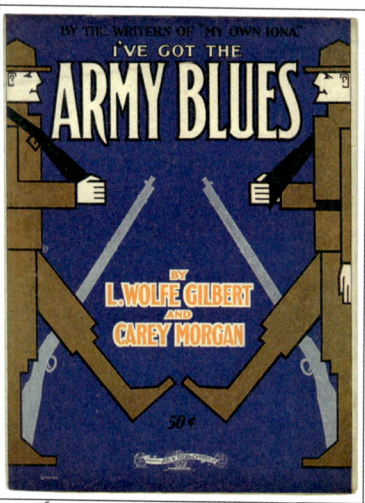
296

297

298

299

300

Additional Covers 337

## 1917

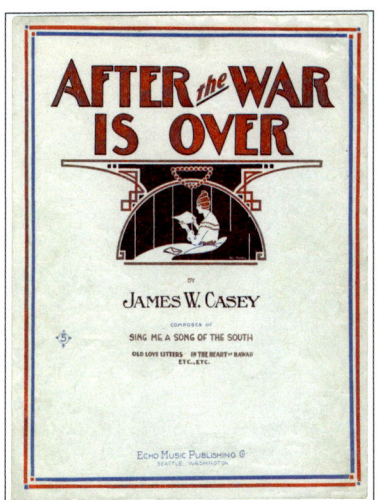
301

302

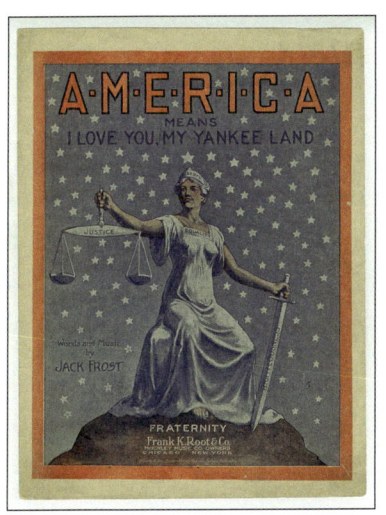
303

304

305

306

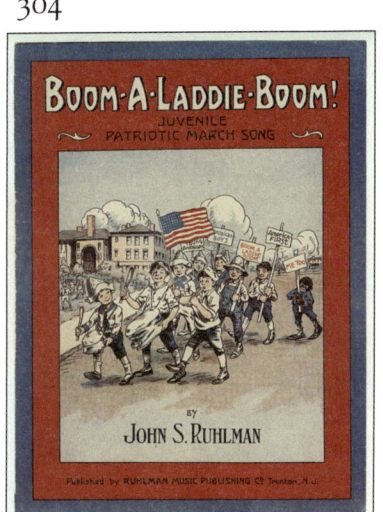
307

308

Color Plates

309

310

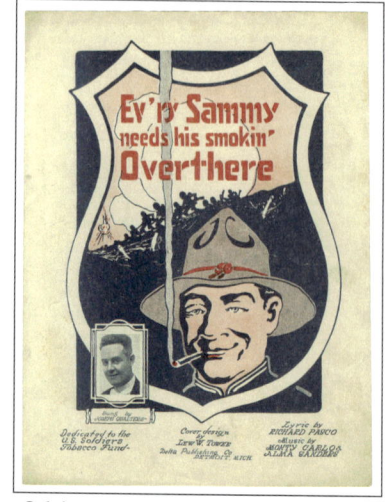
311

312

313

314

315

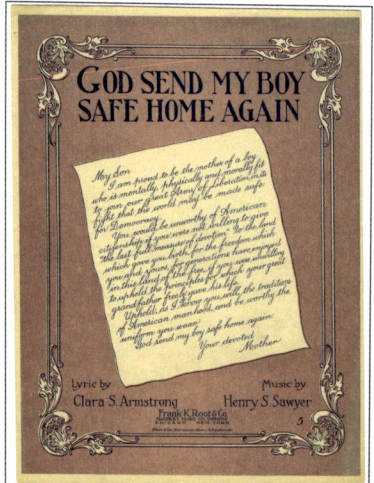
316

317

# Additional Covers

318

319

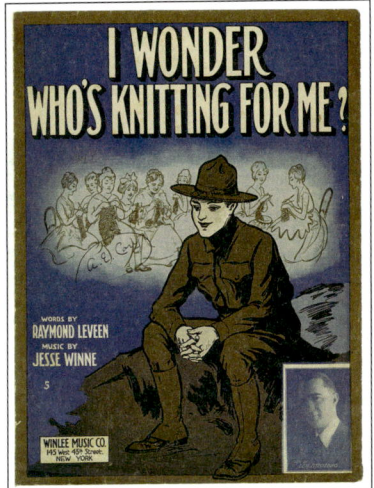

320

321

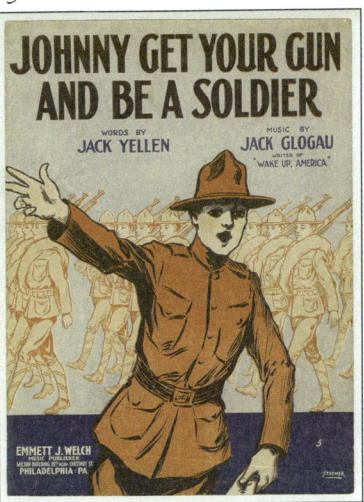

323

324

325

327

328

329

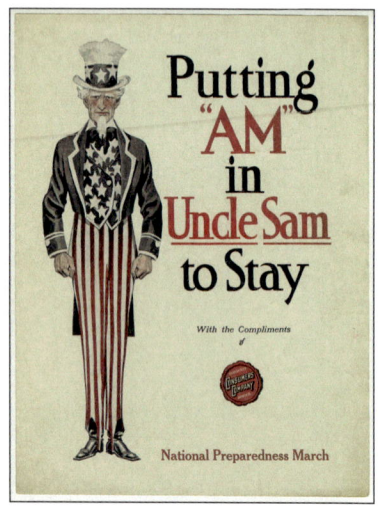
330

331

332

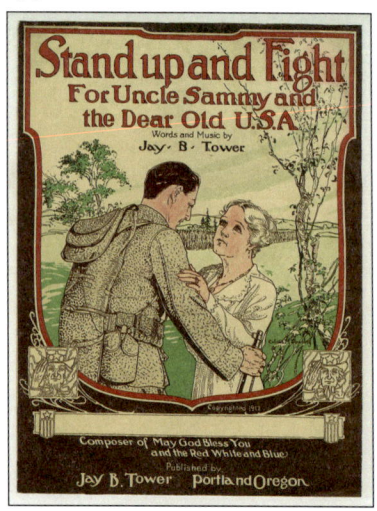
333

334

335

# Additional Covers

336

337

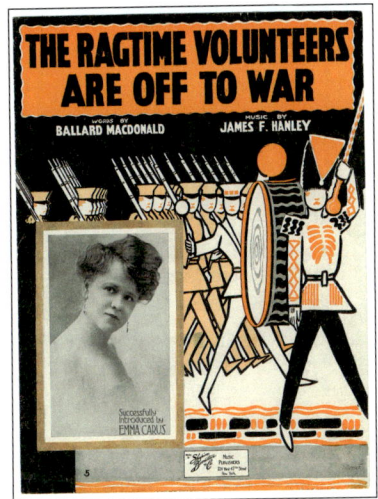

338

339

340

341

342

343

344

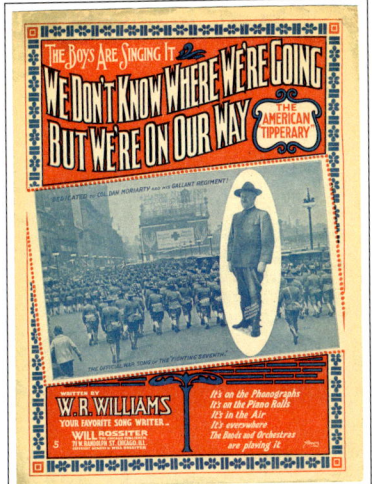

Color Plates

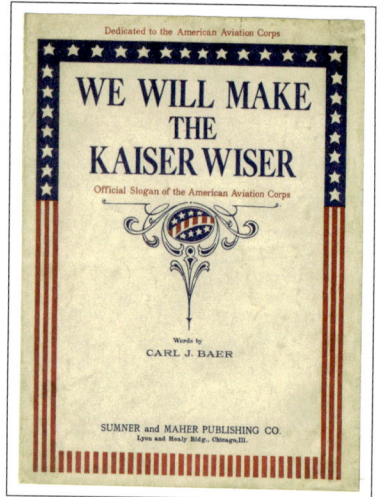
345

346

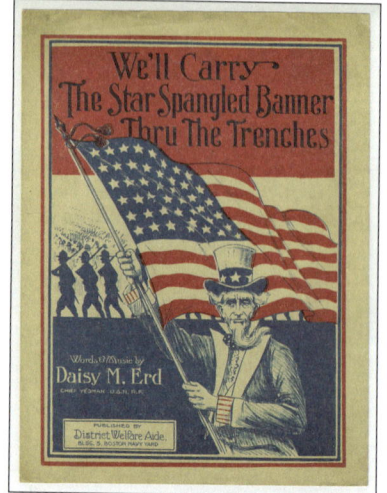
347

348

349

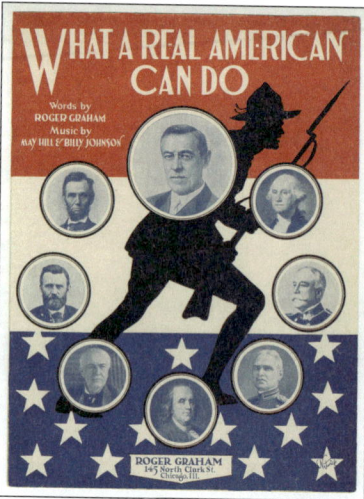
350

351

352

353

Additional Covers

1918

354

355

357

358

359

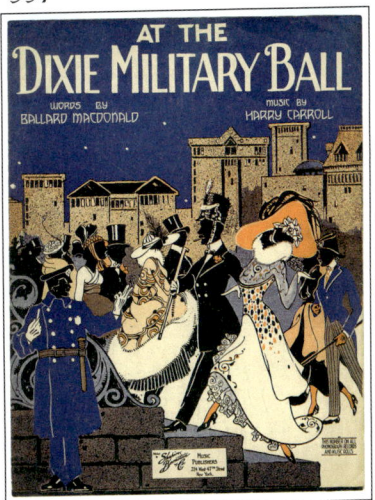
360

361

Color Plates

362

363

364

365

366

367

368

369

370

# Additional Covers

371

372

373

374

375

376

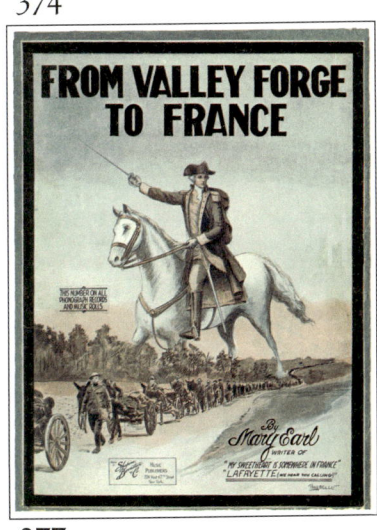

377

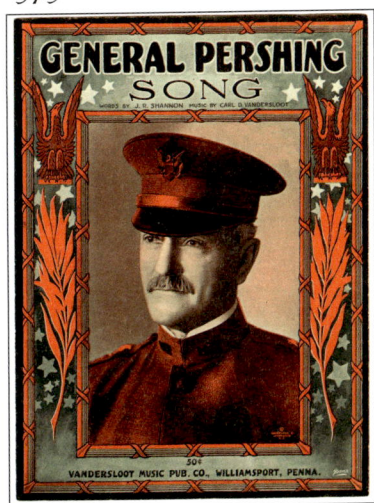

378

379

380

381

382

383

384

385

386

387

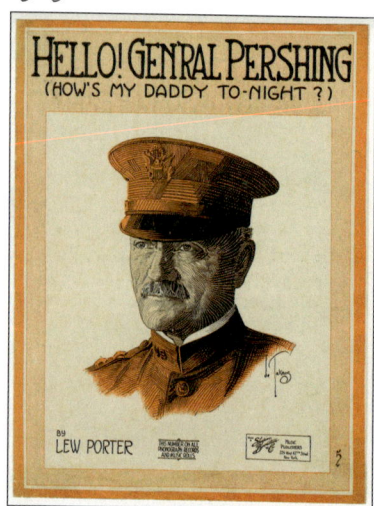
388

# Additional Covers

389

390

391

392

393

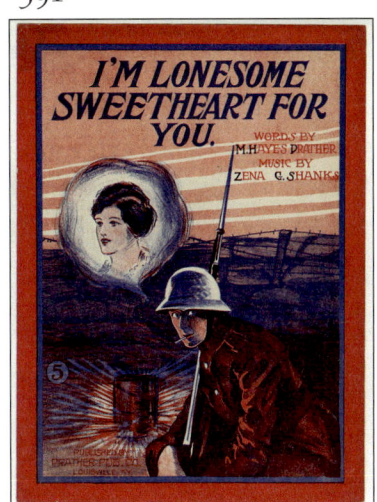
394

395

396

397

398

399

400

401

402

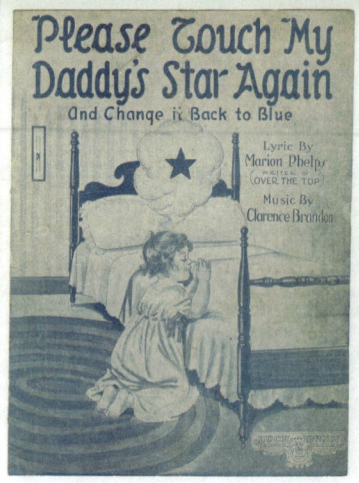
403

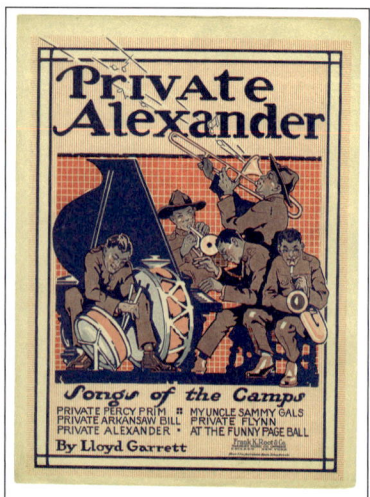
404

405

406

# Additional Covers

407

408

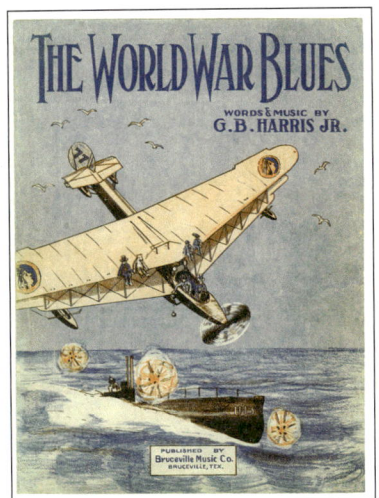

409

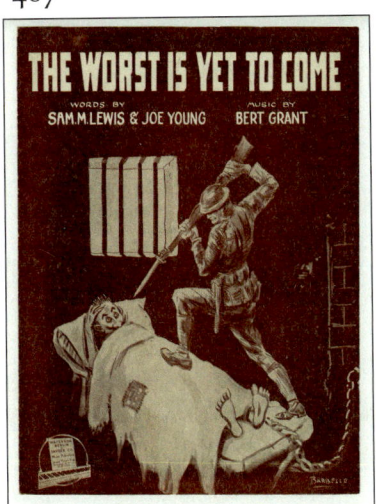

410

411

412

413

414

415

416

417

418

419

420

421

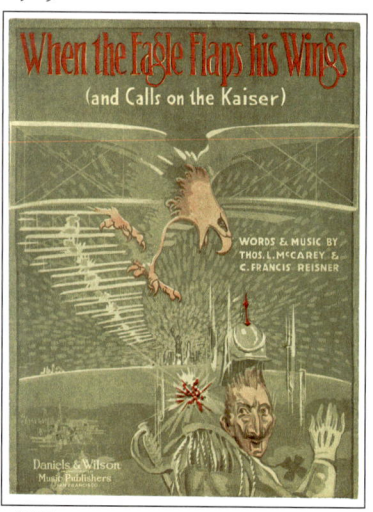
422

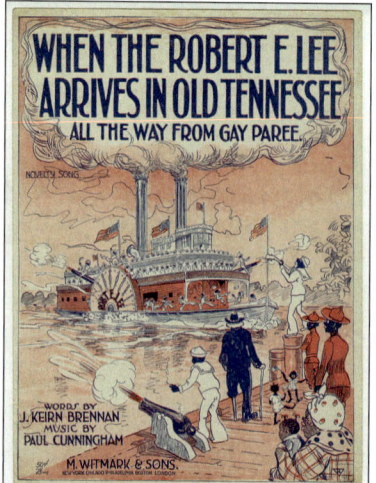
423

424

# Additional Covers

425

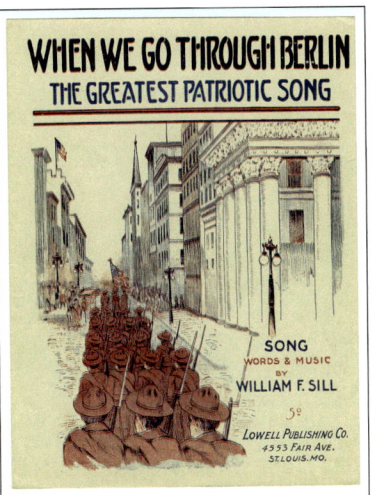

426

427

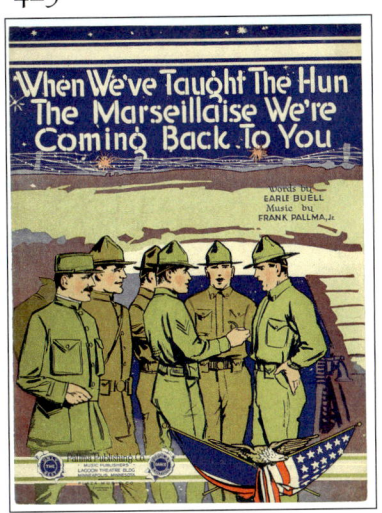

428

429

430

431

432

433

# 1919

434

435

436

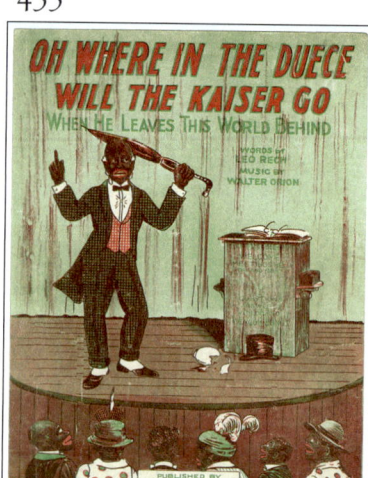

437

438

439

440

441

# Indexes

## SONG TITLES

All references in the indexes are to songs and/or covers, not pages.

A Dash of the Red White & Blue  354
A Letter from No Man's Land  355
A Tale of the Fireside  356
A Tiny Bunch of Violets from No Man's Land  357
After the War is Over  98
After the War is Over  301
Ah Didn't Raise mah Boy to be a Slacker  70
All Aboard for Home Sweet Home  244
All Hail! To Foch!  274
All Together  140
A-M-E-R-I-C-A  302
America, Awake!  134
America First is our Battle Cry!  41
America, Here's my Boy  64
America, I Love You  28
A-M-E-R-I-C-A Means I Love You, my Yankee Land  303
America Needs You Like a Mother  65
America Never Took Water and America Never Will  264
America Prepare  43
America Saved the Day  358
America the Land We Love the Best  359
America To-day  79
America, You for Me  304
America'll Win the War  136
American Crusaders  250
America's Greatest  305
And He'd Say "Oo-la la! Wee-wee"  268
Answer Mr. Wilson's Call  66
Are We Downhearted? No! No! No!  97
Are You Half the Man your Mother Thought You'd be  37
Are You Lending a Hand to Yankee Land?  139
At the Dixie Military Ball  360
At the Yankee Military Ball  306
Attention  361
Au Revoir, but not Good-bye, Soldier Boy  86

Batter up  362
Battle in the Sky  285
Be Brave Little Girl Don't Grieve  363
Be sure to get the Kaiser too!  207
Belgian Rose  364

Belgium, Dry your Tears  21
Big Chief Kill-a-Hun  204
Bing! Bang! Bing 'em on the Rhine  191
Boom-a-Laddie-Boom!  307
Break the News to Mother  120
Bring Back a Belgian Baby for me  222
Bring Back, Bring Back, Bring Back the Kaiser to Me  308
Bring back my Daddy to me  87
Bring me a Letter from my old Home Town  365
Buy a Bond, Buy a Bond for Liberty  166
"Buy a Liberty Bond"  366
Buy a Liberty Bond for the Baby  77

Camouflage  367
Can the Kaiser Teach the Irish to Talk Dutch?  293
Can't You Hear your Country Calling  67
Clap your Hands my Baby  368
Come Across, Yankee Boy, Come Across  143
Come on, Boys  68
Come on, Boys, We're headed Across the Rhine  369
Come on, Papa  227

Dear old Pal of mine  249
Do We Remember Dewey at Manila?  157
Do your Little "Bitty-bit" (Right now!)  73
Don't Bite the Hand that's Feeding You  30
Don't Cry, Frenchy  262
Don't Forget the Boys  270
Don't Steal my Yankee Doodle Dandy  370
Don't Take my Darling Boy Away  15
Don't Try to Steal the Sweetheart of a Soldier  309
Don't Worry, Dearie  310
Don't You Want to be a Soldier  138
Down in the U-17  286

Each Stitch is a Thought of You, Dear  371
Every Boy's a Hero in this War Today  372
Everybody Welcome—Everything Free  373
Ev'ry Sammy Needs his Smokin' Over There  311

Faugh-a-Ballagh  312
"Fill the Flag"  374
Fleur-de-lys, Flow'r of France, Bloom again  253

## Song Titles

For Old Glory  51
For the Freedom of the World  313
For your Country and my Country  53
France We have not forgotten You  375
France, We'll Rebuild your Towns for You  376
Frenchy, Come to Yankee Land  434
From Valley Forge to France  377

Gee! What a wonderful Time We'll have  314
General Pershing  378
Germany, You'll soon be No Man's Land  379
Get Busy "Over Here" or "Over There"  380
Get up and get out  275
Giddy Giddap! Go on! Go on!  127
Give your Hand to Uncle Sam  39
Go Lad and may God Bless You  315
Go Right Along, Mister Wilson  19
God Send my Boy Safe Home Again  316
(Good Bye, and Luck be with You) Laddie Boy  118
Good-bye Broadway, Hello France!  93
Good-bye, Daddy Dear  381
Good-bye, Farewell, Raus mit Kaiser Bill  113
Good-bye, Germany  382
Good-bye, Mother! So long, Dad! Hello, Uncle Sam  58
Good-bye, Sally, Good Luck to You  435
Good-bye, Shot and Shell!  255
Good-bye, Slim  383
"Good bye," That means You  317
Good morning, Mr. Zip-Zip-Zip!  201

Hadn't Bill Forgotten to Reckon with Uncle Sam  256
Hands off the U.S.A.  45
Hang the Kaiser to a Sour Apple Tree  384
Hats off to Uncle Sam  385
He Sleeps beneath the Soil of France  119
He was a Soldier from the U.S.A.  277
Hello Central! Give me No Man's Land  196
Hello! General Pershing  386
Here Comes America  387
Here I am Uncle Sammy, Take Me  318
Here We Are, Lafayette  388
Here's to the Flying Corps  389
Here's to your Boy and my Boy  390
He's had no Lovin' for a long long Time  266
Hoe your "Little Bit" in your own Back Yard  76
Homeward Bound  95
How 'Ya gonna Keep 'em Down on the Farm  261
Hunting the Hun  391
Hurrah! Hurrah for the Christmas Ship  12

I am 100% American. Are you?  392
I Didn't Raise my Boy to be a Soldier  13
I Didn't Raise my Dog to be a Sausage  14
I Don't Know Where I'm going but I'm on my Way  115
I Don't Want to Get Well  123
I Hear America Calling  393
I Hear my Country Calling  319
I Love my U.S.A.  46
I Love the U.S.A.  287
I May be gone for a Long, Long Time  116
I Miss Daddy's Good-night Kiss  237
I Think We've got another Washington  20
I Tried to Raise my Boy to be a Hero  294
I Wonder what's ze Matter wiz my Oo-la-la  269
I Wonder Who's Knitting for Me?  320
I'd be Proud to be a Mother of a Soldier  24
I'd Feel at Home if They'd Let Me Join the Army  59
I'd Like to See the Kaiser with a Lily in his Hand  215
I'd rather be a Newsboy in the U.S.A.  436
If a Mother's Prayers are answered  395
If He can Fight like He can Love, Good night, Germany!  202
If I Come back again "I come back Sweetheart to You"  278
If I had a Son for each Star in Old Glory  62
If I'm not at the Roll Call  169
If Sammy Simpson Shot the Chutes  129
If the Yankees Took Berlin  437
If They want to Fight, All Right  23
If War is What Sherman said It was  288
If We had a Million like Him Over There  168
If You can't Enlist Buy a Liberty Bond  165
If You Want to Fight, All right  23
I'll be over your Way in the Mornin' Bill  208
I'll be there, Laddie Boy, I'll be there  170
I'll Do without Meat, I'll Do without Wheat  163
I'll Make You Proud of Me, Mother  159
I'll See You later "Yankeeland"  321
I'm a Regular Daughter of Uncle Sam  322
I'm all Dressed up to Kill  183
I'm Crazy about my Daddy  184
I'm Going to Follow the Boys  89
I'm Going to Raise my Boy to be a Soldier  36
I'm Gonna Pin a Medal on the Girl I left Behind  224
I'm Hitting the Trail for Normandy  84
I'm Lonesome, Sweetheart, for you  394
I'm off for a Place Somewhere in France  94
I'm Proud to be the Sweetheart of a Soldier  181
I'm Raising my Boy to be a Soldier  69
I'm Satisfied with Uncle Sam  47
In Dutch  48
In Flanders' Fields  149
In the Gloaming, Mother Darling  175

In the Good Old United States  295
In Time of Peace Prepare for War  289
Indianola  131
It's a Long Way to Berlin, but We'll get There  107
It's All over now  242
It's Time for Every Boy to be a Soldier  61
I've got my Captain Working for Me now  271
I've got the Army Blues  296

Jefferson Brown  72
Joan of Arc, They are Calling You  85
Johnny Get your Gun and be a Soldier  323
Just a Baby's Letter Found in No Man's Land  133
Just a Baby's Prayer at Twilight  132
Just a Letter for a Boy Over There  176
Just Give Me a Week in Paris  396
Just like Washington Crossed the Delaware  185

K-K-K-Katy  198
Keep a Steady Heart  160
Keep Cool! The Country's Saving Fuel  164
Keep the Home-fires Burning  33
Keep Them Dropping  209
Keep your Head Down, "Fritzie Boy"  203

Laddie Boy  118
Lafayette (We Hear You Calling)  142
Lay Down your Arms  16
League of Nations Blues  276
Let us have Peace  2
Let's All be Americans now  56
Let's be Ready! That's The Spirit of '76  40
Let's Help the Red Cross Now  324
Liberty Bell (It's Time to Ring Again)  88
Liberty Loan March  167
Liberty Statue is Looking Right at You  158
Like a Baby Needs its Mother  57
Little French Mother, Good-bye!  263
Long Boy  128
Lorraine (My Beautiful Alsace Lorraine)  83
Loyalty is the Word Today  50

Machine Gun March  397
Mammy's Chocolate Soldier  231
Mississippi Volunteers  325
Mister Kaiser, You'll be Wiser, for You'll Dance  211
Mothers of America, You have done your Share!  247
Mr. Kaiser, You'll be Wiser  210
Mr. Sousa's Yankee Band  180
Mr. Yankee Doodle, Are We Prepared?  297
My Aeroplane Girl  398
My Alsace Lorraine  6

My Barney Lies over the Ocean  267
My Belgian Rose  223
My Choc'late Soldier Sammy Boy  272
My Daddy's Coming Home  245
My Heart is in the Trenches of France  399
My Little Service Flag has Seven Stars  174
My Red Cross Girlie  124
My Sweetheart is Somewhere in France  326

Nephews of Uncle Sam  327
Nigger War Bride Blues  71
Now all the World's at Peace  243
Now I'll Raise an Army of My Own  279
Now is the Time to Wake up, America  135
Now that the War is Over  252

Oh! Frenchy  226
Oh! How I Hate to Get up in the Morning  234
Oh! How I Wish I could Sleep  236
Oh, Santa Claus, Send my Daddy Back to Me  130
Oh, Where in the Deuce will the Kaiser Go  438
Old Glory in Berlin  328
On a Battlefield in France  171
On the Battle Field  280
On the Sidewalks of Berlin  216
On to Berlin  206
Ooh la la, I'm Having a Wonderful Time  400
Our Brave American Boys  401
Our Country's in it Now!  137
Our Flag Knows only Victory  329
Our Sammy Boys  81
Our Wilson is the Greatest Man  254
Over the Rhine  104
Over the Top  117
Over There  91
Over Yonder Where the Lilies Grow  146

Pack up your Troubles in your old Kit-bag  32
Paul Revere (Won't You Ride for Us again?)  402
Pershing's Army Song  187
Plant a Little Garden in your own Back Yard  75
Please Don't Take my Harem Away  273
Please Touch my Daddy's Star Again  403
Prepare the Eagle to Protect the Dove  42
Private Alexander  404
Putting "Am" in Uncle Sam to Stay  330

'Round her Neck She Wears a Yeller Ribbon  96
Row on, Woodrow, Row on  151

Salvation Lassie of Mine  260
Say a Prayer for the Boys "Out There"  121

# Song Titles

Say – "You Haven't Sacrificed at all!"  162
Send Me Away with a Smile  331
She's Teaching Me to Parlez vous Francais  405
Sister Susie's Sewing Shirts for Soldiers  11
Soldiers of the Sea  332
Somewhere in France is Daddy  144
Somewhere in France is the Lily  126
Sons of America, America Needs You  80
Stand by Uncle Sam  153
Stand up and Fight for Uncle Sammy  333
Stay Down Here Where You Belong  5
Swat the Bugaboo  334

Take this Message to my Mother  172
That Grand old Gentleman (Uncle Sam)  152
That's a Mother's Liberty Loan  78
That's the Irish in Me  239
That's the Meaning of Uncle Sam  44
The Alcoholic Blues  265
The Angel God Sent from Heaven  177
The Battle Cry of Peace  35
The Battle Song of Liberty  335
The Beast of Berlin  205
The Biggest Thing in a Soldier's Life is the Letter  194
The Birth of a Nation  290
The Boy that is Somewhere in France  406
The Boys Who Fight for You  407
The Call to Peace  3
The Cootie Tickle  259
The Dixie Volunteers  336
The Fatherland, the Motherland, the Land of my Best Girl  7
The Fight is On  141
The Finest Flag that Flies  9
The Girls of the U.S.A.  90
The Girls We Leave Behind  337
The Hero of the European War  281
The Kaiser's Dinner  214
The Kaiser Waned More Territory so We Gave Him H---  439
The Letter that Never Reached Home  298
The Lillies of France  147
The Little Good for Nothing's Good for Something after all  199
The Little Grey Mother who Waits all Alone  29
The Man Behind the Hammer and the Plow  74
The Meaning of Y.M.C.A.  150
The Ragtime Volunteers are off to War  338
The Rose of No Man's Land  240
The Russians were Rushin' The Yanks Started Yankin'  235
The Texans are Ready  408

The U.S. of the World  49
The U.S.A. will lay the Kaiser Away  213
The War in Snider's Grocery Store  10
The World War Blues  409
The Worst is yet to Come  410
The Yankee Boys from Yankee Land  411
The Yanks are Coming Hoo-ray, Hoo-ray!  412
Then I'll Come Back to You  339
There are Just as Many Heroes To-day  282
There'll be a Hot Time for the Old Men  218
There's a Green Hill out in Flanders  340
There's a Million Heroes in Each Corner of the U.S.A.  341
There's a Red bordered Flag in the Window  173
There's a Service Flag Flying at our House  63
There's an Angel Missing from Heaven  413
There's Something 'bout a Uniform  182
They were All out of Step but Jim  200
They'll be mighty proud in Dixie of their Old Black Joe  233
They're on Their Way to Germany  342
They're on Their Way to Kan the Kaiser  105
Those Draftin' Blues  179
Three Wonderful Letters from Home  195
Thtop your Thtuttering, Jimmy  258
Till Over the Top We go  414
"Till the Work of the Yanks is Done"  343
Till We Meet Again  248
Trench! Trench! Trench! Our Boys are Trenching  156

Uncle Sam and his Battering Ram  212
Uncle Sam, Don't Take my Man Away  230
Uncle Sam, Every Man will See You Through  154
Uncle Sam Won't Go to War  4

Wake up, America!  38
We are a Peaceful Nation  34
We are all Americans  8
We are bound to Get the Kaiser  112
We are Hitting the Trail through No Man's Land  415
We are out for the Scalp of Mister Kaiser Man  111
We are Proud of You  251
We Don't Know Where We're Going but We're on our Way  344
We Don't Want the Bacon  189
We Hail from the U.S.A.  82
We Stand for Peace while Others War  1
We will make the Kaiser Wiser  345
Wee, wee, Marie  228
Welcome Home, Laddie Boy, Welcome Home  246
We'll all Make Billy Pay the Bill He Owes  220
We'll be a Big, Big Brother to all Nations  291

(We'll be There) On the land, on the Sea, in the Air 346
We'll Build a Little House in the U.S.A. 292
We'll Carry the Star Spangled Banner thru the Trenches 347
We'll Make the Germans all Sing Yankee Doodle Doo 219
"We'll Follow Pershing into Old Berlin" 103
We'll have Peace on Earth and Even in Berlin 106
We'll Knock the Heligo – into Heligo 100
We'll Never Let our Old Flag Down 22
We'll Put another Star in the Star Spangled Banner 299
We'll Rag our Way thru Germany 109
We'll Stand by You, Uncle Sam 348
We're after You 101
We're All Going Calling on the Kaiser 192
We're All with You, Dear America 54
We're All with You, Mister Wilson 18
We're Bound to Win with Boys like You 155
We're Building a Bridge to Berlin 188
We're Coming over after You 102
We're Custer's Soldier Boys 349
We're Going Over 125
We're going to Celebrate the End of the War in Ragtime 21
We're going to Hang the Kaiser under the Linden Tree 114
We're going to Knock the "Hel" out of Wilhelm 193
We're going to Take the Germ out of Germany 99
We're on our Way to France to Fight for Liberty 416
We're the Sammies from Across the Ocean 417
What a real American can do 350
What are You Going to Do to Help the Boys? 161
What Kind of an American are You? 52
When a Yankee Got his Eye Down the Barrel of a Gun 418
When a Yankee Rolls up his Sleeves 55
When Alexander Takes his Ragtime Band to France 148
When All the World's at Peace 283
When Germany Licks Old England, Old Ireland will be Free 27
When Germany's had her Fall 419
When I Get Back to the U.S.A. 440
When I Gets out in No-Man's Land 420
When I Hear a Gun I'm going to Run 284
When I Send You a Picture of Berlin 217
When I'm Gone Just Write to Mother 171

When Old Glory Floats over the Rhine 190
When our Mothers rule the World 31
When Pershing's Band Plays Dixieland 186
When the Boys from Dixie Eat the Melon on the Rhine 421
When the Eagle Flaps his Wings 422
When the Flowers Bloom on No Man's Land 241
When the Good Lord Makes a Record of a Hero's Deed 232
When the Kaiser does the Goose-step 110
When the *Lusitania* Went Down 17
When the *Robert E. Lee* arrives in old Tennessee 423
When the Sun Goes Down in France 145
When the Yankees Yank the Kaiser off his Throne! 424
When There's Peace on Earth Again 351
When Uncle Joe Steps into France 425
When We go Over the Top 352
When We go Through Berlin 426
When We March into Old Berlin 427
When We Wind up the Watch on the Rhine 353
When We've Taught the Hun the Marseillaise 428
When Yankee Doodle Learns to "Parlez vous Français" 122
When Yankee Doodle Marches through Berlin 108
When You Come Back and You will Come Back 225
Where do We go from Here? 92
Who Put the "Germ" in Germany? 429
Who'll Take Care of the Harem when the Sultan Goes to War? 26
Who's afraid of the Kaiser!!! 430
Who's Who in Berlin? 431
Would You rather be a Colonel with an Eagle on your Shoulder? 238

Yankee Doodle in Berlin 257
Yankee Doodle's in the Fight to Stay 432
You Can't Stop the Yanks 433
You Get Used to it after a While 197
You'll be There 25
You'll have to Put Him to Sleep with the Marseillaise 229
Your Country Needs You Now 60
Your Lips are No Man's Land but Mine 178
You're a Grand Old Flag 300

Ze Yankee Boys have Made a Wild French Baby out of Me 441

# SONGWRITERS

Abrahams, Maurice 18
Allen, Edgar 322
Allen, Thomas S. 282, 290
Armstrong, Clara S. 316
Armstrong, Paul B. 395, 413
Asaf, George 32
Atteridge, Harold 270

Baer, Carl J. 345
Baker, George Clinton 134
Ball, Eva Allen 412
Barron, Ted S. 324
Barry, Joseph J. 292
Baskette, Billy 168
Bateman, Bernice 392
Bayha, Charles 24, 40, 197
Belohlavek, Frances 72, 250
Benoit, George 223, 364
Berlin, Irving 5, 53, 56, 200, 224, 234, 271
Berg, Leon 167
Bewley, Harry 124
Black, Ben 222, 381
Blood, M. V. B. 151
Boyden, George L. 169, 319
Branen, Jeff; 101, 436
Bratton, John W.; 339
Brennan, J. Keirn; 25, 264, 423
Brockman, James 114, 155, 237
Brown, A. Seymour 19
Brown, Fleta Jan 243, 283
Brown, Harry Leslie 358
Brown, Lew 52, 86, 116
Browning, Hiram B. 138
Browning, Mrs. Hiram B. 138
Browning, W. E. 58
Bryan, Alfred 13, 31, 61, 83, 85, 117, 143, 148, 204, 228, 309, 421
Buchanan, D. M. 416
Buck, Gene 67
Buell, Earle 428
Bunce, Harry T. 42
Burkhart, Addison 249
Burtch, Roy L. 414
Bywater, Mary Scott 136

Caddigan, Jack 192, 240, 260, 263, 433
Cahill, Dee Dooling 50, 76
Calhoun, John Clayton 205
Callahan, J. Will 36, 41, 139
Campbell, Fred S. 418
Carey, G. H. 113
Carr, "Kid" Harry 189
Carroll, Harry 10, 233
Carson, D. A. 398
Casey, James W. 301
Cavanaugh, Eddie 289
Chaffee, George B. F. 251
Chantereau, Francis C. 274
Childs, Elizabeth Herbert 43
Clarke, Grant 65, 202, 218, 375
Cobb, Will D. 118, 152, 246
Cohan, George M. 91, 225, 300
Cohn, George C. 209
Conrad, Con 434
Coogan, Jack 376
Cooke, Edmund Vance 313
Cooper, David W. 245
Cooper, Walter 415
Corless, A. G. 3
Cowan, Rubey 40
Cowles, Hal Blake 258
Cox, Charles Roy 213
Crawford, Bob 351
Crisler, J. C. 206
Cronson, Joe 46
Cunningham, Paul 264

Davis, Benny 93
Davis, Edith Ella 374
Davis, Frank 44
Davis, G. Howlett 252
Davis, Joseph M. 165
De Costa, Leon 343
De Haven, Carter 284
De Vaux, Harry G. 440
Delamater, A. G. 365
Dempsey, J. E. 62, 379
Dettling, Jacob 213
Dew, Samuel T. 276
Dillen, Wilson 156

Dillon, Will 15
Dixon, Arthur 68
Doctor, Oscar 84
Donaldson, Walter 383
Dreyer, Dave 217
Driscol, Leone 190
Drowne, F. P. 367
Dubin, Al 60, 281
Duncan, William Cary 332

Earl, Mary 142, 181, 314, 326, 377
Edwards, Gus 264
Egan, Raymond B. 248
Ehrlich, Sam 226, 434
Ellis, Harry 247
Ellison, Jewell 431
Empey, Arthur Guy 137, 158, 178
Erd, Daisy M. 347
Evans, Floyd John 361

Fairman, George 20, 115, 242, 390
Falvella, J. W. 408
Farrell, Joe S. 180
Fay, Frank 217
Ferguson, Joseph 411
Fields, Arthur 107
Fink, Henry 182
Fitzgerald, Zeph 366
Fitzgibbon, Bert 310
Flanigan, Jas. A. 106
Flynn, Allan J. 191, 340
Ford, Lena Guilbert 33
Fortner, Alex C. 94
Francis, George 302
Freed, Arthur 221
Freeman, Harold B. 355
Freese, Mrs. W. A. 401
Fried, Joe 207
Friedlieb, Isabel S. 393
Friedman, Max 57
Frisch, Billy 215
Frost, Jack 23, 110, 127, 170, 269, 303

Garrett, George 45
Garrett, Lloyd 404

Garton, Ted  223, 364
Gaston, Billy  183
Gaskill, Clarence  78
Gilbert, L. Wolfe  6, 296, 430
Gillespie, Haven  315
Goetz, Coleman  21, 95
Goodfellow, W. H.  172, 432
Goodwin, Joe  88, 195, 402
Gordon, C. K.  188
Gould, Billy  66
Gould, Egbert E.  328
Graff, George, Jr.  38, 239, 327
Graham, Roger  350
Gray, Estelle  334
Green, Bud  370, 400
Green, Gene  180
Green, Mort  157
Greene, May  302
Grey, Lawrence  369
Grinnell, O. S.  8
Grossman, Bernard  18, 29, 63, 121, 125, 133, 298, 425

Habelow, Sam  425
Haines, Anna B.  135
Hall, Robert P.  212
Hamilton, E. Paul  140
Hancock, "Hank"  10
Harcourt, S. R.  363
Hardy, Will  287
Harris, Charles K.  120, 321
Harris, G. B., Jr.  409
Hart, Al  70
Hart, Will J.  122
Havens, Jimmie  189
Hazelle, Verne  210
Henderson, Charles E.  102
Herschell, William  128
Hess, Cliff  148
Hiller, Joe  57
Hirsch, Walter  75
Hoier, Thomas  30, 63
Hogan, William  112
Holland, A. C.  427
Holt, Arthur F.  80, 337
Howard, Great  144
Howell, E. M.  171
Hughes, Joseph H.  9
Huston, Frank C.  294
Hyatt, Ralph  407

Irving, Walter  51

Jacobson, Herman  18
Jansen, Walt J.  220
Jessel, George  268
Johnson, Howard  87, 92, 95, 123, 185, 215, 306
Johnson, Philander  126
Johnstone, Gordon  275
Jolson, Al  270

Kahn, Gus  161
Kaufman, Jimmie  26
Keithley, E. Clinton  216
Kendis, James  114, 155, 287
Kennedy, Tom  379
Kinnear, David M.  219
Kissell, Henry F.  171
Klein, Lou  199
Kohn, David  90
Kuhn, Charles  436

Lake, E. J.  48
Lamb, Arthur J.  99, 163, 299
Lange, Arthur  125, 176
Laska, Edward  265, 380
Lawton, J. Fred  162, 277
Lee, Marvin  47
Lefavour, Rosamond H.  419
Leslie, Edgar  28, 56, 148, 204, 227, 298, 336
Leveen, Raymond  320
Levenson, Robert  177, 223, 253, 325, 364
Leventhal, Phil  54
Lewis, Bert  75
Lewis, Henry  215
Lewis, Roger  279, 286, 295, 351
Lewis, Sam M.  132, 196, 236, 261, 262, 341, 410
Lhevinne, Mischa  334
Little, George A.  439
Lloyd, Robert  201
Lockney, Laurence  399
Luxton, J.  285
Lyons, Joe  357

MacBoyle, Darl  34
MacDonald, Ballard  7, 10, 195, 338, 346, 360
Macnutt, Albert E.  22
Mahoney, Jack  59, 191
May, Myron  329
Mayo & Tally  78

Marten, Jimmie  71
Mathewson, F. E.  211
Mayer, Archie  26
McCarron, Charles R.  14, 17, 52, 164, 184, 235
McCarthy, Joe  228
McCarthy, Myles  372
McConnell, J. Edwin  382
McCoy, Katherine Oliver  49
McCrae, John  149
McDougall, Alan  147
Metzger, Adrian  72
Meyer, Daisey Theresa  82
Meyer, George W.  56
Meyers, Charles A.  27
Mitchell, Sidney  231, 238
Mohr, Halsey K.  342
Moore, Herbert  79
Moran, Eddie  77, 308
Morgan, Carey  184, 235, 296
Morgan, Code  55
Morgan, Edward P.  129
Moss, Alcan  280
Mountain, Thomas O.  186
Murphy, Stanley  174

Nathan, Casper  4
Norton, George A.  96
Norton, Hugh  348

O'Brien, John  100
O'Hara, Geoffrey  146, 198
O'Rourke, Kate Beirne  291
Olcott, George  57
Oler, Ann Brown  389

Pascoe, Richard W.  160, 311
Pease, Harry  123
Perkins, C. C.  72
Pfeiffer, C. Arthur  388
Phelps, Marion  403
Piantadosi, Al  331
Pinkard, Maceo  179
Ponce, Phil  130
Porter, Lew  386
Potter, Clinton J.  175
Pourman, E. J.  98
Prather, M. Hayes  394
Pyle, Jr., Harry C.  105

Quirk, Gene  354

Ratcliff, Charlotte 256
Rech, Leo 438
Rees, Thomas R. 429
Rehling, M. A. 3
Reisner, C. Francis 93, 422
Reynolds, Adelbert 254
Rice, Gitz 203
Robe, Harold 249
Robinette, A. M. 424
Robinson, George W. 406
Rockwell, G. Allyn 81
Roden, Robert F. 194
Rogers, Howard E. 89, 202, 241, 375, 391
Rose, Ed 150, 312, 387
Rowland, Adele 308
Ruby, Harry 208, 227, 268, 336
Ruhlman, John S. 307
Russell, Harry 189
Ryan, Ben 217
Ryan, Leo J. 69

Santly, Joseph 351
Sawyer, Henry S. 12
Schaeffer, Lew 54
Seiler, Joe 417
Shadomy, E. L. 293
Shannon, J. R. 141, 378
Shaw, Harold 230
Sherman, Terry 47
Sherry, Bert 35
Sherwood, George G. 187
Sherwood, Ray 97
Sill, William F. 426

Skidmore, Will E. 273, 420
Slattery, Joseph J. 437
Small, Louise 16
Smith, Paul A. 177
Snyder, Charles 84
Solman, Alfred 176
Spray, John. C. 154
Spero, Lou 255
Steege, W. S. 39
Sterling, Andrew B. 64, 108, 125, 176, 229, 288, 317
Stern, Jack 21
Stevens, Alton J. 304
Stevens, Vernon T. 153, 349
Stewart, John Nelson, Jr. 330
Stewart, Paul 193
Story, Chick 260, 263, 433
Strassburg, Ernst von 278
Sullivan, Alex 373, 396
Summers, Charles 111
Sweet, Al 371

Taylor, Tell 119
Tennant, Gilbert C. 145
Thompson, Gordon V. 353
Thornton, J. J. 356
Threlkeld, Erle 166
Tighe, Harry 362
Tomkins, E. J. 109
Tower, Jay B. 333
Tracey, William 87, 266
Trainor, Val 232

Van Alstyne, Egbert 272

Vincent, Nat 17, 155
Von Tilzer, Harry 73

Wakefield, C. Guy 214
Walker, Marshall 273, 420
Warren, Frank H. 131
Wenrich, Percy 92
Wesley, Howard 292
Weslyn, Louis 331
West, Eugene 441
Weston, Charles B. 2
Weston, R. P. 11
Weston, Willie 85
White, James 23
Williams, Frankie 368
Williams, Harry 257
Williams, W. R. 1, 344
Wilson, Al 405
Wilson, Arthur C. 207
Wilson, Emily D. 385
Wilton, Dean T. 318
Wood, Leo 37
Wood. Will 159
Woodruff, Joseph 98
Woodward, Jimmy 384
Woolworth, O. P. 359
Wright, Sidney B. 352

Yellen, Jack 104, 259, 323, 335
Young, Joe 132, 196, 236, 261, 262, 267, 341, 410
Young, R. C. 103

Ziemer, Fred 173

# COMPOSERS

Abrahams, Maurice  18, 204, 341
Ager, Milton  375
Ahlert, Fred E.  270
Allan, Bob  289
Allen, Edgar  322
Anderson, Will R.  365
Andino, J. E.  50, 76
Andrieu, Harry  98

Backherms, Louis E.  399
Baker, George Clinton  134
Ball, Ernest R.  25
Barron, Ted S.  324
Baskette, Billy  93, 168, 371
Bayha, Charles  24, 40, 197
Belohlavek, Frances  250
Benoit, George  223, 364
Berlin, Irving  5, 53, 56, 200, 224, 234, 271
Berg, Leon  167
Bibo, Irving M.  439
Black, Ben  222, 381
Bowers, Frederick V.  99, 163
Boyden, George L.  169, 319
Braham, Edmund  72
Brandon, Clarence  403
Bratton, John W.  339
Brennan, James A.  192, 240
Brennan, J, Keirn  264
Breuer, Ernest  421
Britton, William L.  415
Brockman, James  114, 155, 237
Brookhouse, Win  44
Brown, A. Seymour  19
Brown, Al W.  63
Brown, Harry Leslie  358
Browning, Hiram B.  138
Browning, Mrs. Hiram B.  138
Brunsvold, William  187
Bryan, Alfred  148
Burke, Joseph A.  62, 281, 379
Burtch, Roy L.  414
Bywater, Mary Scott  136

Caddigan, Jack  260, 263, 433
Calhoun, John Clayton  205

Call, Guy  81
Campbell, Fred S.  418
Carlo, Monte  160, 311
Carr, "Kid" Howard  189
Carroll, Harry  7, 10, 233, 360
Casey, James W.  301
Chaffee, George B. F.  251
Chantereau, Francis C.  274
Clay, Ned  416
Cobb, George L.  325, 335
Cohan, George M.  91, 225, 300
Conrad, Con  226, 434
Coogan, Jack  376
Coots, J. Fred  165
Cooper, David W.  245
Cormack, Rennie  60
Cortelyou, Winthrop  332
Cowan, Lynn  396
Cowan, Rubey  40
Cowles, Hal Blake  258
Cox, Charles Ray  213
Crawford, Bob  351
Crerie, E. E. Edwin  3
Cronson, Joe  46
Cunningham, Paul  264, 423

Daly, Joseph M.  282, 290
Daniels, Charles N.  257
Danmark, Ribé  43
Dappert, Merlin L.  304
Darewski, Hermann E.  11
Davis, Edith Ella  374
Davis, G. Howlett  252
Davis, William  353
Dawson, R. Kenneth  34
De Costa, Harry  29, 37, 157, 232
De Costa, Leon  343
De Haven, Carter  284
De Rose, Peter  243
De Vaux, Harry G.  440
De Villar, Julian  408
Demangate, Carl  254
Detling, Jacob  213
Dew, Samuel T.  276
Dixon, Arthur  68
Doctor, Oscar  84

Donaldson, Walter  261, 262, 383
Donaldson, Will  42, 97
Downing, Sam  379
Dreyer, Dave  217
Driskell, C. H.  113
Dulmage, Will E.  162

Earl, Mary  142, 181, 314, 326, 377
Eberley, Lawrence E.  429
Edwards, Gus  118, 152, 246, 264
Egan, Thomas  373
Ehrlich, Sam  434
Elbert, Charles  292
Ellis, James G.  299
Ellison, Jewell  431
Emerson, Arne  135
Erd, Daisy M.  347
Erdman, Ernie  279, 286
Evans, Thomas  411

Fairman, George  20, 115, 242, 390
Farrell, Joe  180
Fay, Frank  217
Fiorito, Ted  405
Fisher, Fred  83, 143, 228
Fisher, Gerrit B.  219
Fitzgerald, Zeph  366
Flanagan, Thomas J.  106
Flatow, Leon  107
Flynn, Allan J.  191, 340
Francis, George  302
Freeman, Harold B.  355
Freese, Mrs. W. A.  401
Friedland, Anatol  430
Friedman, Leo  36
Friedman, Max  57
Frisch, Billy  215
Frost, Jack  23, 127, 303

Garrett, Lloyd  404
Garton, Ted  223, 364
Gaskill, Clarence  78
Gaston, Billy  183
George, William  384
Gilbert, L. Wolfe  286
Glogau, Jack  38, 244, 323, 387

# Composers

Goetz, Coleman  21
Gold, Joe  441
Gottler, Archie  28, 231, 238, 241, 298, 391
Gould, Billy  66
Gould, Egbert E.  328
Grady, Bart. E.  188
Grant, Bert  239, 267, 327, 410
Grant, Charles N.  283
Gray, Eddie  49
Gray, Estelle  334
Green, Gene  180
Greene, May  302
Grey, Lawrence  41, 369
Grimm. C. A.  58
Grinnell, O. S.  8
Grossman, Bernie  18, 125
Gumble, Albert  59, 104, 288
Guy, Harry P.  432

Habelow, Sam  435
Haines, Chauncey  372
Halls, J. C.  256
Hancock, "Hank"  10
Hanley, James F.  195, 338, 346
Harcourt, S. R.  363
Hardy, Will  287
Harris, Charles K.  120, 321
Harris, G. B., Jr.  409
Hart, Al  70
Havens, Jimmie  189
Hawthorne, David H.  305
Henry, S. R.  131
Herbert, Victor  67
Hess, Cliff  148
Hill, May  156, 350
Hiller, Joe  57
Hogan, William  112
Howard, Great  144
Howard, Joseph E.  126
Howell, E. M.  171
Huston, Frank C.  294
Hyatt, Ralph  407

Irving, Walter  51

Jacobson, Herman  18
James, Charles  16
Jansen, Will P.  220
Jentes, Harry  123, 306
Jerome, M. K.  132
Jessel, George  268

Johnson, Billy  350
Johnson, Howard  92, 215
Johnson, Lee  206
Jones, Jean Gilbert  190

Keefer, Ralph  45
Keithley, E. Clinton  170, 216
Kelly, M. F.  22
Kendis, James  114, 155, 237
Kissell, Henry F.  171
Klickmann, F. Henri  4, 269, 395
Kocian, Howard  277
Kuhn, Robert  436

Lake, E. J.  48
Lake, M. L.  140
Lange, Arthur  64, 108, 125, 176, 317
Laska, Edward  380
Lasley, Amber G.  412
Lawrence, Ray  133
LeBlanc, Mitch  71
Lee, Marvin  47
Lefavour, Rosamond  419
Leopold, Walter  75
Leslie, Edgar  56, 148, 227, 336
Levene, Frank L.  177
Levenson, Robert  223, 253, 364
Leventhal, Phil  54
Levi, Maurice  280
Lewis, Henry  214
Lewis, Roger  286, 351
Lewis, William J.  26
Lhevinne, Mischa  334
Lloyd, Evans  101
Lloyd, Robert  201
Lord, Nathan  427
Luxton, J.  285
Lyons, George  310

MacDonald, Ballard  10
MacDonald, C. W.  172
Magine, Frank  357
Mahoney, Jack  191
Marr, Alex  121
Marshall, Henry I.  315
Mathewson, F. E.  211
May, Myron  329
Mayo & Tally  78
McCarey, Thomas  422
McCarron, Charles R.  17, 137, 158, 164, 178, 184, 235

McConnell, George M.  281
McConnell, Lincoln  382
McDougall, Alan  147
McHugh, James  318
Mervine, Ida K.  212
Meyer, Daisy Theresa  82
Meyer, George W.  56, 87, 95, 185, 202, 218
Meyers, Charles A.  27
Miller, Charles C.  109
Miller, Eddie  39
Mincer, Harry H.  295
Mitchell, Sid  130
Mohr, Halsey K.  88, 342, 402
Monaco, James V.  89
Morgan, Carey  137, 178, 184, 235, 296
Morgan, Code  55
Morgan, Jimmie  30
Morse, Theodore  100, 125
Muir, Lewis F.  6
Murtagh, H. B.  214

Nathan, Norman  102
Neander, Harold  110
Nelson, Edward G.  122, 368, 370, 400
Northrup, Theodore H.  293
Norton, George A.  96
Norton, Hugh  348
Novello, Ivor  33

O'Hara, Geoffrey  146, 198, 275
Olcott, George  57
Oler, Elizabeth  389
Olman, Abe  150, 259, 312
Onivas, D.  131
Orion, Walter  438
O'Rourke, Kate Beirne  291

Pallma, Frank, Jr.  428
Payley, Herman  14
Peck, Gerald  255
Perry, Penn  361
Pfeiffer, C. Arthur  388
Piantadosi, Al  13, 221, 244, 331
Pierson, William T.  80, 339
Pinkard, Maceo  179, 266
Platzmann, Eugene  151
Porter, Lew  247, 386
Powell, Felix  32
Powers, Sammy  35

Quinn, W. J.  424
Quirk, Gene  354

Rice, Gitz  203, 249
Richardson, Harry  9
Robinson, George W.  393, 406
Roden, Robert F.  194
Ruby, Harry  208, 227, 268, 336
Ruhlman, John S.  307
Russell, Harry  189
Ryan, Ben  217
Ryan, Mrs. Leo J.  69

Sanders, Alma W.  160, 311
Santly, Joseph  351
Sapp, Kitt G.  94
Sawyer, Henry S.  12, 316
Schaeffer, Lew  54
Seiler, Joe  417
Schwartz, Harry  111
Schwartz, Jean  65, 196
Shanks, Zena G.  394
Shannon, J. R.  173, 356
Shaw, Harold  230
Sherman, Terry  47
Sill, William F.  426
Silver, Abner  182
Skidmore, Will E.  273
Slattery, Joseph J.  437
Sloop, Lon  186
Smith, Walter  209

Snyder, Charles  84
Solman, Alfred  176
Speroy, Robert  413
Spray, John C.  154
St. Clair, L.  392
Stamper, Dave  284
Sterling, Andrew B.  125, 176
Stewart, Paul  193
Stewart, John Nelson, Jr.  330
Stevens, Vernon T.  153, 349
Stern, Jack  21
Stillwell, John  210
Story, Chick  260, 263, 433
Strassburg, Ernst von  278

Taylor, George H.  297
Taylor, Tell  119
Tennant, Gilbert C.  145
Thomas, John E.  49
Thomas, Louis  105
Thompson, Gordon V.  353
Threlkeld, Erle  166
Tice, Blanche M.  139
Tierney, Harry  61, 174
Tours, Frank E.  149
Tower, Jay B.  333

Van and Schenck  309
Van Alstyne, Egbert  161, 272
Vandersloot, Carl D.  141, 378
Vincent, Nat  17, 155

Von Tilzer, Albert  15, 52, 86, 116, 265
Von Tilzer, Harry  74, 77, 129, 199, 229, 308, 362
Voorheis, Gertrude  72

Walker, Barclay  128
Walker, Marshall  273, 420
Wells, Jack  31, 85, 117
Wendling, Peter  117, 236
Wenrich, Percy  92
Weslyn, Louis  331
Weston, Charles B.  2
White, James  23
Whiting, Richard A.  248
Whitmore, Floyd E.  175
Williams, A. L.  90
Williams, W. R.  1, 79, 335
Wilson, Arthur C.  207
Wilson, Emily D.  385
Winkle, Billy  425
Winne, Jesse  320
Wood, Will  159
Woolworth, O. P.  359
Wright, Sidney B.  352
Wuerthner, Julius  397

Young, R. C.  103

Zamecnik, J. S.  313
Zerfing, Harry C.  367

# PERFORMERS

Abbott & White 28
American Comedy Four 13
Austin, Monte 62
Avon Comedy Four 92

Bailey & Cowan 218
Baker, Belle 148, 196
Ballard, George Wilton 42
Barnes & Lorraine 145
Bayes, Nora 21, 91
Beard, Billy 420
Bennett, Murray 28, 65
Bergman, Henry 107
Bessinger, Frank 92
Bowers, Frederick V. 99, 163
Brennan, J. Francis 158
Brenner, Dorothea 92
Brice, Elizabeth 200
Brice & Brazee 47
Brice & King 62, 92
Brooks, Belle 95
Burkhart, Maurice 107, 218
Butler, Amy 28

Cantor, Eddie 227, 234, 238, 269, 336, 425
Carroll, Harry 233
Carter, Frank 196, 224
Carus, Emma 95, 100, 202, 338
Chandler, Anna 28, 122
Cheong, Tang 92
Claire & Dorothea 92
Cogert, Gertrude 121, 341
Cohan, George M. 225
Collins & Harlan 92
Comer, Larry 28, 92
Concerto, Marie 100
Cooper, Harry 95, 100, 196
Courtney Sisters 244
Cowan, Lynn 218, 396
Cross, Wellington 28, 227

Davis, Ben 62
Davis, Josephine 13, 92
Dietrich, Rene 234
Dika, Julia 122

Dooley & Nelson 95, 100
Dream Girls 200, 234
Dunn, Thomas Potter 28

Edah Delbridge Trio 121
Ellis, Harry 91, 92, 247, 387
Elwood, Paul 84

Farrell, Marguerite 40
Fisher, Eleanor 92
Fitzgibbons, Bert 320
Francis, Mae 13
Fuller, Connie Lehr 145

Gilder, Roy 337
Glaum, Louisa 223, 364
Granis & Granis 28
Granville, Bernard 26, 292
Graves, Carl S. 178
Great Howard 144
Greene, Gene 13, 180
Greene, Rita 100
Gunn, Marval 145

Hall, Bob 121, 202, 234
Heider, Fred 13
Herlein, Lillian 441
Herman, Al 223
Honigfeld, D. M. 416
Howard, Clara 65
Howard, Joseph E. 126
Hudler, Stein & Phillips 100
Hussey, Jimmy 65

Jackson & Wahl 92
"Janet of France" 122
Janis, Elsie 122, 400
Jardon, Dorothy 95
Jarrett, Dorothy 241
Jolson, Al 11, 196, 236, 270

Klee, Mel 244
Klein Brothers 92

La Rue, Grace 178
Lambert, Beatrice 92

Leipold, J. Walter 75
Leon, Daisy 28
Lewis, Bert 75
Lewis, Henry 215
Littry, Arthur 200

Maguire, Francis 107
Maitland, Madge P. 28
McCormack & Irving 13
McKinley, Neil 92, 107
Mellinger, Artie 92
Mignon 196
Moretti, Helen 340
Mortan, Eddie 95
Morton, Ed 13, 30, 107
Mullane, Frank 92, 218
Murphy, Elsie 121
Murray, Billy 100
Murray, Elizabeth 23
Murray, Katherine 322

O'Brien, Billie 71

Pielert of Pielert & Scofield 95
Phillips, Evelyn 28
Piotti, Lewis C. 92

Qualters, Joseph 311

Raie, Genia 28
Rayfield, Florence 121
Raymond, Ruby 13
Reilly, William J. 91, 164
Ring, Blanche 191, 312
Roberts, Eshell 28
Rochester, Claire 95
Roland, Ruth 95
Roland, Adele 308
Romano Sisters 244
Russell, Polly 121
Russell Sisters 176

Samuels, Rae 65, 202, 234
Santly & Norton 92
Seeley, Blossom 92
Seymour, Lew 122

Sherman, Mabelle 200
Sisters, Kitty 213
Smith, Willie 241
Smythe, William 196
Starr, Flora 202
Stern, Flora 107
Strollers Quartette 411

Tanguay, Eva 247
Taylor, Tell 119
Temple Quartette 182
Tendehoa, Chief 13

Thompson, Moe 92
Three Romano Sisters 244
Timponi, Florence 100, 107, 234
Toy, Chee 13
Tucker, Sophie 28, 184, 231

Ward, Will J. 13, 107
Wallace, Grace 202
Warner, Frank 145
Warner, Rae 145
Watson, Fannie 28, 213
Watson Sisters 92, 306

Webb, Martin 405
Weston, Willie 100, 298
White, Elsie 28, 244
Williams, Queenie 200
Winchell, Walter 100
Wise, Jack 92
Woodruff, J. 98
Worsley, Billy 65
Wright, Horace 234

Yonge, Jeannette 121
Yvette of Yvette and Saranoff 223

# RECORDING ARTISTS

American Quartet 28, 91, 92, 93, 203
Ash, Sam 28

Bayes, Nora 91, 118, 231, 261, 267
Brown, Edna 196
Buckley, Eugene 198, 201, 238
Burr, Henry 30, 83, 85, 89, 115, 118, 120, 126, 132, 195, 223, 236, 240, 248

Campbell, Albert 30, 118, 223, 248
Cantor, Eddie 271
Caruso, Enrico 91

Dalhart, Vernon 85, 248, 265
Doherty, Jim 29
Donovan, Hugh 240

Elliot, Charles 223

Farber, Connie 200
Fields, Arthur 88, 92, 122, 123, 185, 201, 203, 217, 228, 234, 235, 238, 261

Grant, Rachel 228

Hamilton, Edward 32
Harlan, Byron G. 261
Harris, Marion 148, 231
Harrison, Charles 260
Harrison, James F. 29, 32
Harvey, Morton 13
Hart, Charles 126, 195, 240, 248, 260, 262

James, Lewis 248, 260, 262
Johnson, Murray 32
Jolson, Al 196, 271
Joseph C. Smith's Orchestra 227, 249

Kaufman, Irving 30, 228
Knickerbocker Quartet 32

Lewis, Robert 87

McClaskey, Harry 87
McCormack, John 33, 225, 249
Miller, Reed 33
Murray, Billy 11, 131, 198, 200, 228, 265, 267, 268, 271

Nicholas Orlando's Orchestra 248

Orpheus Quartet 225

Peerless Quartet 13, 86, 88, 91, 93, 115, 116, 128, 185, 189, 201, 217, 224
Porter, Steve 128
Prince's Band 131
Prince's Orchestra 132

Reed, James 29
Rice, Gitz 248

Seagle, Oscar 249
Shannon Four 116, 120
Shaw, Elliot 223, 240, 262
Spencer. Elizabeth 89

Victor Military Band 32, 131
Van & Schenck 123

Werrenrath, Reinald 32, 83
Weston, Willie 85
Wheeler, Frederick J. 33

# ARTISTS

Anderson Art Service 384
Articue 206

B. N. 276
Barbelle, Albert 5, 18, 34, 53, 57, 65, 66, 85, 88, 117, 122, 130, 132, 142, 148, 195, 196, 197, 200, 204, 208, 224, 227, 234, 236, 239, 241, 261, 262, 267, 268, 270, 284, 298, 314, 327, 336, 341, 370, 376, 377, 391, 396, 400, 402, 410, 421
Brooks, H. K. 68
Brown 406
Brown, A. D. 190

Cameron, W. R. 422
Chas. Hanne' Sr. Design 175
Colson, Harold F. 363
Crit Publishing Co. 173, 356
Cronweil, P. W. 160

D 10
Dallin, C. E. 302
De Lappe, W. R. 222, 381
De Takacs, André 6, 15, 16, 21, 24, 64, 83, 116, 143, 165, 168, 228, 317, 386
Denslow 280
Dobinson Engr. Co. 177
Dowling, Colista M. 333
Dulin 286
Dunk 25, 44, 80, 82, 152, 246, 264, 337

Einson 20
Emmons 70
Evans 429

Fisher, E. 287
Fisher, E. S. 3, 318
FSM 248

Gaston, Billy 183
Glazier Lyceum Print 8

H 216, 269
Hager, George 301
Heisman 167
Hurst, E. 45
Hutt, Henry 91, 159, 201, 371

JH 105
JHD 47

K 155, 157, 225, 232, 423
Keller 140
Klinge 207

Ladd-Noon, Eng. 212
Le Morgan 55, 85
Linke 281
Livezey, Will E. 94, 111
LPN 43, 61
L. S. R. 275

Manning, T. C. 399
M'hard, M. E. 295
Mills, R. G. 171

Natwick 156, 179, 350, 420

Pfeiffer, E. H. 7, 26, 50, 51, 74, 76, 77, 81, 84, 96, 99, 115, 129, 145, 169, 199, 217, 229, 252, 282, 285, 294, 308, 353, 355, 362, 389, 405, 425

Pfeiffer Illustrating Co. 98
Plunkett, V. C. 253

R 424
Reiss, Lionel S. 258
Rockwell, Norman 146, 263
Rosenbaum Studios 13, 37, 38, 62, 87, 91, 92, 93, 95, 100, 101, 107, 114, 123, 124, 185, 202, 203, 218, 237, 238, 242, 259, 273, 292, 300, 306, 351, 375
Ross, Penny 324

Sachs 221
Schneider, L. E. 397
Starmer 1, 14, 19, 22, 31, 63, 79, 104, 106, 108, 111, 120, 121, 125, 126, 131, 133, 158, 164, 174, 176, 182, 184, 191, 192, 221, 233, 244, 255, 272, 288, 289, 296, 297, 312, 321, 322, 323, 325, 326, 331, 335, 338, 339, 340, 344, 346, 378, 380, 387, 430, 435, 436

TC 366
Terry Engraving Co. 213
Tower, Lew W. 311

USA 34

Walton, E. E. 86, 161, 181, 194, 205, 226, 235, 266, 368, 434
Williams, Garth 128

# PUBLISHERS

A. J. Stasny Music Co. 66, 122, 370, 400
A. M. Robinette 424
Acme Publishing Co. 291
Advertising Association of Chicago 334
Al. Piantadosi & Co, Inc. 221, 244, 331, 340, 387
Albert Bader & Co. 278
Alton J. Stevens, Music Publisher 304
American Junior Naval and Marine Scout, Inc. 51
American Music Publishers 398
Arthur Dixon 68

Barry, Malmgren & Taylor 297
Beaux Art Publishing Co. 343
Blanche M. Tice Music Pub. Co. 139
Bostonia Publishing Co. 287
Broad and Market Music Co. 98
Broadway Music Corporation 15, 52, 86, 116, 226, 235, 265, 266, 434, 439
Bruceville Music Co. 409
Buck and Lowney 277, 392, 403
Buckeye Music Pub. Co. 213

C. Arthur Pfeiffer 388
C. W. Thompson & Co. 419
Cadillac Music Co. 16
Camp Custer Music Co. 349
Campbell-Shorey Co. 418
Capital City Music Bureau 219
Chappell & Co, Ltd. 22, 32, 33
Charles B. Weston 2
Charles C. Miller 109
Charlotte Ratcliff 256
Chas. E. Roat Music Co. 153, 367, 406
Chas. K. Harris 120, 321, 441
Chas. W. Hatch 230
Church, Paxson and Company 285

Citizen's Liberty Loan Committee 167
Clark-Levy Co. 72
Corbin, James 112
Corless & Crerie 3

D. W. Cooper Music Co. 245, 253, 302
Daly Music Publisher Inc. 35, 192, 282, 290
Daniels & Wilson Music Publishers 55, 257, 422
De Villar & Falvella 408
Dee Dooling Cahill 50
Delta Publishing Co. 311
Dillen & Gormley 156
District Welfare Aide 147
Driscol-Jones Pub. Co. 190

E & S Publishing Co. 373
E. D. Wilson 385
E. J. Lake 373
E. L. Shadomy 293
Eastern Music Co. 46
Echo Muisc Publishing Co. 301
Ed J. Small 372
Edith Ella Davis 374
Éditions Francis Salabert 132
Edw. L. Ballenger Music Publishing Co. 49
Emmett J. Welch Music Publisher 281, 323
Encore Music Pub. Co. 81
Eva Allen Ball 412

F. A. Mills 6
F. B. Haviland Pub. Co. Inc. 42, 97, 194, 243, 283, 368
F. G. Dickerson 8
F. J. A. Forster Music Publisher, Inc. 47, 75, 286, 312
Fisk Pub. Co. 407
Frances-Clifford Music Publishing Co. 72, 250
Francklyn Wallace 34

Franco-American Music Publishing Co. 274
Frank C. Huston 294
Frank K. Root & Co. 4, 23, 36, 41, 110, 127, 170, 193, 216, 269, 303, 316, 395, 404, 413
Frederick V. Bowers, Inc. 99, 163
Freese Music Co. 401
Fried & Wilson Publishers 207

G. Ricordi & Co., Inc. 249
Garton Brothers Music Publishers 169, 364
Gate City Press 151
Geo. Boyden Music Publisher 319
Geo. C. Cohn 209
Geo. Jeffrey & Samuel Habelow 435
George Fairman 242, 390
George B. F. Chaffee 251
George D. Sherwood 187
George R. Garrett 45
Gilbert & Friedland Music Publishers 430
Great Aim Society 76
Gus Edwards Music House 118

H & N Music Publishers 102, 429
H. B. Browning Pub. Co. 138
H. G. De Vaux Pub. Co. 440
H. J. Seiler 417
Hamilton Music Publishing Co. 427
Harold Freeman Music Co. 355
Harold Rossiter Music Company 279
Harrington & Reynolds Publishers 254
Harry L. Brown 358
Harry Von Tilzer Music Pub. Co. 74, 77, 115, 129, 199, 217, 229, 308, 362
Hawthorne Music Publishing Co. 305
Holmes Music Co. 415

Hospe Music Co. 70
Howard and LaVar Music Co. 144
Howland Music Co. 348

Ideal Publishing Co. 90
Independent Music Publishers 27
International Edition Publishing Company 343
Irving Berlin, Inc. 271

J. J. Wuerthner 397
J. N. Stewart, Jr. 330
Jack Mendelsohn Music Co. 177, 240
James Corbin 112
Jay B. Tower 333
Jeff Branen Publisher 101
Jerome H. Remick & Co. 14, 19, 31, 43, 59, 61, 104, 140, 161, 174, 191, 248, 272, 288, 309, 315, 379, 380
Jewell Ellison 431
Joe Morris Music Co. 63, 64, 98, 108, 121, 125, 133, 145, 150, 176, 317, 317, 405, 425, 436
John C. Spray & Co. 154
Jos. H. Hughes 9
Jos. W. Stern & Co. 131, 137, 158, 164, 178, 179, 184, 247, 255, 296
Joseph J. Slattery 437

Kalmar, Puck & Abrahams Consolidated, Inc. 28, 65, 241, 298, 341, 391
Kay-See Music Co. 111
Kendis-Brockman Music Co, Inc. 20, 114, 155, 237
Key Music Publishing Company 145
Kissell & Howell 171

Lang Pub.Co. 433
Leo. Feist, Inc. 13, 17, 30, 37, 38, 62, 87, 91, 92, 93, 95, 100, 107, 123, 124, 146, 185, 192, 198, 201, 202, 203, 215, 218, 223, 238, 258, 259, 260, 263, 273, 275, 292, 306, 351, 353, 371, 375
Leo Rech 438

Lew Schaeffer Music Co. 54
Liberty Publishing Co. 134
Lockney & Backherms 399
Lowell Publishing Co. 426
Lyceum Music Publishers 58, 295

M. Witmark & Sons 25, 29, 60, 78, 89, 126, 149, 157, 225, 232, 246, 264, 310, 332, 339, 365, 423
Mary Scott Bywater 136
Mathewson and Mathewson 211
Maurice Abrahams Music Co., Inc. 18
Maurice Levi & Company 280
Maurice Richmond Music Co. 26, 300
Max Clark Co. 359
Max Friedman Music Publishing Co. 57
McCarthy & Fisher Inc. 83, 143, 168, 228
McKinley Music Co. 12
McMullen-Ince Music Publishing Co. 147
Melody Shop 135
Metropolis Music Co. 324
Meyer Cohen Music Pub. Co, Inc. 252
Midwest Music Publishing Co. 186
Miss Elizabeth Oler 389
Myron May Publishing Co. 329

N. P. Bryan Music Publisher 369
National Music Company 82

Oliver Ditson Company 188
Oxford Music Publishing Co. 160

Pallma Publishing Co. 428
Pearson's 414
Phil Ponce Publications 130
Phoenix Music Co. 299
Prather Pub. Co. 394

Quirk-Dudley Music Publishing Co. 354

R. C. Young Music Co. 103

R. P. Hall & Ida K. Marvine 212
Ralph C. Gillett Publisher 328
Richmond Publisher 421
Roger Graham 350, 357
Rubey Cowan Music Publishing Co. 40
Ruhlman Music Publishing Co. 307
Ryan and Bradley Pub. Co. 69

S. B. Wright 352
S. R. Harcourt 363
Sam Fox Pub. Co. 313
Samuel T. Dew 276
Sapp-Fortner Pub. Co. 94
Seidel Music Publishing Co., Inc. 166, 416
Shadomy, E. L. 293
Shapiro, Bernstein, & Co. 7, 10, 21, 24, 44, 88, 128, 142, 181, 182, 183, 189, 195, 197, 205, 233, 314, 322, 326, 338, 342, 346, 360, 376, 377, 383, 386, 396, 402
Sherman, Clay, & Co. 206, 222, 381
Skidmore Music Co. 420
Smithdeal 361
Snyder Music Pub. Co, 84
Song Review Co. Inc. 152
Song Shop 210
Steege Miller Co. 39
Success Music Co. 113
Sumner and Maher Publishing Co. 344

T. B. Harms and Francis, Day & Hunter 11, 67
Ted Browne Music Co. 382
Tell Taylor Music Publishers 119, 180
Thayer Publishing Co. 318
Theron C. Bennett 96
Thomas and O'Connell Music Pub. Co. 105
Thomas J. Flanagan Music Co. 106
Thos. Goggan & Bro. 71
Triangle Music Pub. Co. 165

United War Work Campaign 162

Unity Music Publishers 220
Universal Music Pub. Co. 172, 432

Vandersloot Music Pub. Co. 141, 173, 356, 378

W. T. Pierson & Co. 80, 337
Wakefield Music Co. 214
Walter Jacobs 325, 335
Waterson, Berlin & Snyder Co. 5, 53, 56, 85, 117, 132, 148, 196, 200, 204, 208, 224, 227, 231, 234, 236, 239, 261, 262, 267, 268, 270, 284, 327, 336, 410
Whitmore Music Pub. Co. 175, 411
Will Rossiter 1, 79, 289, 344

Will Wood 159
William George Music Pub. Co. 384
William Jerome Publishing Corporation 91
Winlee Music Co. 320

Zeph Fitzgerald 366

DEC 1 2 2017